EATING **LESS** IS MAKING YOU **FAT**

Vijay Thakkar is a functional medicine expert and a dynamic, young entrepreneur passionate about fitness. He launched 48 Fitness in 2013 with a vision to redefine and address issues prevailing in the fitness industry. His brand has steadily become one of India's most awarded celebrity fitness clubs, offering personalized services and wellness standards to fitness enthusiasts in the heart of Mumbai. Vijay has written about health, wellness, lifestyle, functional medicine, fitness and nutrition in India for prestigious publications like *Forbes*, *Times of India*, *Hindustan Times*, *Indian Express*, *Femina* and many more.

Praise for the book

'The simplistic view that eating more and exercising less are the primary causes of weight gain, and that weight loss requires you to be hungry and lethargic for life is a lie. Vijay's book provides all of us with a fact-based, clear perspective, vision and interpretation of the true role of calories in losing weight and maintaining health.'

Ranbir Kapoor

'Fitness and health have been one of the cornerstones of my personal and professional lives, and if there's someone who understands and masters this space, it's Vijay. His approach is holistic, authentic and sustainable, and the results speak for themselves. If you're looking to better your life by cultivating a healthier lifestyle, this book will be your friend and guide.'

Anil Kapoor

'Be ready to be surprised, fascinated and lose weight with Vijay while eating good food.'

Tiger Shroff

'Vijay has hit the nail on the head! In my 30 years of being in the fitness industry, never has anyone simplified the relationship between food and body like this. The days of starving are passé; welcome to the millennium, there's no better way to start than to eat, and not just that, eat right with Vijay Thakkar. I know it's hard for most people to believe that we need to eat to lose weight – read this book and learn the secret of HOW to eat and shed those kilos.'

Yasmin Karachiwala, Celebrity Fitness Instructor & CEO of Yasmin Body Image

'*Eating Less is Making You Fat* is well-written, honest and provides good depth to support the thesis. Overall, Vijay has done a great job in providing a straightforward approach to losing weight.'

Dr Nene, Surgeon

'The truth that not many know. The author speaks about what the real causes of weight gain are and how to overcome those problems. *Eating Less is Making You Fat* is a book everyone should read to understand their body and work towards it.'

Warda S. Nadiadwala, Film Producer

'*Eating Less is Making You Fat* is a must-read for all who want to regain their health and increase their healthspan.

Most people don't improve their health because they either don't know where to start and navigate all the conflicting information or how to remain consistent in a world of fast-food marketing, celebratory occasions, and how to fight the couch and remote control. Vijay has spent years creating an easy-to-apply roadmap towards a healthier life for everyone. I consider him a pioneer in India who is paving the way for health, fitness, confidence and empowerment at a time when it's most needed.

Make your life thrive by having *Eating Less is Making You Fat* on your bookshelf.'

Kris Gethin, Celebrity Trainer and
Global Celebrity Physique Transformation Coach

'This book is well-written with excellent scientific references and comes from an extremely knowledgeable author. Read it to be armed with the required knowledge to make informed choices before you think of eating less to lose weight.'

Anand Pandit, Film Producer

'Being fit brings balance to life. In his new book, Vijay Thakkar brings his research and practical way of achieving harmony with smart fitness, the right food and good sleep. Vijay's first-of-its-kind approach to explaining the science behind these three areas, followed by his proven guidance, makes it a must-read book.'

Surendra Tipparaju, Senior Director, Data & AI,
Microsoft Global Delivery, India

'For someone like me, having gone through type II diabetes, the change in my food habits made a big difference. This book could be of immense help for those seeking a healthier lifestyle.'

Ashutosh Sinha, Senior Editor, *Economic Times*

'Inspiring journey into the world of weight loss, diets and food. The author has very intelligently tackled the psychological benefits of weight loss and a balanced diet, which leads to mental and emotional health and feelings of self-esteem.'

Priti Srivastava, Mentor, Advocacy & Corporate affairs,
Reliance Industries Limited

'Only a person of Vijay's calibre, background and education could have written this book. This book is rich with research data and would be a godsend to anyone who wants to stay healthy, not just in a physical way but a holistic way. Vijay is a celebrity in his field and this book shows us why.'

Shiv Shivakumar, Group Executive President –
Corporate Strategy & Business Development, Aditya Birla Group

'Every word by Vijay is fact-based and pushes readers to ensure tangible results in the most sustainable manner. While your fitness coach may appear ruthless in sailing through (high & low tides of) your fitness journey, this book's content is like a lighthouse, avoiding collision course and helping you take the right nautical speed.'

Mukesh Ralhan, Group Head – COE & Strategic Initiatives, Adani Group

'A contrarian, fitness expert Vijay Thakkar turns common fads about weight loss like eat less, burn more do shirshasan. He also deals with heart disease and diabetes in his book which is literally a compendium of information for a healthy life.'

Olga Tellis, Veteran Journalist and Former Editor Asian Age

'Losing weight has been a mystery to many, including me. Like others, I have tried, but every time something changed, and I never got results. Maybe it was age, fast-paced work or just not eating right. This book by Vijay is an eye-opener for many corporate professionals like me. It is a well-researched, self-help guide. This book is a must-read, must-have and must-buy!'

Dr Tanaya Mishra, VP & Head HR (India), Endo International plc

'This book is an urgent call for action. The author provides a deep understanding of food's relationship with the body, nutrition, disease and health. It is also a critical reminder of how evolving food cultures and daily lifestyle choices impact our individual and collective health and well-being.'

Prof. Preeti Shroff Mehta, Professor & Director – Executive Programs, Northwestern University Medill School, IMC (Chicago)

'Vijay Thakkar has always been a pathbreaker and a lateral thinker. This book is another example of how he simplifies the conundrum of weight loss with the help of science, making it an engaging read and an essential on the bookshelves of all fitness enthusiasts and those who are struggling with their weight.'

Dr Niraj Vora, Joint Replacement Surgeon

EATING **LESS** IS MAKING YOU **FAT**

How to Lose Weight Without Starving

Vijay Thakkar

hachette INDIA

First published in 2023 by Hachette India
(Registered name: Hachette Book Publishing India Pvt. Ltd)
An Hachette UK company
www.hachetteindia.com

SRD

All the images used in the text have been provided by the author, with the exception of images from Shutterstock (page 48 & 50) and Freepik (page 59).

Subsequent edition/reprint specifications may be subject to change, including but not limited to cover or inside finishes, paper, text colour and/or colour sections.

ISBN 978-93-93701-55-8

Hachette Book Publishing India Pvt. Ltd
4th & 5th Floors, Corporate Centre,
Plot No. 94, Sector 44, Gurugram 122003, India

Typeset in Calluna 10.5/15.5
by R. Ajith Kumar, New Delhi

Printed and bound in India
by Manipal Technologies Limited

MIX
Paper | Supporting responsible forestry
FSC™ C043100

Author's Dedication

This book is dedicated to my family:
my mom – Hema, my dad – Dinesh,
my wife – Poonam and my brother – Vinay,
for their unwavering belief in me.

The book is inspired by the Fit India Movement (launched in 2019 by the Hon'ble Prime Minister Narendra Modi) with a view to make fitness an integral part of our daily lives.

Author's Note

The references to 'fat' in the title and within the book are for emphasis and refer to the medical state of obesity. The author does not intend to discriminate on the basis of weight, is against body shaming and supports body positivity.

The information given in this book is only for educational purposes and should not be considered medical advice, nor should it override or substitute professional advice from your nutritionist or doctor. Neither the author nor the publisher is engaged in providing professional advice to the individual reader, and they shall not be liable for any damage allegedly transpiring from any suggestion in this book.

While the author has recommended certain products and food items in the book, it is not his intention to promote any particular brands and there is no paid consideration whatsoever.

Contents

Foreword

We are more than eight billion people on the planet, but each one of us is so unique when it comes to not just our personalities but also the way our bodies function. I firmly believed *'body banana koi asaan kaam nahin hai'* until I read Vijay's book, where he explains the science in the most accessible way — what I now call the trick and the truth of being fit.

Personally, I've always strived to give my best to fitness. From a career point of view, walking a challenging path to discover my true inner potential has always been my mantra. Fitness, to me, is not just a professional requirement but something that is essential to my very existence. It has played an integral role in my career of over two decades, from *Kaho Naa... Pyaar Hai* to *Vikram Vedha*, the journey, and beyond. As an action hero, one has to be on one's toes; work is not only demanding but also challenging. Some of my roles demand that I be at the peak of a body type; this requires excessive preparation, but the base must always be ready. The base is nothing but the optimum level of fitness, be it muscular, cardio, flexibility, or mental strength. I believe this is needed in any profession. All you have to do is keep the base ready so that you can enjoy your life, your time with family, and your work challenges to the fullest. Vijay explains in depth, and with scientific backing, how the sync or rhythm in your body is brought to life. His analysis fascinated me, because it is rare to read such extensive research put together seamlessly in one book.

For me, weight gain has not been a major problem, but I have always been a hard gainer, and thus, any role that needs me to be very muscular requires me to work even harder on my body. Some roles even need me to take a beating like an action hero would. To play a flexible dancer and a muscular hero simultaneously, one needs a lot of energy and intensity through the long days and nights, with shoots lasting for months. Hence, I generally deploy various strategies under guidance, such as incorporating the correct nutrients in my meals, exercising according to a program, and following a recovery protocol. This has helped me get fit and repair previous injuries I suffered in my back and ligaments while shooting, and it keeps me strong.

I remember my conversation with Vijay in 2017 at his fitness club, where I was all ears to his thoughts, knowledge, and the tech innovations he had brought to life at the facility. Being a fitness enthusiast myself, I was naturally curious to hear his thoughts on his concept of 'The Human Health Tripod,' on which Vijay has based his book and which I've been following without realising it to stay in shape. I was particularly impressed by his in-depth knowledge of food and how he promotes fitness that is backed by scientific research.

Experts rarely recommend eating optimally rather than eating less. In many discussions, Vijay completely knocked down the ongoing popular model for weight loss — the model of eating less and moving more to lose weight — mandated by various global health organisations.

What I resonated with the most was his unique thought process on why this erroneous treatment framework of dieting, or eating food exceptionally low in calories, invariably harms the health and morale of individuals trying to reduce their weight. I could not agree more with him on this; hence, when he told me he was writing a book to finally take his enormous knowledge to the masses and help millions live healthier lives, I was equally excited to write a foreword for him.

Vijay's book has the power to change the world and reduce the alarming number of lifestyle diseases occurring primarily due to misleading information. By the end of the book, readers will grasp the exact cause of weight gain and why our efforts to prevent it by eating less and moving more are bound to fail. Crucially, this book gives you a tool to manage weight sustainably without starving yourself or feeling lethargic.

I believe this book is a blueprint for curing the most significant health epidemic facing our modern society — an epidemic that the author demonstrates is wholly preventable and potentially reversible, but only if we authentically approach it with the proper understanding of its underlying causes. The truth he elaborates in this masterpiece of a book will one day be acknowledged as self-evident. The sooner that day comes, the better it is for humanity.

Vijay is uniquely qualified to author this book. Enjoy this book. Take charge of your health.

With love,

Hrithik Roshan

(Mumbai, December 2022)

Introduction

'In sciences founded on opinions and dogmas, the use of anticipations and logic is good; for in them the object is to command assent to the proposition, not to master the thing.'

Francis Bacon, *Novum Organum*

The tip of the iceberg

Remember the movie *Titanic*? What did you find most striking, or haunting, in the film? Rose and Jack's love story, the bad-guy Cal Hockley's betrayal, the realistic depiction of the sinking vessel, the emerald necklace that Rose throws into the sea or Celine Dion's memorable song?

Call me a fatalist but what haunts me most about the film is the iceberg, because as a health and fitness professional, I find the iceberg to be the best analogy for our current health crisis.

I like to think of the 'weight problem' as the tip of the iceberg with something deadlier lurking under the surface. Did you know? Only 10 per cent of an iceberg is visible above the water's surface. The other 90 per cent floats beneath it.

Following this analogy, if the tip of the iceberg is the 'weight problem', the remaining 90 per cent is usually a lifestyle-related disorder. And that's the part – the invisible yet dangerous shadow – that usually ends up taking someone's life.

In the last decade, lifestyle-related diseases such as type 2 diabetes, some types of cancer, cardiac diseases, hypertension, stroke, reproductive issues, and polycystic ovary disorders have gone up, especially among the younger population. People are gaining weight too easily and succumbing to the diseases of old age.

Take a look at these numbers:[1]

- Every 12th Indian is a diabetic. India ranks second on the list of countries with the highest number of diabetes patients.
- The number of overweight and obese people in India doubled between 2005 and 2015. Among individuals aged 15–49 years, 20.7 per cent of women and 18.6 per cent of men are overweight or obese.
- More than 1.73 million new cancer cases were likely to be recorded each year in India by 2020, with air pollution, tobacco, alcohol and diet as the primary triggers for it.
- More than 2.7 million people in India die of heart disease every year with 52 per cent of them below the age of 70.

To say that we have a problem is an understatement.

It's also surprising to learn that for 99.99 per cent of our time on Earth, humans have been diabetes-free and obesity has never been this rampant. Of course, we live longer than our ancestors. But given technological and medical advancements, we should ideally be a healthier and fitter population. Yet the data tells us that the opposite is true. Where have we gone wrong? Or, rather, what are we not doing right?

Despite being at the most technologically advanced stage of human history, we are lagging way behind in one fundamental subject – nutrition. It is the most understudied and underrepresented area of healthcare.

Nutrition – A question mark

Is dairy bad? What oils should we consume? Do we need Omega-3 supplements?

Every year there are new theories. One year's superfood is deemed poison a few years later. Think about the reputation of ghee and milk in the 1990s and now. Nutrition science is one giant ball of confusion, but we do know some fundamentals: Vitamin C prevents scurvy. Vitamin D deficiency causes rickets. Smoking causes lung and other cancers.

Research in nutrition is time-consuming and expensive. An ideal research study needs more than 10,000 participants from across the world, who are kept in a controlled environment. They will be divided into groups – some eating only the food that is being studied, some eating everything else but that specific food, and others a mix of both. Some will have to exercise, some will not. And this will be conducted for at least ten years. How many volunteers do you think will sign up to do this? Then comes the cost factor. Studies like these will require blood tests, MRIs and a host of testing procedures for ten years. Who would want to pick up this atrocious bill?

Having said that, these double-blind, randomized control

trials are the gold standard in nutritional research. This method helps researchers make a one-to-one connection between the factors that they are testing. But here's the catch – with a pharmaceutical drug trial, the researchers can convince the control group that their placebo is the real drug, so much so the participants feel the benefits and side effects. We all know this to be the placebo effect. How do we achieve that in nutritional research? Here, we have to control the amounts of proteins, carbohydrates and fats to see the impact of the nutrient being tested. But, simply making the participants consume only protein without fats or carbohydrates to study the effects of protein on human health is not practical and violates the moral grounds of experimentation. The trouble doesn't end here, it's just the start! Dietary carbohydrates or fats have so many types – simple carbohydrates, complex carbohydrates, saturated fats, monounsaturated fats, polyunsaturated fats, and each one impacts human biology in a unique way. Think about this: we want to study the effects of skimmed milk versus whole milk on the health of an adult. The experimental group is given skimmed milk. The control group is given whole milk and told that they are also being given skimmed milk to study the placebo effect. But here's the question – wouldn't the control group know from experience that the milk tastes like whole milk and is not skimmed milk? This would surely hurt the experiment. Now say, after five years of experiments, if some health benefits were observed in the skimmed milk group, say an improvement in blood pressure, even then it is difficult to conclude for sure whether the benefits observed were due to increasing carbohydrates content in the diet or due to decreasing the fat content in the skim milk group. So, a double-blind experiment and making meaningful conclusions is not always possible in this scenario. This is why scientifically precise nutritional studies rarely happen.

Into this fray, 'Big Business' steps in. They work with the government to promote certain foods, fund their own research studies, and pump money into marketing and propaganda. Certain foods are cheaper to manufacture and can feed a large population. High yield = high profits. Then, there are government subsidies.

> Government subsidies, too, tend to favour established grains over uncommon ones. The Indian government subsidizes rice and wheat, up to 86 percent of the cost for the lowest income families, and only recently included millet. In the U.S., from 1995 to 2012, the federal government's agricultural subsidies totalled almost $300 billion, with corn ranking first, wheat second and rice seventh on the Environmental Working Group's top 20 list of subsidized crops.[2]

If we were to also think about the production cycles of plants, crops and trees, it is not difficult to notice that they complete their production cycle sooner for sale in the market over a longer maturation cycle of animal products, which requires higher resources and more time to yield revenues for the farmers and taxes for the government.

Entangled in all these factors, nutrition then becomes

a monster of a problem. And thus, we seem to know less every year.

A three-fold problem

Whenever people meet me – through social media, at my gym and or at social gatherings – I am always asked three questions:

- Why am I gaining so much weight?
- How do I lose weight?
- I lost so much weight. Why am I gaining weight again?

Most of the people who ask me these questions are not completely ignorant about weight gain and the perks of a healthy body. In fact, they know quite a lot. They've spent time Googling for answers, they've had gym memberships – usually in January when the New Year's resolutions are still holding their sway – and they've tried every weight loss trick or diet under the sun: Keto, Atkins, juicing, a calorie deficit diet, the weight loss TikTok dance trends, avoiding foods of a certain colour, and some I haven't even heard of. You name it, they've probably taken a stab at it. And yet they find themselves unable to achieve their goals. When they don't see results for whatever they are trying, they get frustrated, abandon their current weight loss scheme and move onto the next.

What's the other side of this coin? Say, you've committed to a diet, and it's worked. You've shed those kilograms and you've achieved your desired goal. But there's just one problem – how do you maintain your weight now without going into starvation mode for your entire life? After all, life is for living, not denying yourself its pleasures.

Is there a diet that is sustainable for a lifetime?

To this, my answer is: There are no short cuts, but anyone can lose weight and, in the process, reverse their lifestyle-related diseases. The trick lies in knowing the science behind how your body works and responds to food.

If you are suffering from cavities or gum disorders, you go to the dentist. The dentist will fix it and send you home. But what if the dentist sits you down and explains to you the reason behind your dental problems and how to avoid them. He then shows you the correct technique to take care of for your teeth, you'd be better equipped to deal with it the next time. In the same way, through this book, I want to help you lose weight and lead a healthier life by equipping you with a fundamental knowledge of nutrition. Knowledge is power and I want you to have it. Let's move on from Google and trust in the science of nutrition and the human body.

When I conduct workshops on this subject, I ask the attendees to rank the most to least crucial contributor to their obesity problem from the following factors:

- Lack of willpower
- Environment
- Genetics

What was your guess?

In a US poll,[3] over 61 per cent of people responded that personal preferences on food intake and exercise were responsible for the 'obesity epidemic'. I get the same answer in my workshops, that an obese person is weak-willed. I understand where they are coming from. They've been told that eating too much and exercising too little makes people fat.

You will find out how much of this is a lie by the end of this book.

My story

In most Indian homes in the early nineties, there was little to no emphasis on healthy eating. I grew up in a typical Indian household where we ate a standard Indian diet of rice, dal, subzi, fried food made from processed carbohydrates and refined vegetable oil.

This was the time when fat was considered the number one dietary villain. 'Big Business' had been selling cereals, soft drinks and ready-to-eat food in tin cans since the 1950s. I remember every morning before school, I used to devour several bowls of cereal (I wasn't satiated even then!), and every evening after gully games, I used to drink Coca-Cola and similar sugar-rich drinks to 'refuel'.

I admired athletic and lean sportsmen and celebrities and aspired to look like them. But I was a child of the low-fat generation (more on that in Chapter 1), which meant I was an overweight, 6.2 feet tall, seventeen-year-old with a hunched posture. I was afraid to raise my hand and ask questions in class, anxious about approaching girls and embarrassed to be put in the spotlight. To make matters worse, I was frequently ill, always down with flu, fever, diarrhoea or constipation, always on some medication or the other. The medication caused weakness, mood swings, insomnia and weight gain. In 2005, when I was 19 years old, I had an accident. It was a huge wake-up call. I started going to the gym regularly and became obsessed with my own transformation. I began to research how to quickly build lean mass and gain strength to make the most of my time in the gym. I began to talk to other people at the gym and noticed that a large percentage came to the gym for the obvious reasons: to lose weight and become lean. Some people among them were forced to go to the gym by their doctors or family members. They were trying to do damage control when they discovered that they had to reverse lifestyle-related conditions such as high cholesterol, heart problems and blood sugar. That made me think about my symptoms and whether they could've been because of my diet. It was a novel idea to me. It wasn't even on my radar, because it's not something that is explicitly taught, at least during the time I was in high school.

At that time, I was at the London School of Economics studying for my bachelor's degree. But I was more obsessed with researching fitness not only from an aesthetic and athletic enhancement viewpoint, but also from a health point of view – and gain a two-fold perspective. I wanted to understand what was wrong with those who were compelled to go to the gym because of their ill health, why breathing was a challenge for some, and why some of them lose so much calcium in their bones that their bones have become extremely brittle? I wanted to discover why some people were healthy with well-functioning bodies and could easily work towards their fitness goals in the gym, while others were merely surviving through life with disease and experienced sickness frequently.

After LSE, I was at a serious crossroads. I temporarily put my dreams of a career in health and fitness on hold and joined my family business in finance. After a few years, I started feeling the pull of my obsession again. I couldn't stamp out the flame of scientific curiosity that burned within me. I didn't want to take the next logical step of completing my master's degree in finance as I was not truly passionate about it. I thought about how the medical system was failing at eradicating lifestyle-related diseases. Patients were succumbing to them at an alarming rate. Medication only served to slow down the march towards morbidity.

I asked myself:

- Are medicines really enabling individuals to lead a meaningful and high-quality life or simply delaying the inevitable?
- Is there no way to reverse conditions such as high blood pressure, heart disease, diabetes or cholesterol-related issues by tackling root causes?
- Has there been a profound shift in the way that we are eating today compared to what our ancestors ate?
- Did our ancestors succumb to the same unforgiving chronic diseases that we encounter today?
- Could these questions lead us to the reason behind our departure from health, vitality, strength, mental clarity, and healthy body composition?

To find persuasive answers to these pertinent questions, I gave into my inner calling and opted for a master's degree in sports management where I majored in three disciplines – nutrition, exercise science, and public health policies in India, the USA and the UK. For my final dissertation, I investigated the service quality of gyms in India. This research led me to identify many gaps in service elements in the fitness and wellness industry, such as making fitness enjoyable, social, making workout spaces hygienic and giving members neuro- and physical sciences-backed, result-oriented, comprehensive lifestyle solutions along with an individualized adherence plan for each case to fulfil specific needs and objectives. I wanted to create a business with a considerable value-added, win-win proposition that improves the members' quality of life by optimizing one's health with exercise, nutrition and a lifestyle which prioritizes the quality of sleep as an essential factor in maintaining one's health and fitness gains for all the resources employed including their time, sweat and money in working out regularly and following a disciplined nutritional pattern to get the desired outcomes. Most gyms provide a standard one-size-fits-all workout routine to members, unless they pay additionally for personal training. They provide a mundane workout ambience – white tube lights and a music playlist that the front desk executive selected as per his whims and fancies which fails to extrinsically stimulate, energize and excite the members so they regularly turn up for their workout. Add to that: management cutting corners with housekeeping expenses, which sometimes can make the workout space unhygienic.

I wanted to bridge these gaps, so I started my fitness club introducing various disruptive and industry-first proportions by leveraging the power of technology and providing a hygienic workout space with a round-the-clock housekeeping service. Thumping music played by a live DJ and dancing lights integrated with the beats of the music to get all the senses of the members entering the club activated for an energetic workout and providing several formats of group classes for generalized fitness, never letting workout boredom to creep in. The members also had access to a world-class protein and fibre coffee bar and state-of-the-art fitness equipment to make fitness data-driven and focused on standardizing protocols for specific goals to mitigate confusion on the approach irrespective of the staff handling the case and looking at correlations between behaviour and outcome directly. Wellness programmes, too, were provided with services ranging from nutritional counselling to protein shakes, from fitness assessments of body composition, functional movement screening, endurance, and strength tests to individualized fitness programmes. Everything that a member could think of when wanting fitness, everything from A to Z, was available. Based on the knowledge that I gained during my programme and the life experiences I had at that point, I came up with the concept of the human health tripod.

The human health tripod

Think of your body as the vehicle you own. To keep and maintain this vehicle in top condition for years to come, you must use it regularly, provide it with the correct fuel and right oil, and send it for timely servicing. Similarly, your body needs the ignition for health (regular exercise), the right fuel and oil (good macro and micronutrients) to build itself, and adequate rest and recovery (sleep) to be in great shape without having to face lifestyle-related conditions for a long time. I also call this the human health tripod – all three legs of the tripod need to be balanced well. If one leg is shorter than the other or non-existent, then the tripod is imbalanced. The camera – your life – topples over!

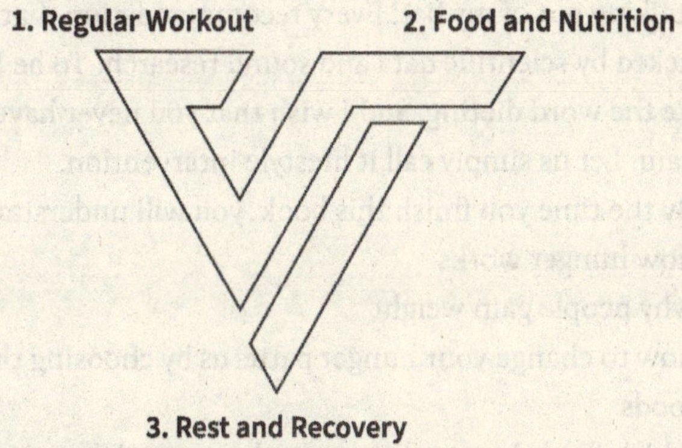

Visual representation of the human health tripod

During my career, I have helped thousands of clients learn and maintain this balancing act. My clients were successfully able to reverse their lifestyle-related diseases – diabetes, autoimmune conditions, Alzheimer's, dementia, thyroid, depression, anxiety-induced psoriasis, and rheumatoid arthritis. You can read their inspiring stories at www.vijaythakkarfitness.com.

Why this book?

This book is a result of a million questions – the ones I asked myself and my professors and the ones that my clients ask me on a daily basis. Throughout this book, I will break down long-held beliefs and bust myths about good nutrition and diets. I will also tell you which foods are good for us and which aren't and why. With this information, you can tweak your food habits to lose or maintain your weight and even reverse diabetes and other lifestyle-related diseases. Much of what I will discuss may seem controversial to you at first, but I am not talking out of my hat! Every recommendation that I make is backed by scientific data and sound research. To be honest, I hate the word dieting, and I wish that you never have to use it again. Let us simply call it lifestyle intervention.

By the time you finish this book, you will understand

- how hunger works
- why people gain weight
- how to change your hunger patterns by choosing the right foods
- which foods keep us hungry and cause weight gain
- why we fall sick and develop lifestyle-related diseases
- how to reverse these lifestyle-related diseases
- how much exercise is good for us

I can promise you that by the time you finish reading this book, you will look at diet and nutrition with a fresh perspective. Let's get started, shall we?

PART ONE

WHY WE GET FAT

1

The Big Fat Lie

'The thing is, it's very dangerous to have a fixed idea. A person with a fixed idea will always find some way of convincing himself in the end that he is right.'

Atle Selberg, Fields Medal winner in Mathematics

The conventional wisdom on why we get fat states that fat accumulation is a result of energy imbalance in the body because an individual gaining weight is unable to remain in perfect energy balance. To get to a healthy body weight one must consume only so many calories that one is able to burn through regular exercise and consume no more calories than that. This implies that individuals gain weight because they fail to count calories in and calories out and balance them. If this conventional wisdom were to be accepted as a reasonable explanation for our observation of an obesity epidemic, then lean individuals who are now gaining weight are gaining so because they have lost their ability to maintain a perfect energy balance. If the conventional notion were to be believed, then it also means that formerly lean individuals who are now gaining weight are lean people who have lost the willpower to exercise and eat in moderation. That is, individuals who are gaining weight have been tempted by gluttony and sloth, and that this can be resolved by telling them to eat less and exercise more.

This assertion that gaining weight results from a calorie imbalance in the body is also known as the calories in, calories out model (CICO) and implies a causal relationship between calories and body weight; that is, excess calories increase body fat, and calorie deficit decreases body fat. However, to make such strong assertions, it's essential to rule out possibilities of a correlation mistaken with causation. In the upcoming chapters, we will explore the question of whether calorie intake is associated with fat accumulation or whether it causes fat accumulation using data from studies. If the two are indeed causally related, then to rule out reverse causation, it's essential to determine in which direction does it work? Does lack of exercise and overindulgence in food cause excess weight, or does gaining excess weight cause an increase in appetite for excess food and a reduction in our impulses to exercise, thereby creating an energy imbalance or a positive energy balance in the body? And what if there are genetic and physiological factors – such as appetite and satiety signalling by hormones involved – which determine how much energy we should consume, what kind of foods we consume and how much energy we burn at complete muscular repose, adjusting our impulses to exercise and our energy intake to create the balance in the body naturally to maintain our body weight homeostatically? And if our weight is indeed homeostatically maintained, then could it be possible that our exposure towards certain foods we find in our kitchens today is disrupting the appetite and satiety signals in our body, which in turn is disrupting this homeostatic regulation of energy and fat in the body? Could the problem of excessive fat gain be a physiological rather than the psychological, moral, or arithmetic problem of overeating that the CICO model suggests? In this upcoming section, we will explore these themes and examine how vital counting calories is to increase our energy expenditure, decreasing our energy intake and, thus, weight maintenance.

Fahim was forty-seven years old when he was diagnosed with type 2 diabetes. He is 5 feet 9 inches and weighed 96 kg. When he came to me in September 2020, his body mass index (BMI) was over 30. He wanted to lose 25 kg, which he thought was an ambitious goal. He had tried everything under the sun – crash diets, cardio, and walking – to create a calorie deficit but failed spectacularly to lose weight and keep it down.

His weight fluctuated between 96 and 89 kg and he asked me, how do I get the motivation to maintain weight? He was frustrated, hungry, irritable, and still overweight! Initially, he didn't want to be put on any kind of regimen as he felt that there was no sustainable way out of his current situation. Every diet plan left him feeling lifeless. He wanted only comfort food, that too mostly at night. Sometimes, he'd wake up in the middle of the night with an urge to eat something sweet.

Once I convinced him that there would be none of that deprivation business on my programme, Fahim came onboard. I also had to factor in his diabetic condition while preparing his routine. In the first three months, he lost around 9 kg. But he wanted to lose more weight, especially around his waist. He wasn't very hungry but still experienced sweet cravings. His body adapted to the new regimen quickly. He has been on this regimen for six months now, and look at his weight loss graph:

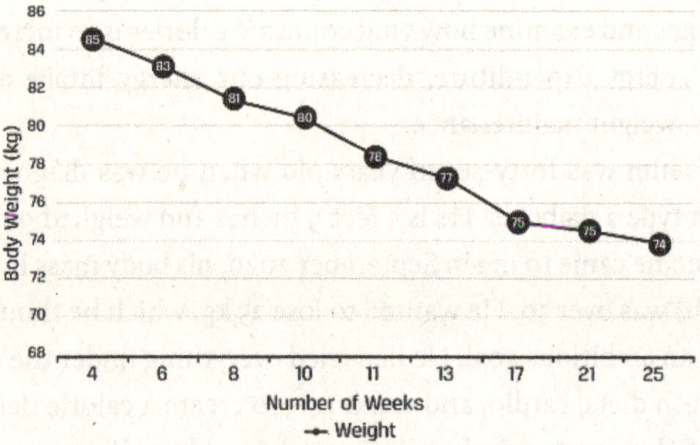

Fahim's Weight

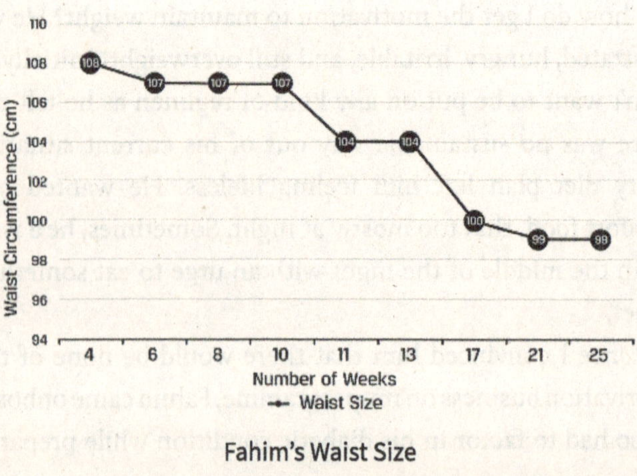

Fahim's Waist Size

Fahim is thrilled that he lost weight without the big three – hunger, deprivation and calorie restriction. So...what did I do different from all the other interventions that had failed Fahim?

Stay tuned and I'll let you in on some of the best-kept secrets of weight loss. And the best part is that you won't have to go hungry again!

The struggles of weight management

Here is a dilemma that has always baffled me: Why do nutritionists gain weight? I'm sure you had the question too! These are experts in human nutrition. They know their energy balances, and the science and mathematics of obesity! As the custodians of nutritional science and authorities on the causes and treatments of obesity, a nutritionist should never be fat! I admit that most of them are self-disciplined and hardworking, and have the huge responsibility of walking the talk every single day. Since no one wants to be overweight (unless we are speaking about a sumo wrestler!), dietitians should possess the dedication and knowledge to remain lean with immense vitality, shouldn't they?

We all have seen the popular prescription for weight loss – 'Eat Less, Move More'. As reasonable as this sounds, it is ineffective. Why does it not work? Is it because they don't stick to the prescription? Maybe the heart wants it, but the mind is weak? It is hard to believe that overweight nutritionists have insufficient willpower to adhere to what they know. Thus, this brings us to the question: What if everything we know about obesity is wrong?

Conventional wisdom says consuming excess calories causes obesity and simply eating less and moving more will solve our problems. But this is more than a century old! More and more evidence against this belief is piling up. Obesity trends are still on the rise. I think this old idea is fundamentally flawed.

Let's start from the beginning, let's understand the history of obesity.

For most of human existence, obesity was sporadic, even when food was abundant. Traditional societies such as the Hazda tribe still don't have obesity. A study revealed that the total energy expenditure of the western population is similar to that of the traditional Hazda hunter-gatherers, where obesity is rare.[1]

Everyone believes that obesity appeared after civilizations developed. Jared Diamond, an anthropologist, reported that in those regions of the globe where populations have transitioned from a society of hunter-gatherers to that of farmers, with the adoption of agriculture, the quality of health and nutrition declined. He described agriculture as 'the worst mistake in the history of the human race'.[2]

What is a calorie?

It is a unit of fuel or energy supplied by our food.

Our body uses it to stay alive and carry out essential bodily functions such as pumping blood, breathing, thinking, building new cells and other metabolic processes. We believe that when the number of calories consumed exceeds the number of calories burned, we gain weight, and when we overeat and exercise too little, we gain weight. These 'beliefs' are so self-explanatory that we never question them.

The history of treatment of obesity and weight gain

1825: Floury and starchy food is bad

Before the concept of calories was discovered, experts adopted a different approach. Based on clinical experience and anecdotal evidence, they suspected that the quality of the food played a role in obesity. Jean Anthelme Brillat-Savarin, a pioneer of the low-carbohydrate diet, wrote in his highly influential book *The Physiology of Taste*, published in 1825,[3] that 'floury and starchy substances', which are the primary ingredients in our food, are directly responsible for fatness. He interviewed hundreds of obese people about the foods they loved the most. They said they couldn't stop dreaming about foods made out of sugar, potatoes, rice, and bread.

1863: Carbohydrates are fattening

William Banting, an English undertaker, rediscovered the flesh-producing properties of dietary starch and wrote a letter addressed to the public called *Letter on Corpulence.*[4] It became the world's seminal weight-loss diet book. Banting was not an obese child and had no family history of obesity. Oddly, he started gaining weight in his mid-thirties, half or a kilogram per annum, and by age sixty-two, he weighed 92 kg. Considering that his height was 165 cm, his BMI was 33.8. He might not be obese by current standards, but at that time, he was portly. So initially, he ate less food, which resulted in extreme hunger, and you guessed it – he also did not lose any weight! Then he took up rowing along the river Thames close to his house in London to increase his physical activity. Rowing invariably improved his fitness, but it resulted in a 'prodigious appetite' that necessitated increased food intake. Finally, in distress, he consulted with a surgeon, William Harvey. The doctor asked Banting to follow a 'low-carbohydrate diet' and told him to eliminate all floury and sugary foods from the diet. So Banting gave up sweets, milk, beer, bread, and potatoes – most of his daily diet, lost his extra weight and found it almost effortless to keep it off! His personal success compelled him to write his famous pamphlet. He believed that weight gain resulted from consuming copious amounts of 'fattening carbohydrates'. You can guess what happened next. For a large part of the following century until the 1950s, diets low in refined carbohydrates became a popular treatment for obesity.

Early 1900s: Eat only 1200 kcal per day

In the early 1900s, counting calories to lose weight became popular after the book *Eat Your Way to Health* was published as a 'scientific system of weight control'. This was followed up by many others with the same message, including the bestseller book *Diet and Health: With Key to the Calories* authored by American doctor and newspaper columnist Dr Lulu Hunt Peters.[5] Dr Peters' programme was simple: a one- to two-day fast at the beginning of the diet, followed by eating only 1200 kcal each day. Slowly, people forgot the fasting step but the 'counting calories' stayed. Even Herbert Hoover, the Director of the US Food Administration from 1917–1919, was convinced that counting calories is the only logical way to lose weight.[6]

Mid-1900s: Dietary fat is the villain

By the mid-1950s, the 'great epidemic' of heart disease hit America. Even US President Dwight Eisenhower succumbed to the disease in 1969. Healthy Americans were suffering from myocardial infarction, or what we know as heart attack, at an alarming frequency. Until then, gastrointestinal infections, tuberculosis, and pneumonia were the only conditions causing death, but suddenly, heart attacks of this kind became prevalent in the first half of the twentieth century.

I think that the experts and government bodies wanted a dietary villain for heart disease and zeroed in on fat in our diet. People began to believe that fat in our food increases cholesterol, a fatty substance circulating in our blood. Doctors, physicians, and public health authorities started to promote low-fat diets. Dietary fat was demonized with immense zest and dubious data. But the unintended result of reducing fat content in the diet meant replacing it with carbohydrates or protein calories. Most high-quality protein foods such as dairy and meat also contain high fat. If we lower the fat, we lower the protein in our food. What we are left with is a high-carbohydrate diet now! And most of the carbohydrates we get in our developed and developing countries are refined carbohydrates. Isn't this a humongous cognitive dissonance?

Not everyone bought into this idea! John Yudkin, a British nutritionist, studied the relationship between nutrients in our diet and cardiovascular disease and discovered no association between fat intake and coronary artery disease. In his 2012 book *Pure, White and Deadly: How Sugar is Killing Us and What We Can Do to Stop It*, he wrote that sugar is the primary culprit for both coronary disease and obesity.[7]

Refined carbohydrates – conflicting opinions	
BAD	GOOD
fattening and affect blood sugar	low in cholesterol and fats

To settle this confusion, public health authorities led by expert nutritionists declared that carbohydrates are not fattening but excess calories are.

Fattening carbohydrates	Calories in, calories out
OUT	IN

Late-1900s: Fat is fattening, carbohydrates are good!

The US Senate Select Committee on Nutrition and Human Needs, led by Chairman George McGovern, convened a tribunal, deliberated on the issue for many days with no new scientific discovery or debate, and concluded that dietary fat is guilty of causing heart disease. They reasoned that because fat is calorically dense and gives more than double the energy per gram of food. So, it's the sole contributor to the excess calories in our body. In 1977, they published a document 'Dietary goals for the United States' directing people to eat less fats and lots of carbohydrates.[8] The entire country, and soon the entire world, started following the dietary advice of a politician! This was a landmark move and a break away from tradition – a government body infiltrated our kitchens and unseated our grandmothers and mothers, who were traditionally the decision makers of what we eat and how much we eat.

Suddenly, the government was telling people:

Eat more carbohydrates
Reduce fat intake
Eat small frequent meals

The formerly 'fattening' carbohydrates were now as innocent as a wolf in sheep's clothes and all its nutritional offences were exonerated. The starch and sugar-rich foods that were formerly known for their fattening properties were now packaged and marketed to be reborn as healthy breakfast foods rich in whole grains and fibre as the better alternatives to eggs and butter to prevent weight gain and heart disease. It was believed that this shift from consuming fat- and cholesterol-deficient foods rich in carbohydrates would help us consume more grams of food, easily filling up our stomachs without significantly increasing energy intake, thereby helping us to not consume excess calories and stay in calorie deficit effortlessly. For instance, sugar is zero fat food so it lacks calorie density per gram followed by whole grains compared to butter and eggs, which are rich in fats and poor in carbohydrates. There was no evidence behind this recommendation and it just didn't matter! Innocent until proven guilty was the standard for the recommended carb intake.

The dietetics paradigm of the globe changed forever in 1980 with the publication of the first Dietary Guidelines for Americans released by the US Department of Agriculture (USDA) and Health and Human Services (HHS), showing a food pyramid based on McGovern's report. This document is revised once every five years, and in its bogus grandeur, the food pyramid still stands tall. Cereals, bread, starchy vegetables and pasta, and low-cholesterol and low-fat foods form the pyramid's base. A heavenly life! Carbonated soft drinks and pasta, thank you, American Heart Association (AHA)!

The pyramid on the facing page tells us – fats make us fat and eating too much without burning it off also makes us fat.

But here's a little conspiracy theory for you: Corn, wheat and rice are cheaper to produce and store than meat, poultry and fish.[9] It's no surprise then that the food pyramid was created by the USDA. Cheaper production and storage of a product = more profits – a fantastic proposition for 'Big Business'. Was this dietary guideline created to help people get healthy or was there a vested interest?

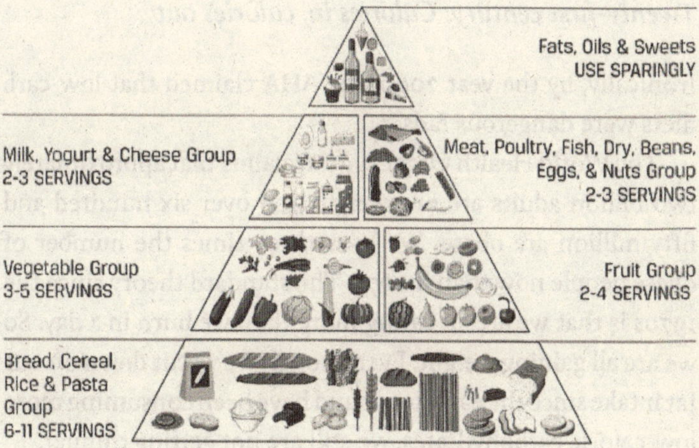

Food pyramid

Cut to the year 2000, sugar intake rose to unprecedented levels. Everything was about lowering cholesterol and fats in the diet and big processed food brands saw this. The added sugar content went up in processed foods to preserve flavour. What do people do when more carbohydrates are recommended to reduce fat intake? They do not consume salads of iceberg lettuce, and green leafy vegetables, they eat more refined carbs and sugars! In India too, we turned away from natural fat sources such as butter, whole-fat dairy, ghee, and coconut oil and embraced refined low-fat, high-carb food such as pasta and bread and polyunsaturated fat-rich, refined vegetable oils.

Twenty-first century: Calories in, calories out

Ironically, by the year 2000, the AHA claimed that low-carb diets were dangerous fads.[10]

The World Health Organization claims that approximately two billion adults are overweight and over six hundred and fifty million are obese. We have three times the number of obese people now than in 1975. The standard theory since the 1970s is that we are all eating more than we burn in a day. So we are all gaining weight. Even though we've cut down on our fat intake since the early 1970s and have been consuming more low-calorie carbohydrates, we still are not getting thinner.

The idea is that the number of calories consumed and expended cause our weight to change. Weight is gained if calories consumed exceed calories expended, and weight is lost if calories consumed are less than calories expended. This idea has triggered an interest in recommending an eating less and moving more approach towards weight loss because it is believed by CICO theorists that staying in a negative energy balance (calories in < calories out) will cause fat tissues to shrink and the body weight would be lost. Thus, their explanation for the weight problem and its solution is adopted from the first law of thermodynamics, which states that energy can neither be created nor destroyed; it can only be converted from one form to the other. Thus, the stored fat weight in the body is a result of excess calories consumed or overeating, translating into a positive energy balance (calories in > calories out). Excess energy consumed through food but is neither exercised out nor burned gets converted and stored as body fat.

Their Solution: Follow the first law of thermodynamics aka the Calorie Deficit Diet

Jean-Pierre Flatt, Professor Emeritus of Biochemistry at the University of Massachusetts Medical School, was the first scientist in the 1970s to promote the calorie deficit theory[11] to combat obesity and lose weight. A generation of researchers on nutrition and dietetics believed in his energy balance equation. The premise of his theory is simple:

> *the more calories we consume, the fatter we get,*
> *and thus, the less we consume, the more weight we lose.*

WHO continues to back this: 'The fundamental cause of obesity and overweight is an energy imbalance between calories consumed and calories expended.'[12]

This theory seems so logical that it's become the bedrock of understanding weight loss. In its essence, this theory is based on the school of thought where gluttony and sloth are the reasons for obesity. These experts were simply borrowing from the literature published in England since the 1960s. That is, the laws of thermodynamics and the energy balance equation (CICO – *see box*) are the root cause of obesity.

And voila! The laws of physics have been used to explain the biochemical mechanism of fat generation and fat loss. This drove home the point that excess calories in the body are converted into fat. And this in turn made everyone believe that obesity is the direct result of gluttonous and slothful behaviour.

Calories in, calories out

The first law of thermodynamics, otherwise called the law of energy conservation, states that energy is neither created nor destroyed. So the calories we consume should be burnt, stored or expended.

What does this mean for you and me?

Changes in body weight = calories consumed – calories burnt

If we consume and burn the same amount of calories, we maintain our current body weight or if we consume more than we burn, we gain weight. If we consume less than we burn, we lose weight.

In other words, it says that you need to move as much as you eat to maintain your current weight, and if you lead a sedentary life and consume more calories than you burn, you gain weight.

A lot of people believe that this *calories in, calories out* equation in weight management is an unchangeable fact.

Is obesity a psychological condition?

Louis Newburgh, an American physician and a professor at the University of Michigan in the 1930s, and Jerome Groopman, Professor of Medicine at Harvard Medical School in 2017, are among the prominent scientists who believe that obesity is a psychological condition caused by eating more because of 'unresolved emotional conflict'.[13] Basically, stress eating or emotional eating! Another lobby said that the psychological condition is a lame justification for overindulgence. They believed that lean individuals eat in moderation, have greater control over their appetite, and instinctively absorb calories only to the extent that they burn. Essentially, their body is so intelligent that they effectively combat semi-starvation and energy balance. These experts described obesity as 'the conviction of gluttony's primacy',[14] 'a disorder' of eating habits, 'a perverted appetite', a lack of 'willpower' and a perceived character flaw.[15]

Think of it like this: Say you're in a long conference meeting. Three hours later, an assistant brings in coffee and a plate of cookies. Someone reaches out and takes one cookie. Another has two. And a third, who is feeling very hungry, may eat three. According to the above obesity theory, the lean individuals in the meeting room will refrain or consume in moderation and the individual predisposed to be obese cannot simply help themself from over-consuming. Thus, reaching for food is a conscious act, a behaviour. Here, a person's willpower apparently determines their obesity problem.

Do you see the problem with this argument?

By this assumption, all calories are tolerated and processed identically in different bodies. If it were as simple as this, why don't we also grow taller if we consume more calories? Why does this assumption only apply to a horizontal growth pattern? Can we conclude that a child grew to be shorter than the average because he consumed fewer calories than he burnt or that his brother grew to be taller than him because he must have consumed more calories than he burnt? No, we cannot conclude that because genetics, the growth hormone and sex hormones influence the growth and fusion of the epiphyseal plate, which determines the individual's height rather than energy balance.

If the food pyramid works, why are we getting fatter and sicker?

The number of people who are overweight and obese in India doubled between 2005 and 2015.[16] One in five men is either overweight or obese in 18 of India's 22 states and union territories.[17]

Are we not following advice or are we simply getting bad advice?

Let's summarize what we've learnt till now.

We've learnt that the way to enjoy good health is by eating more whole grains, fruits and vegetables, and reducing fatty foods. We've also learnt that if we want to lose weight, we must reduce calories and burn any extra calories.

All this looks simple and convenient on paper. So no one addresses the elephant in the room: why are we getting fatter and sicker? Is it because we aren't following advice? To answer this question, I once again return to data because as the saying goes 'numbers don't lie'.

The image below shows the changes in annual food availability in the US published by the USDA.[18] It estimates how much of a particular food is consumed by the population each year. It is calculated by how much is produced countrywide, adding imports, subtracting exports, and estimating or adjusting for waste.

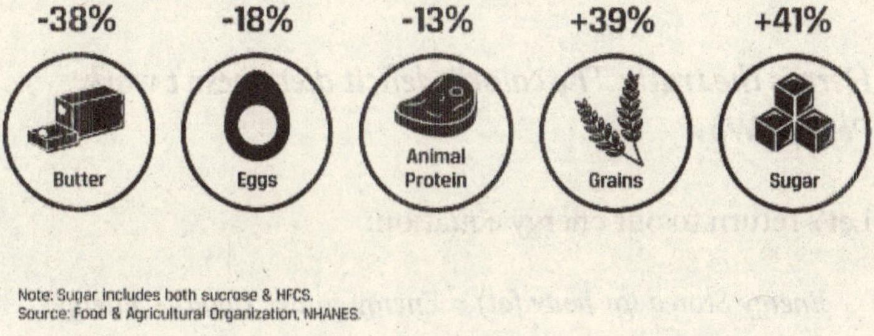

Visual representation of change in food availability in the US

This is where I'd like to stop and scratch my head. If the data indicates that we are indeed playing by the rules, then where are we going wrong? If it's not us, then what is it?

The big fat lie

What if I told you that everything you know, or have been told, about losing weight is a lie? That the diets you've tried and the fitness regimes you are currently on will work only till a certain limit, after which, there's a good chance that you'll gain everything you've lost and some more.

Does that sound terrifying to you? Or does that make me seem like a quack? Like a conspiracy theorist on the sidewalk, holding up a placard proclaiming that the world is coming to an end.

What if I told you that weight loss is simpler than it looks and that you can achieve your fitness goals and enjoy good health with a few tweaks to your lifestyle – does that sound more appealing?

Here is the truth: The calorie deficit diet doesn't work. Period. Why?

Let's return to our energy equation:

> *Energy Stored (or body fat) = Energy Intake (food) – Energy Expenditure (exercise or excretion)*

By this logic, we gain weight because we have overeaten, that is energy in > energy out. But we do not know how much eating is overeating. We know that we overate only because we gained weight. This equation does not give meaningful information about why people gain weight. Essentially, this is a tautology which is the round-and-round logical reasoning of an event. It's saying the same thing in two different ways without any explanation being offered for either. In fact, Edwin B. Astwood, a Bermudian-American physiologist and endocrinologist, and professor at the Tufts University School of Medicine, and Roxane Gay, an American writer, professor, editor and social commentator, along with many influential European clinical researchers in Germany and Austria, consider the CICO line of reasoning for obesity as *circular logic.*[19]

Here's a puzzle for you to solve.

A. What makes a person an alcoholic?
   1. They drink too much
   2. They drink every day
   3. They lack self-control

B. What will make them stop being an alcoholic?
   1. By drinking less or moderately
   2. By stopping drinking completely
   3. By exercising self-control

Unfortunately, none of these answers are correct. If they were, the implication would be that alcohol is the problem. Alcohol is not the problem because everyone who consumes it, even in small quantities such as a glass of wine, would be termed as an alcoholic or would one day become one. The drive to consume more alcohol than what the body can excrete (alcohol in > alcohol out or a positive alcohol balance) stems from the baseline neurochemical states and an abnormality in the brain triggered by emotions from events, relations and life situations, genes and childhood experiences. Willpower is also not an acceptable answer because alcoholism is generally a symptom of an underlying disorder. To treat this disease, a counsellor will first identify and work on correcting the underlying disorder. Advising an alcoholic to reduce alcohol intake is not effective.

The root cause of alcoholism usually lies in our circumstances – social, economic, and emotional. It has deeper, more nuanced roots. Children from troubled families may become alcoholics because they weren't given a safe and secure foundation to grow and flourish in. Children of alcoholics are four times more likely than other children to become alcoholics themselves.[20] They grow up lacking self-esteem and have a deep need to be loved, resulting in poor relationship choices, or they rebel and end up mimicking their parents. So when treating an alcoholic, we need to get to the root cause, and therapy is usually the best proven method.

Now let's apply this logic to food, eating and obesity.

If we've spent years trying to eat in moderation or eat less and have ended up diabetic and obese anyway, as many have, then perhaps the problem is not overeating.

In the next chapter, I'm going to deconstruct the calorie deficit diet to conclusively show you why it doesn't work with the help of our trusted friend – math.

2

Calories Don't Count

'The complicated mechanism of the body must be taken into consideration, and the ways it takes to reach its goals are not always the straight paths envisioned in our calculations.'

Max Rubner,
The Laws of Energy Conservation in Nutrition

The math doesn't add up

In his 1936 book, *Basal Metabolism in Health and Disease*, the American physician and teacher Eugene DuBois, stated: 'There is no stranger phenomena than the maintenance of a constant body weight under marked variation in bodily activity and food consumption.'[1] In other words, maintaining one's weight (or energy balancing) is an astounding feat because it's a complex biological process. Most lean people are probably not doing anything consciously to stay lean. He proved this by the following math:

First, let's establish the basics.

- 1 kg = 2.2 pounds (lb)
- 1 pound of body fat = 3,500 kcal of energy

DuBois had argued that if this hypothesis of the calorie balance equation was true, then by that logic a twenty-year-old who would gain 10 kg of fat in ten years would do so by simply overeating 21 kcal every day.

Thus, the amount of excess calories consumed over 10 years would be

22 lbs × 3500 kcal = 77,000 kcal of fat

The amount of excess calories consumed per annum would be

77,000 kcal/10 years = 7,700 excess calories

The amount of excess calories consumed per day would be

7,700/365 days = 21 kcal

The average basal energy requirement for an adult is 2,000 kcal/day.

This means that eating just 21 kcal over your daily calorie requirement would make you gain 22 pounds (10 kg) of fat in a decade! According to this explanation, eating a piece of chocolate after your meal would add nearly 1 pound of fat in 6 months, and thus 2 pounds in a year, which is equivalent to 1 kg of fat.

By this logic, it would mean that people who are thin or maintain a constant body weight for decades are math geniuses to be able to safeguard themselves against such a small margin of error (1.05 per cent)! 'The average human consumes one million or more calories per year, yet weight changes very little in most people. These facts lead to the conclusion that energy balance is regulated with a precision of greater than 99.5 per cent.'[2]

Do you see your lean friends and family doing this kind of math to stay the way they are?

I bet you they don't.

Research shows that calorie deficit diets are a hoax

The best research area to examine whether calorie deficit diets work is diabetes because the first treatment recommended for a type 2 diabetes patient is weight loss.

In one study, 699 patients were observed in a controlled setting for 60 months.[3] One group was given less food and was restricted from consuming foods high in fat and sugar. The diabetic group that ate less, exercised more and was administered the drug metformin to control their blood sugar did not lose weight for over 60 months!

In another diabetes prevention programme, 3,234 patients were observed in a controlled setting for 5.7 years.[4] All the participants lost only 2 kg (on average) after five years of lifestyle intervention including calorie deprivation and increased physical activity.

One of the most expensive and ambitious weight loss programmes conducted by the National Institutes of Health, US is the Women's Health Initiative, a study that focuses on the effect of a low-fat diet and increased exercise on women's health.[5] The study followed nearly 50,000 women for an average of seven and a half years in a large-scale randomized controlled trial. The participants were divided into two groups: the intervention (or experimental) group and the control group. The participants in the control group were given an educational leaflet on the importance of a low-fat, low-calorie diet and exercise, whereas the experimental group was observed under a strict and regulated environment, where they had to follow a reduced-calorie, low-fat diet and increase their physical activity.

In the first year, the average weight loss was around 2 kg. So the researchers calculated that the participants in the experimental group would lose around 13 kg by the end of the study. But by the end of the study, none of the participants in the experimental group lost any weight and there was no significant difference between the average weight of participants in the two groups!

Why and how did this happen?

One probable reason could be that by increasing the exercise regime, women gained muscle weight and lost fat. So the numbers on the weighing scale did not change. However, interestingly, the researchers looked at their waist to hip (WHR) ratio. The WHR matters because it would change if the women in the experimental group lost fat and gained an equivalent amount of muscle, as fat is typically carried around the waist. As it turned out, the average waist size of the women increased from 89 cm to 90.1 cm, resulting in an average WHR increase from 0.82 to 0.83. This means that not only did these women not lose any weight, they actually gained more fat than before the intervention![6]

The UK General Practice Research Database of 2004–14 shows that the probability of reaching a normal weight range through a low-fat, low-calorie diet and exercise is 0.6 per cent and if one is morbidly obese, 0.1 per cent.[7] Dr Elliott P. Joslin, the first doctor in the US to specialize in diabetes, wrote in his book *Joslin's Diabetes Mellitus* – considered the bible of diabetes – that the calorie deficit diet 'is the cornerstone of any therapy for obesity'. However, 'none of these approaches has any proven merit'.[8] In the *Handbook of Obesity*, the authors write, 'dietary therapy remains the cornerstone of treatment and the reduction of energy intake continues to be the basis of successful weight reduction programs', yet results of such diets are 'known to be poor and not long-lasting'.[9]

So the 'eat less-burn more' approach doesn't work and is bound to fail.

This is why if you've gone on a diet and lost some weight, you'll know better than me why it's so hard to maintain weight loss.

The Minnesota Starvation Experiment of 1945

In 1945, in the city of Minneapolis, US, a bizarre experiment was conducted by Dr Ancel Keys.[10] During this time, famine had ravaged Europe.

Keys wanted to understand the physiological effects of starvation. 'He convinced the military that a study of starvation could yield information that would have both humanitarian and practical benefits – because knowing the best rehabilitation methods could ensure the health of the population and thereby help democracy grow in Europe after the war. Having secured his funding, Keys set out on his novel experiment.'[11]

Thirty-six lean men volunteered for the study. Their energy intake was gradually reduced from 3,200 kcal/day (normal) to 1,570 kcal/day. The participants continued to exercise – walking a minimum of 22 miles/week. Their diet comprised carbohydrate- and starch-rich foods and lacked protein and fats. This diet followed the national guidelines at that time. The experiment ran for twelve months. These were Keys' findings:

- drastic drop in strength and energy
- fatigue and a feeling of being old
- mental apathy
- decline in concentration, judgement and comprehension
- the strong political opinions held earlier faded to irrelevance
- food became their overwhelming priority
- some men obsessively read cookbooks and stared at pictures of food with an almost pornographic obsession
- tantrums (scientists called this condition 'semi-starvation neurosis' developing into 'character neurosis')
- mealtimes became the high point of their day, and they were irritable if food was not served on time
- cheating on the mandated meal plan
- heart rate slowed drastically (55 to 35 bpm)
- their heart sizes shrank
- they felt cold all the time
- their metabolic rate dropped to conserve energy

- frequency of bowel movements fell to weekly
- blood volume dropped 10 per cent

When these men were allowed to finally eat properly, they consumed up to 10,000 kcal/day and regained 1.5 times the weight they had lost. Keys called this 'post-starvation obesity'.

Consider this: when we first went into lockdown in 2020 due to the COVID-19 pandemic, we hoarded food and supplies. We feared that we would not have access to food, and our natural instinct for survival kicked in. In many cases, people who could afford it spent way more than they naturally did on their monthly household budget. It's human psychology to indulge in things that we've been deprived of to compensate for ill feelings.

This Minnesota Starvation Experiment of 1945 is the best example to show that sometimes we are victims of poorly done research and struggle to differentiate between correlation and causation. Just because overeating is correlated with weight gain, it does not necessarily mean that *overeating is a cause of obesity*. If you've gained a few inches around your belly over time, it does not necessarily imply that it is a consequence of you eating too much and that you need to cut all calories as though they homogeneously affect fat tissues.

To become lean and reverse lifestyle diseases, we need to shift our focus to what is making us fat. In the next chapter, I'm going to let you into two aspects that affect how our bodies process fat and how we can use this information to better understand our bodies.

3

Metabolism Matters

> 'The literature on obesity is not only voluminous, it is also full of conflicting and confusing reports and opinions. One might well apply to it the words of Artemus Ward: "The researches of so many eminent scientific men have thrown so much darkness upon the subject that if they continue their researches we shall soon know nothing.'
>
> Hilde Bruch, *The Importance of Overweight*

The truth about *The Biggest Loser*

Have you watched *The Biggest Loser* – the hit American reality TV series that ran for fourteen seasons? In the show, contestants needed to cross a bunch of hurdles to lose weight and win a big cash prize. An inspiring watch that was also critiqued for its ruthless and schadenfreude attitude.

A study looked at the participants in Season 8 (2009) and compared the weight changes of the participants during and after the show.[1] The truth is that in the first 30 weeks after the show, they lost both fat and fat-free mass (water, bone density, and muscles), but the loss was concentrated on fat mass. The average weight loss was 91–149 kg and body fat 28–49 per cent. However, after the show, thirteen of the fourteen participants regained the lost weight, and four were heavier than before. A participant, Erinn Egbert was the only one who maintained her new weight even six years after the show. Everyone else gradually regained their weight to what it was pre-contest. Almost all the contestants burned fewer calories at rest than they did six years ago.[2] Why did this happen?

What is fat? Fat is an organ.

The idea that obesity is caused by overeating and weight is lost by undereating still seems to be a popular notion in the medical community. Doctors and nutritionists are invariably seen as the authorities who become the formal agents of propagating this knowledge in their practice. The first lesson given to aspiring medical school doctors is physiology and anatomy. In these lectures, all the different organ systems such as the cardiovascular, pulmonary, gastrointestinal, urological and endocrine systems are examined and dissected for a clearer understanding of their functions in the maintenance of the body, the pathophysiology of how they get diseased and how to treat these diseases. These lectures cover all the diseases that their patients would encounter. However, there is one significant omission: none of the organs examined and dissected sufficiently explain obesity – a condition that ails a quarter of the global population and leads to type 2 diabetes, cardiovascular diseases and blood pressure.

When the cadaver is dissected to understand the anatomy of the human body, the first layers of the body, the skin and the fat, are discarded for eventual incineration. A vital omission here is that the fat, a critical part of the body that orchestrates our metabolism, is rejected and trashed. The fat tissue is an organ that controls our appetite and metabolism. It interacts with the body and stores our energy reserves. As the students actively learn and dissect the organs such as the heart, lungs and kidneys, this crucial organ is ignored, discarded, and thrown into the dustbin.

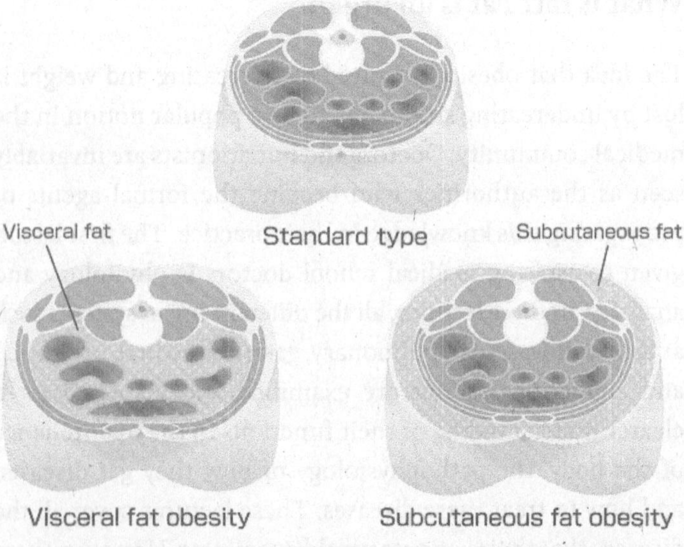

This image offers a cross-sectional view of the placement of fat around the key organs in the abdominal area

Even today, obesity-related training for doctors has not changed and is stuck in the 1980s. The researchers and experts in obesity are thus self-taught, and their outlook often differs from doctors, who still are dependent on the limited understanding they received in medical school. In this book, we will admit ourselves to my *virtual obesity school* to cover the subject that unfortunately remains ignored.

Fat – the energy store of the body

Fat, medically known as the adipose tissue, is a life-preserving and critical organ of our body. Fat regulates our energy. Fat cells (also known as adipocytes) assume a crucial responsibility in the survival of every mammalian species – from bats to elephants to humans.

It has three significant properties:

1. It is lighter compared to bones, muscles or organs. Thus, its transport in the body is energy efficient.
2. It insulates the organs and muscles against cold temperatures and inhibits significant loss of thermal or heat energy, particularly in cold climates. Mammals such as seals are covered in a thick layer of fat, which enables them to swim in ice-cold oceans. However, fat is stored only in a camel's hump, allowing the rest of its body to breathe in the 40° Celsius heat of the desert.
3. Fat can store a humongous amount of energy. Fat is a voluminous, light, and insulating energy material held in the body.

Every fat cell can store energy when there is famine or when the food supply is low. The more energy it stores, the larger it becomes, and the more swollen the fat cell becomes in size. In the initial phase of the fattening process, the body does not grow more fat cells. The number remains the same but every cell grows almost six times its original volume and becomes bloated with its stored energy. This phenomenon is called hyperplasia. When there is no more room left in the fat cell to store more energy, more fat cells are produced in the body and the number grows from an average of 40 billion to, in extreme cases, over 100 billion. The sad news is that if these fat cells are sucked out using surgical techniques such as liposuction (it's a common practice and only a short-term fix), the body simply rebuilds the fat cells as fat is deposited back in the body. This mechanism is the body's compensation as it aims to maintain homeostasis (more on this in the next chapter).

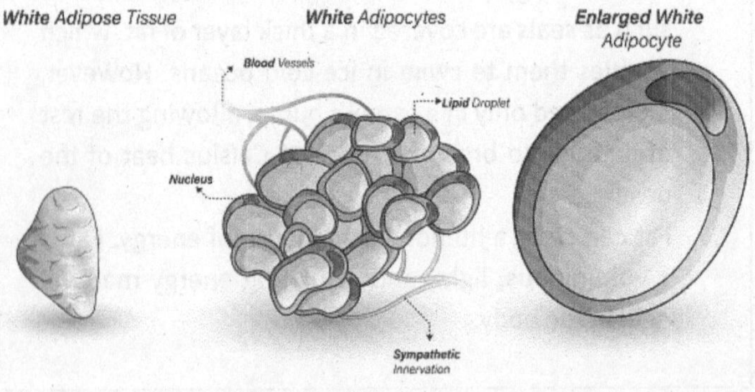

White Adipose Tissue

Energy storage is the most critical function of the fat organ for the survival of the human species during food shortages and famine. For example, the brain requires a steady supply of fuel (glucose) in the blood to function. When the food intake plummets, our fat cells and liver replenish the glucose levels to be readily available for the brain to use. There need not be an actual famine for our fat stores to be called upon for rescue. The body perceives a low-calorie diet as a famine. It cannot differentiate between the two. In cases where the energy requirements of the body are the same, but the food intake is reduced, the body relies on fat cells to provide the energy for our daily activities to make up for the energy deficit. Having a storage fuel tank of reserve energy in the form of fat, just like the one in our vehicles, is vital to our ability to survive, reproduce and raise the next generation. But here's the caveat: having larger fat stores isn't in our best interests because carrying around an oil tanker's worth of energy will significantly limit our ability to perform regular day-to-day activities. So the body controls the size of these fat reserves through self-regulation, very efficiently and cleverly via a negative feedback loop. I'll tell you more about this in the next chapter.

Circling back to *The Biggest Loser*, to understand why the participants on the show gained back all their weight (and more!), we need to unpack the meaning of metabolism.

What is metabolism?

Metabolism is the process by which your body converts what you eat and drink into usable energy. This energy is called adenosine triphosphate (ATP). This is our 'energy currency'. Even when you are at rest, your body needs energy for all its 'hidden' functions such as breathing, circulating blood, adjusting hormone levels, and growing and repairing cells.

Say you eat white rice, daal and subzi for lunch. Your body breaks it down to ATP. At the molecular level, all plant food is essentially a chain of glucose molecules bonded together. White rice is essentially a starch complex. Starch is a very large molecule and is broken down into glucose to get assimilated in the blood and reach each cell in our body. This process starts from the mouth, where the saliva containing salivary amylase (a digestive enzyme) is released by the salivary glands. It chemically breaks down the starch in white rice into smaller chains of glucose, assisted by chewing which breaks it down physically. After this, when the food is gulped down, it reaches the stomach, where hydrochloric acid and other enzymes and gut bacteria in the stomach break it down into glucose. This glucose then travels to the intestines and is absorbed into the bloodstream from the small intestine and becomes available for use by the body. This glucose is used constantly by the body and is stored in the form of glycogen in our liver and muscle tissues.

Basal metabolic rate (BMR)

Seventy per cent of our daily energy expenditure goes into bodily activities – maintaining heartbeat, controlling chemical reactions in the body, breathing and temperature control. Basal metabolic rate (BMR) is the number of calories required by the human body to sustain itself. In humans, it can vary from 1,500 kcal to 4,000 kcal depending on gender, age, body structure, genetics and muscle composition.

For example, if someone's BMR is 2,000 kcal per 24 hours, the individual burns 83 kcal per hour on average to ensure their body is functioning optimally. Suppose they go on a 1,500 kcal diet, their body will adjust to the low food intake by reducing its energy output (i.e., BMR) to 1,500 kcal per 24 hours. This means that the body will store more energy rather than using it for generating ATP, and the person will feel sluggish and slow.

Individuals usually think that they only burn energy or calories when they move and exercise. That is why the 'energy out' component of the energy balance equation is often misunderstood. In fact, most of the energy we expend in the day does not require us to move or be active and is not within our conscious control.

The concept of the 'basal metabolism' of an individual organism was pioneered by Adolf Magnus-Levy in 1893.[3] Basal metabolism is the energy an organism expends while at 'complete muscular repose', having fasted for at least twelve hours. As explained before, this energy that we use subconsciously is known as the BMR.

Approximately five out of seven parts of our daily calorie expenditure are not within our conscious control. This means that more physical activity is ineffective in tipping the energy balance towards 'energy out' to lose fat. It's grossly inadequate to think that one is storing fat because of not exercising more.

The remaining two parts (approximately 30 per cent of the energy) that we expend can be divided into two parts:

1. **Passive energy expenditure** = the calories we expend to get through our everyday lives
   Your energy could be expended for digesting food, cleaning, walking to work, doing a hobby, or moving around in the office. For most of us who don't have a manual job or don't exercise, this will make up most of the remaining 30 per cent of energy expenditure.

   Diet-induced thermogenesis
   Calories are burned to digest food via many chemical reactions and to store nutrients in the body. Max Rubner wrote in his 1902 book *The Laws of Energy Consumption in Nutrition* that heat is produced by the 'thermochemical tangle of breakdowns' that occur during digestion, that is 'diet-induced thermogenesis'. Researchers in the field of metabolism measure the resting metabolic rate (RMR) or BMR after twelve to eighteen hours of fasting, during which time the diet-induced thermogenesis that causes an elevated rate of calorie burning plays itself out. Max Rubner discovered that protein causes the highest diet-induced thermogenesis among the three macronutrients.[4] The larger the amount of protein digested to support tissues and organs, the greater is the heat production. The 'specific dynamic effect' of protein, as Rubner called it, is generally invoked as the justification to consume protein-rich diets for fat loss. It is believed that the process of

breaking down and utilizing protein requires more calories, which would ensure that those calories can't be used as fuel or stored as fat.

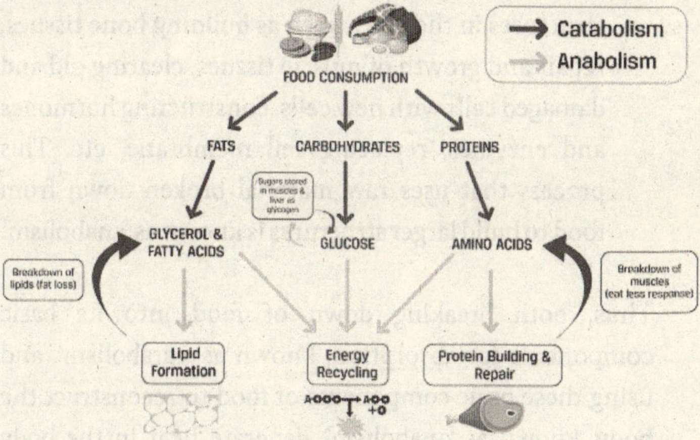

Diet-induced thermogenesis

As seen in the figure above, breaking down food takes energy and releases heat (*thermo* + *genesis* = heat production).

1) Heat is released when the food is 'catabolised' (breaking down food into its basic components for absorption) in the stomach from carbohydrates to glucose, proteins to amino acids, and fats to fatty acids.
2) Heat is released when glucose, amino acids and fatty acids are converted to ATP – the energy currency of our body through the process of cellular respiration, which leaves carbon dioxide and water as waste.

3) Metabolism not only refers to breaking down food and producing ATP but also encompasses the process by which the body also uses glucose, amino acids and fatty acids from food to make more complex structures in the body, such as building bone tissues, repair and growth of muscle tissues, clearing old and damaged cells with new cells, constructing hormones and enzymes, replacing cell membrane, etc. This process that uses raw material broken down from food to build larger structures is known as 'anabolism'.

Thus, both breaking down of food into its basic components for absorption, known as 'catabolism', and using these basic components of food to reconstruct the body, known as 'anabolism', generate heat in the body leading to thermogenesis, and together they are a part of our 'metabolism'.

Excessive post-exercise oxygen consumption (or afterburn)

When we do a workout with high intensity, resistance and speed, microscopic tears occur in our muscles. The repair and growth of these muscles require nutrients such as fat and oxygen and help in burning more calories throughout the day. This repair work lasts beyond the workout period and even for several days. During this time, our body experiences an increase in metabolic rate and energy requirements, even in the absence of mechanical or muscular movement.

2. **Active energy expenditure** = energy expended by active exercise
   For some individuals, energy can be expended during a run or workout session in the gym. For others such as construction workers, hunters and rickshaw drivers, active energy expenditure is a part of their lifestyle. For those living a sedentary lifestyle, like most of us working in metro cities, active energy expenditure may involve climbing a few flights of stairs or running for a bus, which contributes to just two or three per cent of our daily energy expenditure.

Myth: Basal metabolic rate is constant

Measuring 'calories in' is easy; however, measuring moment-to-moment 'calories out' is complex. A convenient yet baseless assumption made is that calorie expenditure stays constant.[5]

No two individuals have the same RMR/BMR. Total daily energy expenditure (TDEE) is based on exercise, excess post-exercise oxygen consumption, non-exercise activity thermogenesis, thermogenic effect of food and BMR. It can vary by as much as fifty per cent and goes up or down based on food intake and other factors. On average, men expend more calories than women and larger men more than smaller ones with huge variations. The average energy intake of humans is approximately 2,065 kcal/day. This translates to 8.64 million joules of energy each day (a day consists of 86,400 seconds). Using this information, we can calculate the energy power (or rate) that an average male utilizes each day. The power required to run a human body is approximately 100 watts – that's the same power needed for an incandescent light bulb. However, as stated, it is the average. The energy used can vary from 60 watts to over 240 watts. Just think of an individual's metabolism variability as a regulator connected to a bulb. It can be adjusted to make it shine brightly or glow dimly or anything in between.

Understanding the changes in metabolism is the key to controlling fatness or leanness. But metabolism is a complex and dynamic feature of our energy-modulating system. Researchers are unclear about how these metabolic alterations occur. Having treated hundreds of obese patients and studied the literature on metabolic differences, I believe that the two mechanisms responsible for metabolism are

1. Autonomic nervous system – sets the level of metabolic stress on one's body
2. Thermogenesis – generates heat from chemical energy

Stress and relaxation response of the central nervous system

We have no deliberate control over the autonomic nervous system (ANS). Our subconscious brain will ascertain whether we are in a comfortable or threatening environment and adjust our body's fuel regulation. If the brain perceives a threat around us, it will activate the fight-or-flight response. Say you are taking the bus to an all-important, life-altering meeting that you cannot afford to miss. As you approach the bus stop, you see the bus leaving the station. Irrespective of your fitness

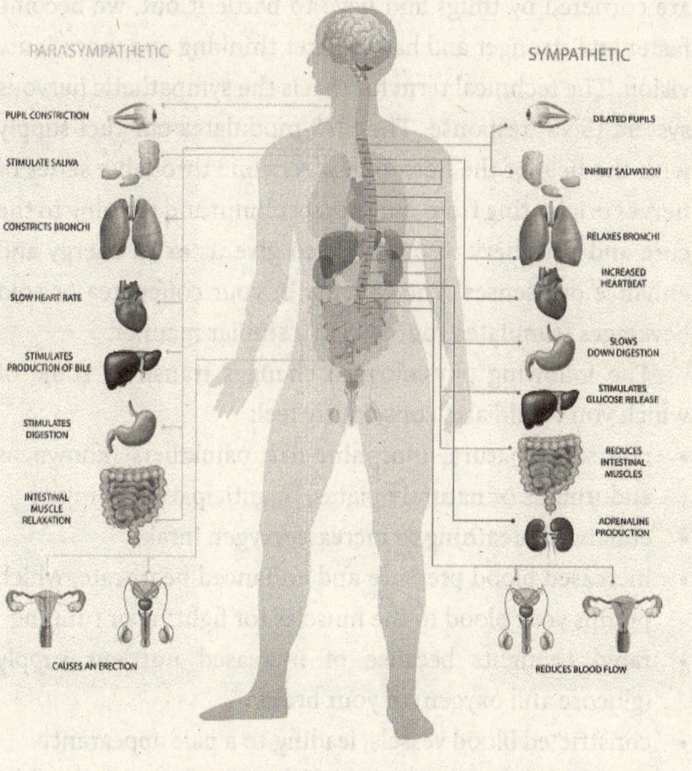

Responses of the central nervous system

level, you run after the bus like a professional athlete to catch it. When you look back on the incident, you will realize that you have achieved a superhero-like feat. How did it happen? Have you heard of the term adrenaline rush? If it hadn't been for your ANS response, you wouldn't have been able to do it. Once your body senses a life-deciding threat, it has an intrinsic ability to switch on the turbochargers, which is the fight-or-flight response. Whether we are running to save our lives or are cornered by thugs and have to battle it out, we become faster and stronger and have clearer thinking and more acute vision. The technical term for this is the sympathetic nervous system (SNS) response. The SNS modulates our fuel supply with the help of the hormone adrenaline through a series of nerves originating from our spinal column and running to the core and periphery of our body to give us extra energy and enhance our senses. The caffeine in your coffee, tea or cold beverages stimulates your SNS in a similar manner.

The following physiological changes transpire, some of which you would also consciously feel:

- release of natural morphine-like painkillers (known as endorphins or natural opiates) in anticipation of injury
- enhanced breathing to increase oxygen intake
- increased blood pressure and enhanced heart rate, which pumps your blood to the muscles for fighting or running
- rapid thoughts because of increased nutrient supply (glucose and oxygen) to your brain
- constricted blood vessels, leading to a pale appearance
- excessive sweating to cool the body down during the predicted exertion
- dilated pupils for enhanced vision

All these actions are part of our fight-or-flight response, which uses up a lot of our energy and the body can't maintain it for a long time. Eventually, the parasympathetic nervous system (PNS) is activated, which triggers a relaxation response. When this system is more dominant, our bodies focus on food digestion and relax into a more fuel-conserving state. When the brain perceives a safe environment, our breathing becomes more relaxed, which is an indication to our brain to reduce blood pressure and heart rate. In other words, the ANS supervises our body's energy distribution during perceived danger. What if this system also adjusts our energy expenditure to counteract energy excess or deficit (i.e., overeating or undereating)? When you change a car into a lower gear while driving, more fuel is consumed. Just like this, our body could increase energy expenditure after overfeeding by activating the SNS.

These two systems are orchestrated by hormones and nutrients that act like a messenger for our body to gauge whether it is time to be physically and metabolically active or time to be sedentary, rest and reduce the overall energy expenditure by reducing heat generation, anabolism and catabolism. In the next section, we will understand how hormones orchestrate these signals based on the energy available to it. Each cell in our body possesses nutrient sensors that are responsible for constantly gauging the nutrients available in their environment, and thus, the metabolism within the cell is altered accordingly to either initiate cell repair and inhibit growth when nutrients are difficult to come by or initiate cell growth and inhibit repair when nutrients are in abundance. For instance, hormones such as cortisol and adrenaline activate the SNS and make more fuel available to the body to think and exercise when we are well nourished, whereas serotonin and melatonin activate the PNS and make less fuel available (conserve energy) for the body when we are nutrient deprived and indicates drowsiness preparing the mind and the body to get lethargic, rest and sleep. Let's understand how nutrients, ANS and hormones are interlaced.

Hormones: The key to your weight loss

Here's a question to mull over: When we are asleep, how do we stay alive or rather, how is energy being released in our body?

One word: hormones.

To fulfil its energy needs, the body constantly toggles between using food energy and stored energy. Hormones decide whether our body should use food energy or stored energy. When we are at rest, energy comes from a stored reserve aka 'internal energy'. After a meal, our internal energy stores are blocked and our body uses the energy broken down from that meal. Whenever our hormonal balance goes haywire because of wrong or irregular food intake, the body spends a significant amount of time using food energy while keeping the fat stores locked. This eventually leads to fat gain. The amount of time our body spends using food energy while storing the excess energy versus the amount of time our body uses our stored energy makes all the difference to our net weight gain or loss. We assume that losing or gaining weight is easily adjustable and is within the conscious control of our behaviours. However, that is not the case. The fat stores, our body's energy system, are regulated intricately by our hormones like all other systems in our body including the parasympathetic, respiratory, gastrointestinal, sympathetic, adrenal, parathyroid, thyroid, circulatory, hepatic and renal.

In the 1890s, scientists believed that all the calories we consume will either be oxidized or metabolized and used as fuel or they'll be excreted or stored as muscle or fat. This gave birth to the 'calories in = calories out' equation, implying that fat stores are fundamentally unregulated, inert, and a trash can of excess calories. It was believed that calories are removed from the stores when calories in <calories out and more calories are stored when calories in > calories out. Then, scientists learnt about hormones. For instance, blood sugar is regulated by the hormones glucagon and insulin. Among others, growth in height is orchestrated by the growth hormone, free thyroxine and thyroid stimulating hormones modulate the temperature in the body, and the list goes on. We were told that fat cells are not intrinsically regulated, that our overconsumption and an immoderate and sedentary lifestyle will make us gain weight, and that underconsumption or moderated consumption and overactivity will result in weight loss. Ultimately, this assumption has been documented as untrue.

Now let's get back those participants on the show, *The Biggest Loser.*

When you go on a calorie deficit diet, two forces are working to make you regain your weight:

1. your BMR goes down
2. you are increasingly hungry as your body is trying to compensate for your drastic weight loss

For example, you lead a sedentary life. As we've discussed before, you do burn calories even if you aren't doing anything.

Let's say you burn 1,800 kcal/day when lying on your sofa and watching TV all day. One day, you decide, 'Enough is enough. I need to take control of my life, lose weight and get into shape.' You seek out a nutritionist and go on a diet. The nutritionist's advice to you is reduce your calorie intake to 1,200 kcal/day, creating a calorie deficit of 600 kcal/day. You go on a diet and lose weight. You are happy now, and you go back to your old daily routine because while you were underfeeding your body, you were also left hungry and dissatisfied. But your new body requires only 1,200 kcal/day to fuel your daily energy needs at this lower weight. The extra 600 kcal will get stored as fat for future use. And that is why the participants on the show gained back their lost weight.

In another experiment aimed at studying the relationship between calorie intake and BMR, the results were shocking.[6] When the participants were fed more than what their body needed (they gave each participant a milkshake every day!), they had an average weight gain of 10 per cent. Their bodies generated more heat to burn the excess calories, i.e., the metabolic rates of their bodies increased. When the participants maintained a calorie deficit, they lost weight but their BMR reduced by approximately 20 kcal/day even after they went back to their initial weight. For those participants who lost 10 per cent and 20 per cent of their initial body weight, BMR reduced by almost 300 kcal/day.

This means that their new bodies required less energy at rest than before. This also means that calorie deficit diets don't work! Your body simply adjusts its BMR based on your daily calorie intake.

To grasp this idea better and appreciate why calorie deficit diets don't work in the long run, it is vital to understand how the body likes to maintain a constant supply of energy in the short term to fulfil its energy requirements and, at the same time, perpetually anticipates and calculates the energy required in storage to ensure its future survival. The body juggles between these two questions and slowly adapts to the data points it receives from the environment through our actions to physiologically orchestrate our behaviours by hormones that signal hunger and satiety to maintain a 'homeostasis' of energy.

4

Our Bodies Don't Like Change: Homeostasis and Hunger Hormones

> 'Everything in food is science. The only subjective part is when you eat it.'
>
> Alton Brown

If it ain't broke, don't fix it

You'd be surprised how similar the human personality and human molecular biology are. If there's one thing most of us dislike, it is change. A change of jobs makes us uncomfortable on the first day. A change in routine is unnerving. Moving to a new city or country makes us anxious. Quitting smoking seems almost impossible. The first week of gym training is always both mentally and physically brutal. If we could, we would prefer to preserve our status quo indefinitely because it means we live in a comfort zone of predictability. And predictability means less stress and less anxiety.

Even though the human body has evolved and adapted quite efficiently, it is not a fan of change. It tries to maintain fairly stable conditions necessary for survival. We call this state *homeostasis*, which comes from the Greek words *homoios* meaning similar and *stasis* meaning standing.

'Homeostasis is the tendency not to stray from the range of favourable or ideal internal conditions. Such conditions must remain constant. Maintaining a stable internal condition is crucial to any form of living thing. Different physiological strategies are employed to maintain the proper functioning of a system despite the external environment's dynamicity. In fact, this capability is one of the hallmarks of being alive.'[1]

What does all this have to do with weight loss?

My answer: a whole lot.

Homeostasis: our body's negative feedback loop

The calorie balance equation and energy conservation are commonly cited as the root cause of obesity. But eating less and exercising more is utterly ineffective at fighting this, as we have seen, because there are metabolic forces at work in our body called the 'negative feedback system'. This is hardly understood or talked about.

Negative feedback systems can be found in any system – mechanical (e.g., machine), office policies and procedures or biological (e.g., humans). In these systems, a switch is connected to a sensor that detects the internal environment of the system. If any change occurs in the system, the sensor will detect it and the system will try to get back to its normal state from the changed state. An example of a negative feedback mechanical system is the air conditioner (AC) at home. When you set it to an automatic mode at 20 °C, the sensor in the AC will constantly monitor the room temperature and reduce the cooling effect when the room is cooler than the desired temperature and increases it when the room is hotter than the desired temperature. Similarly, the feedback mechanisms in our body protect our organs and keep itself on an even keel. Any harmful changes are immediately sensed and automatically counteracted to maintain health and order.

In the mid-1800s, the legendary French physiologist Claude Bernard noted that the primary feature of all multicellular living organisms is the interdependence of the organs and systems in the body to the whole. He proposed that living organisms are a 'harmonious ensemble'[2]; therefore, all physiological systems must collaborate to ensure the survival of the whole. To maintain the normality of our internal environment, the *milieu intérieur* as Bernard phrased it, the body maintains a fasting blood sugar level of 80–100 mg/dl, postprandial (after a meal) blood sugar level of below 200mg/dl and a body temperature of 36.5–37.5°C regardless of external factors. Bernard noted that every critical process in our body has only one aim: to conserve the internal environment. He also said that the body continuously adjusts all the parts of its biological ensemble to compensate for any external alterations.

In 1926, American physiologist and chairman of the Harvard Medical School, Walter Cannon[3] rekindled Bernard's idea of homeostasis and re-termed it as 'the wisdom of the body'. He noted that the volatile elements in our body have understood 'the trick of maintaining stability'. Technically, 'homeostasis' implies 'standing the same' but both Bernard and Cannon envisaged an idea similar to what systems engineers call dynamic equilibrium. That is, living systems alter with time and change in response to the forces exerted on them but perpetually work to reinstate the same equilibrium point, for instance, the approximate body temperature (37°C). Our body is an extraordinarily complex network of these interdependent homeostatic systems: maintaining a set level of energy stores and blood sugar and stabilizing blood pressure, body temperature, and mineral and electrolyte concentration (pH) in the blood – all adequately stable to sustain the moment-to-moment alteration of the external environment. Any lifestyle choice that will disturb this harmonic ensemble will trigger immediate compensatory responses throughout our body to reinstate the dynamic equilibrium.

Do we count the water we drink?

If we understand how our body regulates its water content, we can better understand how it regulates its energy content and energy requirement, i.e., fat release and storage. Our energy storage mechanism and hydration are indistinguishable.

Our kidneys produce at least 710 ml of urine each day to purify the blood. If the quantity of urine is below the standard amount, we may develop kidney failure. To maintain a margin of safety, our kidneys signal us to drink about double the amount of water as an insurance mechanism, i.e., if our survival requirement is 710 ml/day, our thirst switch is turned on to drink 1,500 ml/day. But the amount of urine produced is still the same. If we go without any water intake for a few hours, the kidneys sense this and signal the switch in the part of the brain that controls thirst and activates the 'water-in' switch. You start thinking about drinking water. The signal gets stronger the more dehydrated you get. At the same time, the kidney communicates with the brain to ratchet down the 'water-out' switch. During this time, you would pass a lesser amount of dark, concentrated urine to counteract your dehydration. Suppose too much water is available in the body (over-hydration), the sensor works in the opposite direction and switches off the first signal to the brain. Your desire to drink more water will be gone and you would pass loads of diluted urine. With less 'water-in' and more 'water-out', over-hydration is corrected.

In a heralded 1943 lecture, American physiologist Curt Richter called our body's tendency to adjust its behaviour in response to physiological requirements as complete 'self-regulatory' functions.[4] He said that one of the basic systems by which humans and animals maintain homeostasis is through behavioural adaptation. Thirst and hunger are manifestations for replenishing fluids and essential nutrients and calories. He also argued that physical activity is another example of this behavioural modulation. Our body dictates the level of physical activity – expends excessive energy in surplus or conserves enough energy in deficit – to maintain internal balance.

Fortunately, all doctors know about the hydration system

in our bodies as this is taught in medical school. Unfortunately, when it comes to a disease like obesity, the standard theory is 'calories in' versus 'calories out'.

Negative feedback loop of obesity – understand this to lose weight

When there is abundant energy available to the body, our metabolism rate is boosted (more calories are burned) and appetite is suppressed. When the body is in energy deficit, appetite is stimulated and metabolism plummets (calorie burning is reduced to preserve our fat stores). This system exists to maintain your fat reserves at a constant level. This might seem odd at first but is an important part of most biological systems.

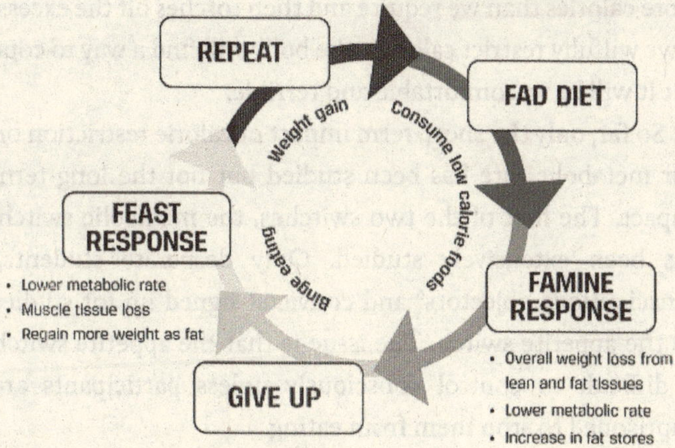

The vicious eat less cycle

How does this work?

If we consider that our fat regulation mechanism mirrors our hydration system, it would have two switches and a sensor. The sensor would monitor the energy stored in our fat tissue and when it detects a change in the quantity of fat stored (more or less), it releases a hormone that communicates messages to two switches:

1) our basal metabolism – the energy we burn
2) our appetite – the calories we consume

Just like our hydration system, the fat regulation system would also signal for higher calorie consumption than required. To recap, even though our body needs only 700 ml of water per day to survive, our built-in insurance system compels us to drink 1.5 l, that is, double the amount. Similarly, perhaps our energy-regulating mechanism guides us to eat more calories than we require and then torches off the excess. If we wilfully restrict calories, the body will find a way to cope but it will be uncomfortable and terrible.

So far, only the short-term impact of calorie restriction on our metabolic rate has been studied but not the long-term impact. The first of the two switches, the metabolic switch, has been extensively studied. Only desperate students,[5] conscientious objectors[6] and convicts[7] signed up for studies on the appetite switch. The issue is that the appetite switch is difficult to control consciously unless participants are imprisoned to stop them from eating.

We accumulate fat even when we don't eat too much

Australian endocrinologist and clinician researcher Dr Priya Sumithran and her team put fifty overweight or obese patients on a calorie deficit diet.[8] During the first eight weeks, they witnessed drastic weight loss – from an average of 98 kg (baseline) to 83 kg. After that, something surprising happened. The subjects hardly lost any weight, which stagnated for the next ten weeks. After that, they began to regain the lost weight.

There have been countless experiments like this to show that calorie deficit diets don't work.

Now, let's understand why it happens.

Think back to the lockdown days. What did you feel when you read about shortages? Did it make you anxious? Did you rush to the shops to stock up? Our body feels the same way when we start reducing the amount of food we normally eat and becomes vigilant. As we have learnt in the previous chapter, when we deprive the body of food or when we are at rest, the body sources its energy (or ATP) from the fat tissue. Think of it as a fixed deposit. When the body realizes that its fixed deposits are suddenly being depleted, it goes into preservation mode because it doesn't like change. It wants to re-establish the homeostasis of fat storage. So it will adjust basal calorie expenditure – by reducing body heat and breaking down muscle tissue – to regain its fixed deposits to former levels. This is one of the reasons why folks with less body fat feel colder than those with more.

When you lose a drastic amount of weight following the

CICO method, the body's fat reserves drop tremendously and quickly. So it finds ways to compensate this energy imbalance and lower weight by:

- slowing your heart rate
- reducing your blood pressure
- increasing your obsession with food
- reducing the frequency of your bowel movement
- shrinking your heart muscle

On a reduced calorie regime, the body prioritizes sending calories into storage. This triggers a bunch of ripple effects. If the calories are being hoarded for storage, then there is not much being released by the body to fuel other vital functions such as heat regulation, muscle, bone tissue and immune cell synthesis, or energy utilization at the organs and muscles. What will that do to your heart, lungs, brain, which need ongoing calories to operate? They will not function optimally.

After all this, your metabolic rate is lower at your new weight and if you start eating normally, you gain weight.

So up until now, we have understood the important ideas and concepts involved in the body orchestrating our energy expenditure by switching between its two autonomic systems which are SNS, when food intake increases and PNS, when food intake plummets. Along with this when we follow a calorie deficit diet, the body not only dims our metabolism, but it also simultaneously strengthens its appetite signals so that we are preoccupied with trying to find food, intensifying our urge with time to consume food. These two switches in our body are orchestrated by a censor that assesses the energy available for use and in storage to maintain the homeostasis. So, our body is an intelligent and adaptive being, rather than a passive and isolated being, that adapts quickly to the amount of calories it is provided and in fact gets very uncomfortable when food supply drops with uncertainty transpiring and thus prioritizes energy storage over expenditure to ensure future survival. The popularly held belief that energy is largely burned, and calories are expended through our conscious actions and behaviour of exercising regularly is untrue. The major portion of calorie out or energy expenditure is not due to our conscious actions, but it is orchestrated through the subconscious mind that controls the autonomous functions in our body by driving our sympathetic and parasympathetic nervous systems. Thus the homeostasis function in the body of energy balance is the most crucial element in energy expenditure which in part is dictated by the composition of nutrition intake. In the next chapter, we will see and debunk some of the popular notions surrounding the energy balance equation and some implicit assumptions that are famously invoked to explain obesity, weight gain, maintenance and loss of weight.

5

The Calorie Hysteria

'We can begin [the treatment of obesity] by looking at the situation as it exists and not as we would like it to be.'

Albert Stunkard and Mavis McLaren-Hume

The conventional wisdom on fat regulation argues that the energy balance equation predicts fat accumulation and fat loss in the body. That is, if we keep our calorie intake (energy in) constant and increase exercise (energy out) so that energy out > energy in, we will slowly lose weight. This idea and concept is a well-accepted law in physics in closed systems; for instance, say if you have 1,000 millilitres of gasoline filled in your vehicle's fuel tank and after using your vehicle, it has come down to 500 ml, and no gasoline is added. It can be reasonably concluded that 500 ml has been utilized. So indeed, the equality criteria is fulfilled, and we have 500 ml (energy left) = 1,000 ml (energy in) – 500 ml (energy out). It must be true! However, as we have seen in previous chapters, our body is not a closed system, and we do not consciously control our appetite (energy in) and basal metabolism (energy out). If we do not feed the body when it requires energy, then it will ratchet down our metabolic rate to compensate for and replenish our fuel reserves. So, our body is an open system that regulates itself on the basis of the energy it receives and the environment in which it finds itself. Our biology does that to maintain homeostasis through hormones to alter our metabolic rate and appetite for food. The following pertinent question is the biggest test for energy balance theory in predicting the rate and magnitude of gain or loss of body fat.

The energy equation – Can fat be equal to zero?

You decide to go on a week's vacation to your favourite destination. All week, you laze on your bed and watch your favourite TV shows and movies. You order your favourite food off the menu and count calories based on what is written on the menu. Every day, you have a calculated intake of 2,200 kcal. After the vacation, you feel lazy and think you have gained weight. You consult a dietician, and the first thing that they do is calculate your BMR using the Mifflin-St Jeor formula. Medical and dietetics students are taught to use an individual's weight, height, age, and sex to calculate this BMR. This will estimate the energy that your body burns per day, and from that, your dietician will tell you how many calories you need to consume each day to maintain your weight, lose it or gain more. This is estimated using the first law of thermodynamics, that is, energy stored = energy in – energy out. Many smartphone apps and health websites also use this formula to let you know your estimated caloric requirement.

Say your BMR is calculated as 1,700 kcal/day.

This equation will give you the fat you think you have gained during your vacation:

2,200 kcal – 1,700 kcal = 500 kcal/day

For a week, it is 500 kcal x 7 days = 3,500 kcal/week

This roughly calculates to 1 lb of fat tissue in your body (which means around 0.45 kg because 1 kg equals 2.2 lbs). Scientists have calculated that 1 lb of fat in your body has approximately 3,500 kcal of energy. You will be recommended to create a calorie deficit of 500 kcal per day, that is, a negative energy balance, by eating less and moving more to bring your weekly weight down by 1 lb until the desired weight is achieved. If you continue to eat 2,200 kcal per day, you will be asked to burn 2,700 kcal per day – 1,700 kcal used by your body at complete muscular repose and 1,000 kcal burned through exercise. However, this approach has a problem: in theory, it is possible to bring down the pounds of fat even to zero by this math. But that's not truly possible because your metabolic forces[1] are working to keep your weight within a constant range. There is a reason why humans, as a species, have been able to evolve and survive over millions of years. Our homeostatic survival mechanisms have evolved through numerous cycles of feast and famine and prevented body weight fluctuations beyond specific points of hunger and satiety by fine metabolic tuning to ensure our survival.

In this chapter, I will be busting some calorie-related myths, all of which centre around this CICO equation.

A calorie is NOT just a calorie

Are all calories equally fattening? 'A calorie is a calorie' suggests that the only significant factor in our food and weight gain is the total calories consumed. Every food we consume is ultimately mapped down to its energy value. For more than three decades, nutritionists and public health officials have used this logic.

In 1878, Max Rubner[2] first demonstrated that a calorie of protein supplies the same energy as a calorie of carbohydrate or fat to the body. He originally called it the isodynamic law of macronutrients. Nutritionists distilled this notion over the years to the famous phrase 'a calorie is a calorie.' Rubner also identified that fat possesses more than twice as many calories per gram as carbohydrates or protein. He also suggested more than a century ago that 'the effect of specific substance upon the glands' was perhaps a more important component in weight regulation. He said that the impact of each macronutrient on hormones secreted by the glands is markedly different and this determines how the body commissions those nutrients. He also said that the caloric equivalence of the foods themselves is irrelevant to the fattening process.

A 2004 study[3] concluded that 'a calorie is a calorie' and yet admitted that an isocaloric diet (having approximately the same calorific value each day) of high protein and low carbohydrates may lead to more weight loss than a low-fat diet.

Does a beer calorie cause an identical metabolic or hormonal response as a calorie from ghee? Of course, the answer is no. Anyone who has studied basic physiology and metabolism knows this for a fact. These two foods have different metabolic consequences. Beer, which is full of carbohydrates, will elevate the blood sugar level and trigger an insulin response through the pancreas. Ghee, which is a fat, will not increase your blood sugar or insulin because fat is absorbed and transported to the liver.

How do we convert the food we eat into energy?

Food has to be broken down to its simplest chemical form, which happens during digestion. After we chew our food, it reaches our stomach, where it is mixed with stomach acid and slowly released into the small intestine. Nutrients are drawn out of the small and large intestines as the food slowly travels through them and the remainder is excreted. Carbohydrates, proteins and fats are broken down into their component parts of glucose, amino acids and fatty acids, respectively. Amino acids are primarily utilized to develop and repair organs and muscles, and the rest are used to synthesize hormones, enzymes and neurotransmitters. Fatty acids are directly absorbed into the body and are stored in every single cell, a significant portion of which is stored in the nervous system. All these macronutrients provide energy for the body but have different metabolic pathways and so elicit different hormonal responses – whether the food goes into storage or is released for use by the body.

Calorie intake and expenditure are NOT independent variables

This is a critical mistake. The conventional notion is that calorie intake and calorie expenditure are independent variables, as mathematicians would call it, that is, a change in one will not affect the other. But many experiments and anecdotal experiences have confirmed that this assumption is wrong. Have you heard of the concept of working up an appetite? When we want to be hungry to enjoy an all-you-can-eat buffet, we work up our appetite by eating less food before and doing more physical activity. In reality, energy in and energy out are interlinked. Change in one drives a corresponding change in the other. Because our body weight is regulated, the energy stored in our body is fixed at a specific range based on our physical environment and genetics. When we increase our 'calories out' with exercise, it influences our 'calories in' as we get hungry and build up an appetite. When we decrease our calorie intake, we feel lethargic (less 'calories out') because the body wants to conserve energy for essential bodily functions, just as any practical person would do if they lost their job and have to cut down on their expenses. The outcome is the stalling of weight loss.

We DON'T have conscious control over our calorie intake or expenditure

We assume that because eating is an intentional act, we have control over when we eat and hunger signals have only a tiny role in it. The reality is that many imbricate hormonal pathways dictate our choice of food intake and food abstinence. Satiety is a state of 'no appeal for food' because our body already has sufficient energy to burn. For instance, we feel hungry at mealtime, and the smell of grilled food stimulates our appetite to drive us to consume food. But, after we have completed a meal and have acquired all the calories and nutrients we require from the feast, those same scents of food make us feel somewhat nauseated. Our bodies possess an innate mechanism to steer us to consume food (or not). Like our heartbeat, the body-fat store regulation is automatically controlled.

Wrong: The fat or energy stores in the body grow because of overeating, not exercising enough, indulging in the comforts of the modern world, being greedy and not caring for the body.

Right: Hormones decide both energy intake and energy expenditure. Thus, the ultimate cause of weight gain is an imbalance of hormones in the body and not an imbalance of calories.

Obesity is NOT because of excess calorie consumption

We have made a fundamental error by confusing correlation with causation. The law of conservation explains that calorie is neither created nor destroyed, and the energy we consume through food will either be stored, expended, or excreted. These laws only explain energy balance without the mechanisms and individual differences. These laws don't explain why an obese individual does not adjust his intake to his expenditure.

Traditionally we have believed that the fat stored in our body is the difference between what we consume and what we burn.

Energy or fat stored = energy in – energy out

But that is only one way to look at the equation. An alternative view is that the fat stored (the left-hand side of the equation) causes a change in 'energy in' and 'energy out' (the right-hand side of the equation). If more energy is pulled into the fat stores, they grow in size and less is available for the body to use. If this alternative view holds true, a growing fat tissue will increase appetite and reduce energy expenditure, whereas a reducing fat tissue will increase satiety and energy expenditure. Both the conventional and alternative cases are equally possible because both satisfy the rule of equality in the energy balance equation. There is no arrow of causality in one specific direction. The cause for 'calories in > calories out' could actually be due to an abnormality in our fat tissue regulation (energy or fat stores). That is, the amount released for the body's use versus the amount stored for the growth of the fat tissue. It could be like a cancer cell that lives for itself. This could lead to increased appetite and indolence in the obese.

Conventional view: 'Energy in – energy out' causes weight gain or weight loss
Alternative view: Weight gain or weight loss causes 'energy in – energy out'

Think of your metabolic forces as a software that drives your body, the hardware. If the software is configured to store energy rather than release it, you will have eaten food frequently for energy. If your software is configured to release energy from its fat stores, you will hardly need to eat frequently. The best example is the hormonal changes that drive pregnant women to accumulate fat. In this scenario, increased fat stores would ensure the availability of necessary fuel to carry the baby to term and nurse it after birth from an evolutionary point of view. The mother's weight loss postpartum may also be modulated by hormonal changes. The experts have failed to grasp this fact and perpetuate misconceived notions and practices in the field such as undereating for weight management.

Doctors are taught that height growth is driven by the growth hormone but the growth of fat tissue is driven by excess eating or inactivity. Imagine a world in which excessive height growth was the issue! In this scenario, we would certainly not be looking at the calories that the person consumes but the abnormality in growth hormone secretion and its treatment. The obese have a genetic predisposition to amalgamate slight excesses of fat in their adipose tissue[4], which prompts compensatory responses from their bodies to consume slightly more calories or use slightly fewer calories than the lean. Their set body weight and body fat storage levels will be higher than the lean. They will gain fat until the underlying abnormality is treated.

The fundamental question then is: what are the hormonal and metabolic deviations that make them store a higher amount of fat?

Patients with type 1 diabetes, due to their physiological condition and abnormality, feel hungry frequently until treated with the proper medication. The underlying defect is that neither the body can use the sugar for cellular energy nor is the body able to convert it into fat. As a last resort, the body excretes the excess sugar in the body via urine to bring down the blood sugar levels from near toxic levels. This results in frequent urination and glucosuria (that is, sugar in the urine). Imagine if doctors tried to treat this condition with psychological counselling rather than medicine to correct this physiological defect. What would be the success rate of such a treatment? Do we question the morality of a diabetes patient for frequently drinking water and wanting food? No we don't, because we discern their problem in the body and correct it with insulin medication to control their blood sugar and reinstate the normal physiology of glucose metabolism. We should take a similar deep view to understand the physiological dysregulation in individuals who are gaining weight but want to lose it to treat it correctly and have better treatment outcome.

What looked like a cause could actually be the effect. German-born American psychiatrist Hilde Bruch,[5] who treated obese children in 1940, noted that 'emotional experiences' and 'life situations' such as 'overprotection' and 'maternal rejection' aroused 'increased desire for food' in a specific type of individual. Such a stimulus leads to fat gain only when an individual has a 'special tendency to store fat' in higher quantities than others and does not simultaneously increase calorie expenditure. Further, she noted that the efficacy of any therapy for obesity could be valued only by the 'permanence of the results'.[6] She was intrigued by the apparent ease with which some children could lose weight once she gained their trust and cooperation. Having tracked such cases over two decades, she was even more galvanized by the 'speed with which they will regain lost weight and by the tenacity with which they maintain their weight at an individually characteristic high level'.[7] When she tried forcing the weight below one's individual level, she found 'such efforts are usually short-lived.' She realized that the typical explanation for this phenomenon is that excessive calorie intake is a symptom and not the cause of obesity and that the conventional treatment of a calorie deficit is not the solution. She studied and tracked many obese individuals over a prolonged period and concluded that food is essential for 'the maintenance of life in general' and 'for obesity'. Even though overeating was common in obese individuals, it 'is not the cause'. Instead, 'it is a symptom of an underlying disturbance'. A compulsion for 'overeating' and the alterations in 'weight regulation and fat storage' system are the primary disturbances. In her 1973 book, *Eating Disorders: Obesity, Anorexia Nervosa and the Person Within*, she wrote that she suspected that a 'primary metabolic or enzymatic disorder' is the cause of obesity based on a growing body of literature. She acknowledged that clinicians must study human obesity to recognize the nature of this disorder and should clearly differentiate between the 'cause of obesity' and 'the result of it'.

All my clients acknowledge that their obesity leaves a psychological impact. A 1973 *New York Times* article[8] suggested that the obese eat very fast, do not take time to chew their food, and are inordinately sensitive to external prompts that entice them to eat, while not being responsive to the internal signals of satiety. During that time, obesity was classified as an eating disorder, and the treatment for obesity had transformed into a subdiscipline of psychology and psychiatry. Whatever the terminology, all of these behavioural treatments try to correct a defect in willpower. Every effort to treat obesity involves making the person eat less and move more, which attributes a psychological-behavioural cause to the disease. If that were true, then wouldn't it 'cause obesity in everyone?', observed endocrinologist Hugo Rony.[9] After all, everyone has a pleasure-seeking outlook towards life, even those who are non-obese. Obviously, such a mental state in itself is insufficient for causing obesity. Those who are obese evidently have an innate 'tendency to obesity'.

In 1940, Rony wrote that an obese individual who sustains his weight at 136 kg is in a 'caloric equilibrium' similar to any individual of regular weight. An 'energy in > energy out' might help us understand his weight gain but does not tell us why the individual maintains that weight, why his body counters any attempts to lose weight, and why the individual tends to regain weight after successful weight loss. The obesity-research community has largely neglected the scientific and logical insufficiencies of 'overeating and sedentary behaviour' theory. When we allege that obese people 'eat a lot' or 'overeat', I want to ask you: compared to whom?

A frequent observation in obesity research is that overweight individuals consume no more than lean individuals. British physiologists R. Passmore and J.V. Durnin wrote in 1967[10] that obese individuals might not eat as little as they think or claim they do but also don't consume any more than others. When the food consumption of a group of obese individuals was studied, it was observed to be 'no greater than' a control group of individuals of normal weight. Some obese individuals naturally ate less and were not gluttons. However, these scientists didn't ask the question: how such abstinence would make a person fat? The only viable explanation for obesity despite moderation is the mysterious conservation of calories. If not, how does one explain why they stay fat while others easily stay lean on the same diet? Why would somebody overeat or be sedentary if the outcome is obesity? Only two possible explanations exist:

1) obesity is driven by a hormonal or metabolic disorder
2) obesity is within their control and the obese lack the willpower that lean individuals possess

Irrespective of the accepted wisdom, terming obesity as a behavioural problem is infinitely paradoxical. In 1978, Susan Sontag noted in 'Illness as Metaphor'[11] that the notion that a disease is a result of 'mental states' and can be remedied by 'willpower' is always an indication of how much is not understood about the 'physical terrain of a disease'. This is definitely the case with obesity.

Consider this: as losing weight plummets total energy expenditure, many obese individuals blame slow metabolism as the cause of their weight gain condition. However, research[12] shows that obese individuals possess a higher metabolism. The average total energy expenditure of lean volunteers was 2,404 kcal, whereas obese volunteers, despite the less physical activity, had an average total energy expenditure of 3,244 kcal. This is because an overweight body does not try to gain weight but attempts to lose it.

Our bodies will work to restore the lost fat stores by increasing our hunger levels through the action of the hormone ghrelin and suppressing the satiety hormones, peptide YY, cholecystokinin, and amylin. Suppose the food is still difficult to come through. In that case, our bodies will reduce overall calorie expenditure by lowering metabolism and regulating heart volume, blood pressure, body temperature and heart rate in a distressed attempt to preserve calories. As a result, fatigue, cold and hunger are experienced – a situation that all dieters are well versed with. This is better understood by researchers who study malnutrition than experts who specialize in studying obesity. Prakash Shetty, former director of Nutrition Planning, Assessment and Evaluation Service at the United Nations' Food and Agriculture Organization, explained that a change in the secretion of hormones such as insulin and glucagon changes the metabolic response to calorie restriction.[13] He also said that these physiological changes are metabolic adaptations aimed at improving the 'metabolic efficiency' and fuel distribution to the tissues during energy deficiency in the body.

Keith Frayn, professor of human metabolism at Oxford University, wrote in his 2010 textbook on metabolic regulation[14] that 'it is a fight against mechanisms which have evolved over many millions of years precisely to minimize its effects. As food intake drops, the thyroid hormone level falls, and metabolic expenditure plummets. Food intake has to be reduced further to drop below the energy expenditure level. Hunger mechanism, including the feeling of an empty stomach, results in a search for food.' The conventional response to the inability of semistarvation diets to generate long-term weight loss results has been to criticize the overweight individual for lack of focus and willpower. However, obesity has nothing whatsoever to do with any kind of moral failure or a lack of willpower.

Hugo Rony, Hilde Bruch and others have said that the failure of semistarvation informs[15] us that overeating or positive caloric balance is not the cause of obesity. Whether we exercise more or eat less, it will only decrease our basal energy expenditure and/or make us hungry to compensate for lack of energy entering the body. So the change in our fat stores is not the consequence but rather a cause of the disease. Overeating does not cause fat gain, but getting fat makes us eat more and move less. Excess calorie intake is not a personal choice but it is because of elevated hunger hormones. Just like in type 1 diabetes, high blood sugar, chronic weakness, urination, thirst and hunger are symptoms and not the cause of the disease, similarly hunger and indolence are symptoms not cause of fat accumulation.

The critical point is not how many calories are eaten or

how much is burned but how the energy or those nutrients from food are dispensed and used. It's not the calorie balance that is driving our system but the demand and distribution of energy at the cellular level. Proposing that our energy stores are under our voluntary control because we can control our eating behaviour is like thinking that breathing is under our voluntary control because we can consciously exercise holding our breath.

For instance, when we move to the mountains from sea level, the air becomes thinner, the subconscious brain will recognize the environmental change and automatically adapts by breathing more deeply for us. In the same fashion, I believe that for some of us, the quantity and quality of calories we consume will affect how our brain calculates how much energy should be stored and how much to distribute in the body.

Obesity is not caused by excess food intake but by excess fat accumulation.

The real questions to be asked are:

1) Why do fat cells accumulate fat?
2) What drives the body's choice to store certain amount of calories as fat? The body could have easily used all the energy from food to generate body heat, build and repair muscle tissue or excrete the excess.
3) Can our food environment and genes influence how hormones in our body interact with our fat tissues?

So, in this chapter, we have understood that the conventional treatment of obesity or weight gain is an energy deficit lifestyle using the energy balance equation, which is popularly applied to cure the disease. Still, its implications and inherent assumptions do not apply to an open system such as our biology. A low-fat, high-carbohydrate caloric deficit diet is prescribed along with an exercise regime as a remedy to weight gain. The primary rationale for adding exercise to the weight gain intervention is not to improve fitness but to burn calories and maintain a deficit further. This leads to less 'energy in' and more 'energy out' creating an energy deficit in the body. The abrupt and sudden change in energy balance also means that our body starts to initially give up more fat than it is used to but eventually becomes uncomfortable at the rate at which it is losing energy. As a result, it adjusts to the new low level of energy input and a higher level of energy output by reducing our BMR to compensate and go into an energy conservation mode, like an electrical appliance at our home in standby mode. Though it is powered, it does not do anything.

Additionally, the increase in appetite as a result of less 'energy in' will encourage food-seeking behaviour, leading to stalling of your weight loss goals and the weight coming back up as increased fat stores. When this inevitable failure happens, the approach or treatment protocol is not criticized for its failure to reap results, but the dieter is blamed for lacking the willpower to see the plan through and achieve the set objective. Thus, obesity is treated as a disorder of motivation and willpower, which are psychological aspects in the treatment through counselling. Deeming the weight gain problem as being a psychological condition that can be treated by bringing the focus back and realigning behaviours to eat less and exercise more is problematic and ineffective. A better and more effective manner to treat the problem of weight gain would be to treat the disease as stemming from a defect in the physiology of energy systems orchestrated by our hormones and our subconscious brain. Weight gain problems should not be treated to instil motivation and correct other psychological issues but to understand the physiological differences between individuals and consider treating it through good nutrition and other lifestyle factors. The underlying abnormality of hormones in the body can be corrected which in turn will correct the fat tissue regulation through the brain - will reduce overeating and could correct energy regulation in the fat tissue - thus the body will get the energy from its stores for daily activity.

Recently, various theories and mechanisms implicate our genes and our environment in the aetiology of weight gain. Then at the same time, the theorists who believe in the CICO model of obesity treatment dismiss the role of genetics and food environment and believe without any reservation that as long as we eat less and exercise more, weight loss is inevitable. They argue that there is nothing incredibly fattening about the processed foods rich in ingredients such as white flour, added sugar and refined oils we find in our urban environment because a calorie is a calorie, nor there are genes that decide our body size. Only overeating is a factor in obesity and weight gain. So, what is the truth? Do genes and food environment play a role in determining our body size?

Let's find out the answers in the next chapter.

6

Are Genetics or Toxic Food Environment to be Blamed?

> 'A colleague once defined an academic discipline as a group of scholars who had agreed not to ask certain embarrassing questions about key assumptions.'
>
> Mark Nathan Cohen,
> *Health and the Rise of Civilization*

Are there any external and autonomous factors that cause fat accumulation? Yes. Is it the fault of the modern world where we consume toxic foods day in and day out? Is it a genetic problem? Yes and no. Read on to find out.

Should we blame snacking?

French fries, cheese curls, chocolates, candy, soft drinks, potato chips, cheeseburgers, drive-throughs and supersized portions – all of these have become a fabric of our life just as trees, grass and clouds. Experts at Harvard School of Public Health[1] credited the manufacturers of TV shows and computers as abettors of a sedentary lifestyle – few children bike or walk to school, and there is a lack of physical education which is keeping children inside and inactive to play video games and watch TV.

As per a WHO report,[2] as populations became more urban and incomes rose, there has been a nutritional transition from diets high in complex carbohydrates to diets high in sugars, added fats and saturated fats. The report also noted that the accompanying shift towards physically less rigorous job profiles, passive leisure pursuits, enhanced use of technology at home and automated transport led to the tremendous growth in obesity globally. But the real question is, why do we all not grow obese? Ultimately, most of us continue to be guarded against obesity, although some of us hoodwink our hunger by consuming wine and cocktails with our meals and remain lean.

Is all of this because we have more money to spend? Hence the snacking on processed foods and gaining weight. But why do the poorest people in many countries have higher obesity trends? As per the US National Health and Nutrition Examination Survey (NHANES) data for 1971–2000,[3] the poorer the population, the more obese they are likely to be.

A diabetes survey in Jamaica in the early 1960s[4] reported high rates of obesity, specifically in adult women. The dual burden of obesity in mothers and malnutrition in their children in the lower-income segment is present across the globe in both poor and wealthy nations. How is that possible? According to a 1960 report[5] on the Zulu tribe from Durban, South Africa, 40 per cent of female adults were corpulent and women in their forties averaged around 79 kg. In the 1950s, diabetes and obesity were highly prevalent among Asians and

Africans in Durban despite engaging in 'physically active work' and consuming a low-calorie diet rich in 'highly refined sugar, foods containing highly refined flour, and polished rice'.[6]

In the previous chapter, I have argued that obesity is not because of overeating but because of fat accumulation. With what we are observing here, this fat accumulation may also be linked to the changes in the nutrient profiles of what we regularly eat. Anywhere in the world where populations ate their indigenous native diet, obesity was not observed. Consumption of refined food products rich in added fats and sugar are causing obesity. But is this the whole explanation?

Can we blame our genes?

Don't we regularly hear such anecdotes that some people eat whatever they want under the sun and do not get fat while others, even after counting their calories, don't do so well? Ageing people often talk about how they used to maintain a healthy body weight effortlessly when they were younger and that now it is difficult to maintain the same. How does that fit into the energy balance theory? Did these people possess a greater willpower in their youth to maintain an energy balance?

Jane Wardle, an epidemiologist at University College London, published a persuasive study[7] on twins who had been separated at birth and adopted into different homes. She analysed more than 2,000 twins and compared their sizes using BMI. Identical twins share identical DNA. They have the same hair, eye colour and complexion and nearly identical heights. What if one was brought up in a home with little physical activity and loads of refined convenience foods and the other in healthy surroundings? The outcome may come as a shock to many. The study revealed approximately 75 per cent consistency in the BMI despite different surroundings and upbringing. She also found that if a child was obese, 75 per cent depended on their genes and 10 per cent on the home environment and parental upbringing. Later studies also confirmed that 70 per cent of our propensity to gain fat is dictated by our parentage.

Diabetic mothers are known to give birth to heavier babies. If women of childbearing age are obese and diabetic, they pass their metabolic results on to their children through an intrauterine environment.[8] If the mother has chronically high blood sugar, then the growing pancreas in the foetus will reciprocate to this environment by over-producing insulin-secreting beta cells.[9] This makes the baby produce more fat, which is why diabetic mothers have a propensity to give birth to fatter and bigger babies,[10] setting them up for lifelong weight issues.[11] Besides, if one's mother happened to be obese and diabetic during pregnancy, she would pass on her gene, increasing one's predisposition for obesity by 50 per cent because the genes were incubated within an obese body.

The good news is that 30 per cent is in our control. We can make good choices with the help of science. It is important to remember that if we are predisposed to obesity, we may not become as thin as we wish, but we can fight it by making the correct lifestyle choices. Our habits play a role in activating or silencing the expression of our genes (this field is called epigenetics) for health or disease and obesity or leanness.[12] American psychologist William Sheldon invented the concept of 'morphology'[13] of body types in the 1940s. He stated that people are of three main body types, namely ectomorphs, who are likely to be lean and long; mesomorphs, who are muscular and broad; and endomorphs, who are fat and round. As an endomorph, if you starve, you might lose weight and look emaciated but you will not transform into a mesomorph or ectomorph.

Can childhood obesity treatment programmes help with this situation? In 2010, a controlled trial[14] for eight- to ten-year-old African-American girls was conducted in which they were encouraged to 'reduce consumption of sugar-sweetened beverages and high-fat high-caloric foods, increase the intake of water, vegetables and fruit.' The message is very untidy but reasonable. It isn't clear what effect was measured – reduction in sugar, reduction in fat intake, reduction in calories, or the increase in vegetable and fruit intake? The curriculum reduced calories from 1,475 to 1,373 in the first year and then in year two, further to 1,347. In year two, the control group was asked to increase their calorie intake from 1,379 to 1,425. Were the girls able to lose weight? No. The average body fat per cent of subjects in the experimental group rose from 28 to 32.2 per cent as the second year concluded. For everyone involved in the experiment and invested in the theory that reducing calories would lead to weight loss, it was a staggering failure and yet one more confirmation of the dominant role of the calorie deficit in damaging our metabolism. This result drives home the point that quantity of food intake does not navigate bodyweight, so decreasing food intake will not result in losing fat stores.

In the 1950s, prominent physician George Campbell[15] noticed that 80 per cent of the diabetic patients that consulted him belonged to the Natal Indian community in South Africa. Their predecessors migrated to South Africa in the latter half of the nineteenth century and worked as indentured labourers on local sugar plantation fields. He observed that seven out of ten Natal Indians lived below the poverty line.[16] As per his study, the contrast in diabetes rate he saw in Natal Indians and the numbers in India was approximately 1 per cent versus 2.48 per cent in Natal, ruling out a genetic predisposition. Campbell attributed this to sugar. Sugar consumption in India per capita was twelve pounds per annum as opposed to approximately eighty pounds for Natal Indians. The fat content of the diet may have been low, which rules out fat as the culpable factor. According to Campbell, excessive calories cannot be blamed because few of these imperious Natal Indians survived on less than 1,600 calories each day, a level which in various countries would be considered as nearly 'a starvation wage', and yet they were 'enormously fat' and proven by blood tests suffered from undisputed diabetes. This shows how our diet can trigger epigenetics to attract diseases that were uncommon with our ancestors.

> Epigenetics – '*epi*' in Greek means on or above and 'epigenetic' describes elements beyond the genetic code. It is a field of science that studies how our environment and behaviours can affect which of our genes are activated and which are not, without changing the DNA sequence. Obesity being a hormonal imbalance is a reliable explanation considering this kind of genetic influence.

Does food deprivation in our mothers make us obese?

At the end of the 1960s during the Nigerian civil war, a devastating famine occurred. Researchers studied 1,300 infants born prior to, during and after the war.[17] Infants born during the famine were more susceptible to suffer from diabetes, central obesity and high blood pressure. How would starvation in the womb result in babies having a higher risk of developing diabetes and obesity in the future? Let's view this problem from a different perspective. How would it benefit a baby born to a starving mother to have a more dynamic appetite and gain weight more effortlessly than usual? We now know that an overweight mother may endow her child with an obesity-prone body through a highly sensitive pancreas for insulin release, but why would an under-nourished mother predispose her baby to gain weight easily? This appears to be counter-intuitive. This answer lies in the lack of micronutrients found in the body of starved mothers. When food is restricted, the individual will develop deficiencies in protein, minerals, and vitamins. The genes in the foetus detect the deficiencies in the mother, and their genetic expression is modified to ensure that sufficient food is consumed in the future environment to mitigate similar deficiencies. Later studies[18] confirmed that taking vitamin supplements during pregnancy profoundly modified how the baby looked. Some genes influence obesity or leanness in the body. For example, individuals having the fat mass and obesity-associated (FTO) gene are 3 kg heavier on average than those without the gene. Some genes encode for appetite and others for fullness, whereas some encode for metabolism (the amount of energy that one would burn off). If we can switch on and off such epimutations (modifications) in our genes that control appetite, satiety and metabolism using the power of our lifestyle habits, we will make significant progress in fixing the issue of obesity without starvation.

Our eating behaviour and hunger are driven by the energy requirements of the body. Our brain needs fuel to think. Building muscle requires energy. All the organs need a constant supply of vitamins, minerals and energy to function. This energy can either be supplied by eating while awake or removed from the fat stores. This is known as the diurnal cycle of energy balance, satiety and hunger.[19] We fill nutrients in our body when we are awake and put them to use during fasting periods. Unlike sheep or cattle, we are not continuously grazing. Instead, we eat periodically. As long as this energy is continuously provided, your body is least concerned with where the energy is coming from. But if your epigenetics programme your fat cells to be extremely sensitive to food deprivation and fat reduction, your fat cells will hold on to more fat rather than release it for the body's fuel. Obesity, in this sense, is not the problem of an imbalance between energy intake and energy expenditure but an imbalance between energy available to the body to function normally and energy stored in the fat tissue; a problem of energy trapped in the fat tissue.

Does everybody get obese when they overeat?

Claude Bouchard, the Director of the Human Genomics Laboratory at Louisiana State University's Pennington Biomedical Research Center, published a study in 1990[20] in which he and his colleagues overfed twelve pairs of identical twins (twenty-four young men) by 1,000 calories per day, six days per week for three months to study its genetic influence on fat gain. The eventual weight gain was 4.1–13.64 kg. Their body fat also increased differently by a factor of three. They noted that both twins added equivalent fat and weight and so 'genetic factors are involved', which controls our tendency to store calories as either muscular, lean tissue or fat.

James Levine from the Mayo Clinic conducted a study in 1999[21] in which he overfed sixteen healthy subjects by 1,000 calories each day, all days of the week, for two months. Levine noted that 'fat gain varied ten-fold among the volunteers' – some of the subjects managed to add not even a pound of fat while others added almost 4.1 kilograms. The results were not isolated findings. Almost every overfeeding study has yielded the same outcomes.

But if we ask most doctors or nutritionists about this metabolic adaptation to overeating, they will be unaware of such a mechanism. This is not covered in their obesity training. Why is that so? One would rightly expect the medical profession to discern something so nuanced and critically essential. It should have been recognized as common knowledge. Some researchers in the field would argue that a physically larger body would have increased energy expenditure after weight gain, that is a larger body burns more energy. This hypothesis doesn't add up when we look at the change in the body composition after weight gain. Most individuals who gain weight in overfeeding experiments and in regular life add the excess weight as fat and not metabolically active tissue such as muscle. Unlike muscles, fat expends minimal energy and is an efficient organ. So the thermogenic effect in overfeeding is a significant contributor to improved metabolism than increased mass.

German physiologist Carl von Voit[22] speculated that the metabolic rate of our cells depends on the energy available. More energy is generated when more fuel is provided. He said that excess calories increase the energy available to our cells, tissues, and muscles and increase our 'impulse to move' or 'impulse to physical activity'. This restless feeling is the manifestation of the body having more energy to burn. The inescapable conclusion is the same elementary outcome of how our bodies operate when overfed. We have frugal metabolisms when we are low on energy reserves and undernourished. So our bodies are required to efficiently burn the calories that we consume. When high on energy intake and over-nourished, we have spendthrift metabolisms to mitigate the excessive increase in weight and fat stores. Our cells may have a specific ideal or maximal faculty for metabolizing nutrients. However, the quantity that is actually metabolized is finally dictated by the quantity and maybe the quality of the nutrients provided. This resolution is made on a hormonal and cellular level, not a conscious or cognitive level. The idea is encapsulated in a German word *luxuskonsumption*, meaning a spendthrift metabolism that splurges excess energy as physical exercise or heat.

Does voluntary food deprivation (dieting) make you obese?

Regular calorie deficit dieting episodes are a potent way to train your mind to induce obesity. We not only regain the weight but also overshoot it. It is because, with this diet, we add new data points for our brain to recalculate our set point weight.[23] The brain perceives this shortage as caused by an environmental catastrophe such as famine, a negative energy balance of eating less and moving more. These instances are factored in when the brain is calculating how much energy to store for survival, which drives our food-seeking behaviour: more hunger, less satiation, and lower energy expenditure (metabolic rate). The higher the frequency of these less-eating episodes in the past, the higher will be the body's set point weight. Research in this area confirms this explanation and, more importantly, my patients tell me the same thing about their weight loss, weight regain and weight settling at a higher point.[24] This also implies that the body utilizes less energy in a pre-obese condition[25] than those who stay lean, suggesting that low-calorie expenditure is a risk factor for obesity. This means that pre-obese individuals do indeed have a retarded rate of energy expenditure. Since we understand type-2 diabetes better as a disease than weight gain and obesity, let's draw a parallel between the two to clearly understand the underlying problem in obesity and weight gain and the direction of treatment protocol to sustainably maintain healthy weight. Pre-diabetes condition is defined by abnormally high insulin levels and thus it is a risk factor for developing the disease of poorly managed blood sugar. Similarly, lowering metabolic rate is a pre-obese condition and an effect of gaining weight. In type 2 diabetes, to cure or reverse the problem sustainably, we need to correct high insulin levels aka insulin resistance. Similarly, to reverse and cure obesity or to lose weight sustainably we need to treat low metabolic rate not just transiently but on the long run. Elevating your metabolic rate is the treatment we should be looking at and it can be done through simple lifestyle interventions that I'll be revealing and elaborating on in the final section of this book. Also, by now you would have guessed what is the most effective way to pull down and reduce your metabolic rate? It's by reducing food intake.

To explain the pattern simply:

- Insulin resistance causes high insulin levels and diabetes
- Pre-obese condition causes lowering of metabolic rate and weight gain

Can we influence our body's energy expenditure?

During the First World War[26] in the outskirts of Paris in a draughty warehouse, the French government had just discovered how to concoct extra-strong dynamite. The labourers primarily comprised women who mixed two chemicals, picric acid and dinitrophenol (DNP), to concoct Trinitrotoluene (TNT) explosives before packaging them into metre-long artillery shells and shutting them to secure them. The job was challenging and exhausting; however, the supervisors noted that the workforce was not producing the expected output. The workers complained of too much heat, developed fevers and were sweaty despite it being winter and a cold warehouse. After a while, it became clear that many women were losing considerable weight too. Then disaster struck. One day, a young worker in her twenties collapsed with muscle convulsions. She had a raging temperature. Her body eventually turned hard like a rock and she died. She could not breathe due to paralysis and died on the factory floor of asphyxia. Scientists from Stanford University in the 1920s[27] analysed the effects of DNP on metabolism and discovered that exposure to the chemical enhanced the resting metabolic rate by a mighty 50 per cent. The fat reserves pull out copious amounts of energy to feed the muscles and organs for conversion into ATP. The heat produced in the muscles elevates the body temperature, and the body compensates by sweating to cool the skin. DNP acts on the power plant of the cells – the mitochondria. The mitochondria typically convert the fuel circulating in the body (fatty acids, ketone and glucose)[28] to cellular energy (ATP) to enable the cell to carry out its functions. For example, muscle cells build muscles.

> Regular pathway: Food energy enters the cell → produces the cellular form of energy, ATP
>
> When DNP enters the cell: Food energy enters the cell → DNP inhibits ATP production → cell loses this energy as heat

Researchers have been striving to find its natural alternative within our bodies for a half-century. If DNP-like compounds could be found and be somehow safely leveraged, this could result in a very enticing weight loss drug. This search started by analysing the effect of 'brown fat' on fuel use. Unlike white fat, which stores energy, brown fat transforms food energy into heat with the help of a protein called UTP-1, just like DNP. Sadly, there is not enough of it in the adult human body to make any meaningful changes to increase energy burning. So recently, the attention of scientists has shifted to our muscles. Studies hot off the press[29] have documented that muscle cells possess a DNP-like compound known as sarcolipin, a protein with the ability to burn those surplus calories, not through exercise or movement but just by converting the calories into heat energy, or *luxuskonsumption*. This heat is then effortlessly lost into the atmosphere. The excess calories are utilized easily. Contemporary thinking about obesity[30] is slowly shifting. Researchers are describing obesity as not only a condition of excess fat accumulation but also as a condition characterized by a lack of muscles to burn excess energy for maintaining a healthy body weight.

In short, obesity is a result of a combination of problems – our genes, our food environment, our mothers' food environment during pregnancy, and our own attempts at crash diets. Simply put, we would categorize people in our current world into one of the three categories:

- Obesity proof – still regular size and able to sustain this size easily

- Obesity susceptible – normal to overweight, conscious that if they overeat processed food or don't exercise regularly, they will increase in size
- Obesity prone – overweight or obese individuals who struggle with size even when they exercise and watch their calories

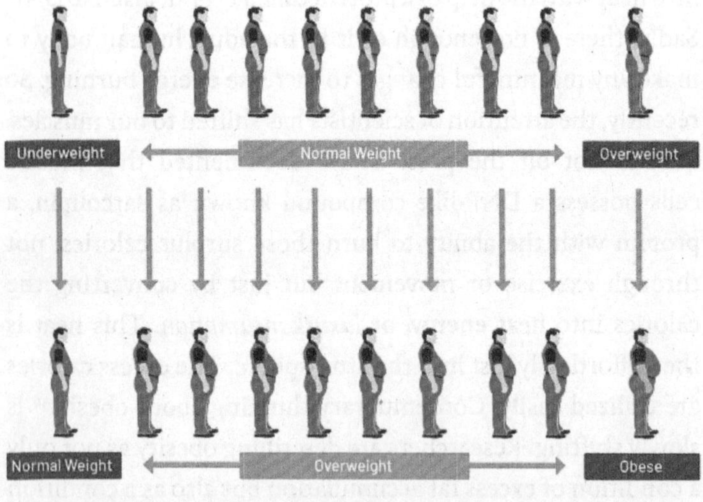

If processed food affected everyone similarly, everyone's weight would shift upwards equally

For those who suffer from obesity, two primary predetermined factors play a role: a genetic predisposition combined with a processed food diet. Are all human tribes, races and populations equally or distinctly susceptible to becoming obese when exposed to a processed food diet? Take a look at these numbers:

- Only 6 per cent of the population on the island of Nauru (in the Pacific Ocean) are normal weight, while the remaining 94 per cent and 71 per cent are overweight and obese, respectively.[31]
- In the United States, the obesity level is around 42 per cent.
- In Europe, nearly 60 per cent of adults are overweight and obese.

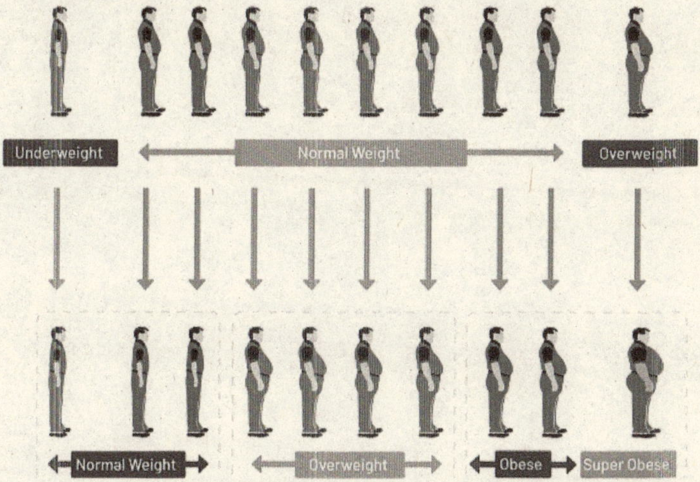

Actual change in weight of population after switching to a western diet. One third of the population is resistant to weight gain, one third is likely to get obese and one third is highly vulnerable to obesity.

So now that we have seen that the lion's share of our body size is determined by our genes and the type of food we consume, we also have the answer to the question, 'do autonomous and external factors make us gain weight?' Let us now deep dive into and see how our external food environment interacts with our body's internal environment, that is our hormonal system, to regulate our weight and specifically the reserves of fat we hold at any given point in time.

7

Understand Your Hormones for Weight Loss

'Concepts [in scientific theories] should relate as directly as possible to observation and measurements, and be distorted as little as possible by explanatory elements.'

Max Kleiber, *The Fire of Life: An Introduction to Animal Energetics*

In 1917, the American chemist, physiologist and nutritionist Francis Benedict conducted a study called the 'Human Vitality and Efficiency under Prolonged Restricted Diet'.[1] In the study, the daily caloric intake of the volunteers was reduced from 2,100 kcal to 1,400 kcal, that is, by 30 per cent. It was observed that the volunteers were unable to keep warm despite covering up with an excessive amount of clothing, were hungry and grumpy most of the time and their BMR was reduced by 30 per cent. After the end of this experiment, the volunteers immediately started consuming excess amounts of food and regained their lost weight.

Hunger is such a terrible thing that it is justifiably and

typically cited as one of the three worst burdens of humans alongside war and pestilence. Individuals who are on a low-fat, low-calorie diet tend to feel hungrier. It isn't any form of psychological voodoo or loss of morality or willpower but a natural consequence of increased hunger because of a hormonal response to weight loss. Losing weight prompts two crucial responses in your body:

1) a drop in TDEE instantly and indefinitely to conserve the body's energy
2) hunger signals by hormones

I am shocked at times to witness the self-control of a few of my patients who can starve themselves for weeks uncompromisingly. For someone who has lost tremendous weight, the power of the hunger signal can be similar to that of an unquenched thirst. Its psychological effects can steer your decisions and life. If you live in an environment where advertisements, smells and images of delicious, highly flavourful, high-calorie foods surround you, there will only be one winner – your hunger. It is a regular hormonal fact of life. We experience hunger, get tired, depressed and cold when we restrict calories to lose weight. These are all tangible and assessable consequences of a reduction in caloric intake. Thus, increased hunger and decreased metabolism are not the cause but the consequence of weight gain. The homeostatic mechanism operates to balance calorie input and output and sustain a seamless fuel supply to your cells and a constant body weight. It is exceptionally complex and concerns the entire body.

Here's how your body works:

Our appetite and satiety hormones are generated in the fat tissue (where the energy reserves are sensed) and produced by the stomach and intestines. The organs in the gastrointestinal tract (the stomach and intestines) and the fats in the body are regulated by a negative feedback loop. Different hormones sense food in our stomach, small intestine or the fat tissue and send signals to the brain to ensure that we don't undereat or overeat. These feedback mechanisms are known as the gut-brain pathway and the fat-brain pathway. The gut-brain signalling pathway orchestrates our short-term (hour-to-hour and day-to-day) hunger and satiety regulation. The fat-brain pathway orchestrates our long-term (months and years) of calorie intake and expenditure.

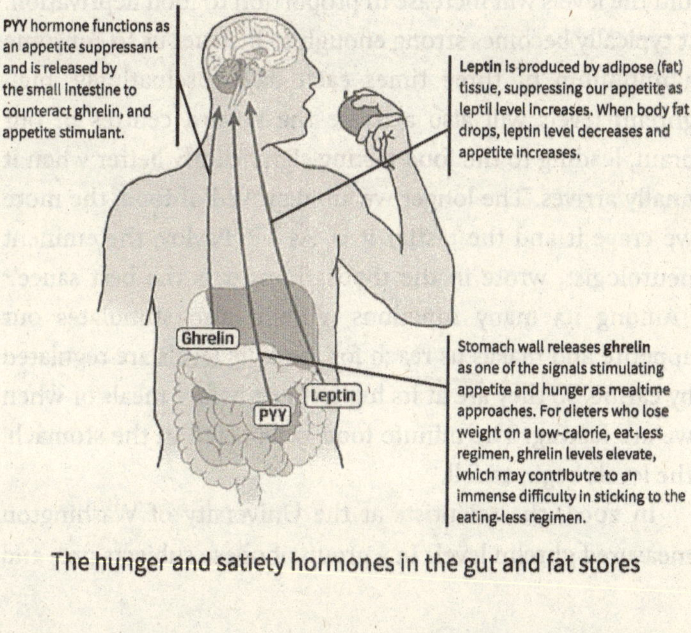

The hunger and satiety hormones in the gut and fat stores

The gut-brain pathway – Hunger and satiety hormones, ghrelin and PYY

There is a constant communication network between the gut and the brain. They communicate through the vagus nerve which originates in the brainstem, going down the neck and to the gut. It carries an extensive range of signals between the digestive system and the brain. When there is a calorie shortage in the body, the gut and the brain reason with each other – 'Of course, we need more food to supply sufficient energy to the organs because the lion's share of what is coming into the body is increasingly going into storage for the future!' They come up with a plan. The brain communicates to the gut by releasing the hunger hormone called ghrelin. It is generated in the stomach's upper region, and the levels will increase in proportion to food deprivation. It typically becomes strong enough to instruct us to consume a minimum of three times each day. Fascinatingly, high ghrelin levels will also activate the reward centres of our brain, leading to the food tasting significantly better when it finally arrives. The longer we are deprived of food, the more we crave it and the tastier it is. As I.P. Pavlov, the eminent neurologist, wrote in the 1890s, 'hunger is the best sauce'.[2]

Among its many functions, ghrelin also stimulates our appetite and makes us reach for food. Its levels are regulated by eating, so they are at its highest just before meals or when we are fasting. The minute food is detected in the stomach, the levels begin to fall.

In 2002, the scientists at the University of Washington measured ghrelin levels in a group of obese subjects pre- and post-prescribing a low-calorie diet.[3] The diet was prescribed for twenty-six weeks and an average of 17 per cent weight loss was observed. Ghrelin levels were measured throughout the day and as predicted, peaked just before mealtimes and subsided after a meal. This pattern was sustained even post the study.

Ghrelin signals were elevated by 24 per cent throughout the day post-weight loss compared to pre-weight loss. The ghrelin levels were at an all-time peak post-weight loss. In fact, the lowest ghrelin levels post the mid-afternoon meal post-weight loss matched with the highest ghrelin levels pre-weight loss. The group on the calorie deficit diet admitted that they were voraciously hungry throughout the day, even post-meal. This perfectly fits with what my patients tell me, that they get ravenously hungry after a calorie deficit diet and find it difficult to concentrate on anything but the subsequent meal. It can be specifically depressing if the next meal is a low-calorie, low-fat meal.

> The dieters were perpetually ravenous because their afternoon ghrelin level, even after consuming food on a low-calorie diet, is the same as the pre-lunch peak in appetite before dieting.

We all have an eating threshold – that moment when we feel we've had enough. But how do we know that? It doesn't occur magically. As we eat our meal, another hormone is being produced by the small intestine and is gradually released into the bloodstream. This hormone is called peptide YY (PYY) – the satiety hormone. PYY is generated by the small intestine cells in response to food inside the small intestine and sends a signal to the brain to generate a feeling of satiety. Another satiety hormone, glucagon-like peptide (GLP-1) is also released by the small intestine into the bloodstream after consuming food. It sends a satiety signal to the body via the hypothalamus to cease food consumption. GLP-1 also improves the insulin sensitivity of organs and muscles, which instructs the body to burn more glucose, making insulin function better. When GLP-1 is present in the stomach, the food content is gradually emptied and nutrients are gradually absorbed, leading to a slower rise in blood glucose and the fat-storing hormone insulin. PYY and GLP-1 function to switch on satiety and switch off appetite. The message is more instant and intense if the intestine detects protein. A 2010 study[4] measured the effects of four distinct proteins (whey protein supplement, tuna, turkey, and eggs) on the insulin levels of the participants. Whey protein elicited the highest insulin levels. Four hours later, the volunteers were treated to a buffet lunch. The group of volunteers that consumed whey protein were unable to eat a lot of food because they were still satiated.

Protein from animal sources results in prolonged satiety, with whey being the most effective. When two meals with the same number of calories but with vastly different nutritional profiles are given to an individual, say two whole eggs and sugared soda, which food do you think will create more satiety? The undisputed winner is the eggs. PYY and GLP-1 post egg consumption simply allow it to 'sit' in your stomach, slowing down the energy release from the stomach. However, food contents that instantly exit the stomach such as in the case of soda which does not 'sit' in your stomach long enough for extended satiety levels, quickly makes you hungry and compels you to reach out for the next snack or meal prematurely, making you overeat.

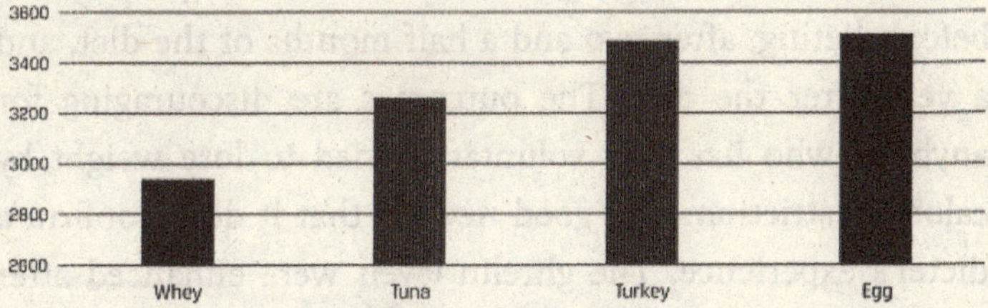

Calorie consumption four hours after consuming a protein-rich meal

When overweight people go on diets, they are asked to live life with increasing hunger indefinitely. The feeling of deprivation is not just emotional but is a specific biochemical response triggered by a starving body that wants to revert to a

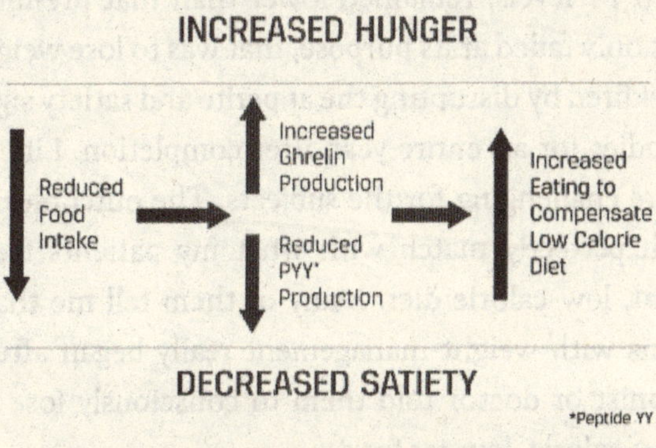

The science of how eating less makes you fat

state of homeostasis. You can stop yourself from binge eating when you feel hungry, but you can't possibly stop yourself from feeling hungry or control your hormones! That's just physiology and not under your control.

Consider this: What does a diet do to the PYY levels? Do these signals alter over time, even after a diet? A study[5] observed the PYY and ghrelin levels of the participants before dieting, after two and a half months of the diet, and a year after the diet. The outcomes are discouraging for anybody who has ever voluntarily tried to lose weight by calorie restriction. The good news is that it does confirm a dieter's experience. The ghrelin levels were enhanced after the completion of the diet, as we saw in the previous study. PYY's satiety signals to the brain also drastically plummeted. The dieters felt miserable and hungrier even after the meal, with a lower feeling of satiety than that before dieting. This is typical and expected. Here is more bad news. A year after completing the diet, the group regained most of their weight, appetite (ghrelin) levels remained elevated, and the satiety feeling (PYY levels) remained lower than that pre-diet. The diet not only failed at its purpose, that was to lose weight, but also backfired by disrupting the appetite and satiety signals in their bodies for an entire year after completion. Life indeed got more challenging for the subjects. The outcomes of this research perfectly match with what my patients feel after a low-fat, low-calorie diet. Many of them tell me that their problems with weight management really began after their nutritionist or doctor told them to consciously lose weight with low-calorie, low-fat food.

I've laid out all the science behind why we get hungry, how calories are distributed in the body, and how hormones affect our hunger and satiety. Are you convinced yet that eating less is just not sustainable in the long run? The only meaningful way to lose weight is to understand our appetite and metabolic systems and use that to your advantage to maintain your weight at a healthier long-term level.

The fat–brain pathway – Leptin and hypothalamus

I have introduced the two hunger-controlling switches to you before – the metabolic switch and the appetite switch. The hypothalamus, a small pea-sized area at the base of our brain holds the key to these switches. It controls the entire body's homeostatic regulation. It is connected to our ANS, which in turn controls the endocrine system aka our hormones. The hypothalamus also literally holds the key to our heartbeat. All the hormones in our body have some direct or indirect influence on fuel utilization in the short run and fuel hoarding for the long term.

In the 1990s, scientists found a hormone called leptin that was generated by our fat cells and that appeared to work on the hypothalamus to switch the metabolism higher and lower and hunger on and off. Its name is derived from the Greek word *lepto*, which means 'thin'. Leptin is perpetually released by the fat cells, not because of any signal. It indicates to the hypothalamus how much fat is present in the fat stores. You can think of it as the fuel gauge in your vehicle notifying you how much more you can travel and how much fuel there is in the tank. With the discovery of this messenger hormone leptin, we know that fat in our body is not a garbage can for excess calories, but it plays a vital role in the negative feedback mechanism for energy distribution and storage mechanism, and as predicted, it functions like the negative feedback for hydration. After overeating, the volume of fat in the stores increases and leptin is produced from fat cells and released into the bloodstream. The hypothalamus, the weight control centre in the brain, detects the leptin and the message that there are sufficient energy stores and realizes no more is required. A message is sent to the body to decrease appetite and increase both the body's metabolic rate and satiety. This is the fundamental and potent fat-neuron signalling pathway. These elements act to sustain body weight within a predetermined range of weight-set points.

Leptin is also potent in halting weight loss. When drastic weight is lost during a famine, calorie-restricted diet or sickness, the fuel stores (fat and glycogen) in the body get depleted and leptin circulation is reduced. The hypothalamus detects this and acts to halt the additional loss of energy by decreasing satiety, increasing appetite and reducing calorie expenditure. These steps slow down and stop further weight loss. When calorie intake finally increases (food becomes readily available), the individual gains weight. This mechanism shows us how people have effortlessly maintained their weight for decades without counting or restricting calories. The following figures show you why we easily lose those extra pounds after vacation and why we gain weight after a drastic weight loss post-illness or crash dieting:

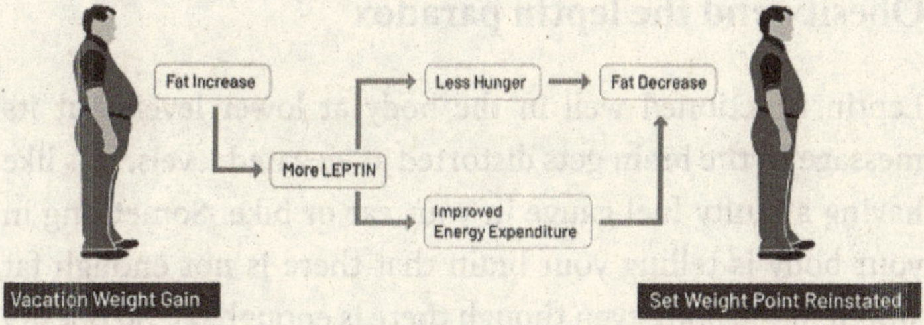

Leptin's action of facilitating fat loss to the set weight point

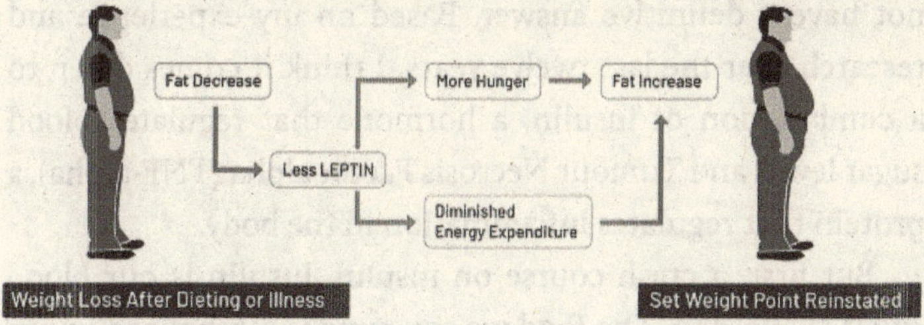

Leptin's action on facilitating fat gain to balance out weight loss through dieting

You might ask me: but why couldn't there be a leptin drug that would help obese individuals lose weight? In 1994, researchers at the Howard Hughes Medical Institute in New York discovered the hormone leptin and a team of scientists led by Jeffrey M. Friedman proved that leptin injections cured obesity in mice.[6] But it didn't work in humans. Doctors prescribed higher and higher doses of leptin to obese patients in a medical trial. The patients did show elevated levels of leptin but they just weren't losing any weight. This puzzled everyone. What is this paradox?

Obesity and the leptin paradox

Leptin functioned well in the body at lower levels but its message to the brain gets distorted at elevated levels. It is like having a faulty fuel gauge in your car or bike. Something in your body is telling your brain that there is not enough fat stored in the body even though there is enough fat. So obesity is not a state of leptin deficiency but leptin resistance. But what is the reason for this? The scientific community does not have a definitive answer. Based on my experience and research over the last twelve years, I think it comes down to a combination of insulin, a hormone that regulates blood sugar levels and Tumour Necrosis Factor alpha (TNF-alpha), a protein that regulates inflammation in the body.

But first, a crash course on insulin. Insulin is our blood sugar chaperone. The food we consume is catabolized in our digestive system into its simplest forms for absorption into the bloodstream. Carbohydrates are chains of sugar bonded together in complex structures which are catabolized into simpler forms, such as glucose, fructose and galactose in our digestive system. Dietary fibre is also a carbohydrate made up of very complex structures of sugars that cannot be broken down by our digestive system and thus moves through the digestive tract without being absorbed into the body. Fats are broken down into fatty acids, and proteins are broken down into amino acids. Specific foods such as processed and refined carbohydrates such as white flour, starch and sugars break down faster and raise blood sugar levels quicker than other foods. As soon as our body detects this, insulin is released from our pancreas and it chaperones the sugar from the blood into the cells for burning it as energy or storing it away as fat. Protein and dietary fats don't raise the blood sugar as much as carbohydrates, which are literally made up of sugars. If we don't have proper insulin production in our body, we are in trouble! Glucose, that is, the sugar in our blood will rise up to toxic levels. Even if insulin were working correctly, if we have too much sugar in our bloodstream and our cells already have enough glucose, we are still in trouble. The excess sugar is converted into fat. This newly produced fat is stored around the organs (see chapter 3) known as visceral fat (in the liver leading to fatty liver disease) and subcutaneous fat (stored underneath the skin). Under typical conditions, elevated insulin levels promote sugar and fat accumulation in the body. Low insulin levels promote the release and burning of sugar and fat energy and chronically elevated levels of insulin result in elevated fat storage.

Elevated insulin and leptin resistance

Both insulin and leptin signal the same cells of the hypothalamus. The cells have distinct receptors for insulin and leptin, like post boxes. But once the message is delivered, the signal pathways within the cell overlap. The cell is unable to read both the messages from leptin and insulin simultaneously. When insulin[7] functions on the cell receptor, there is no room within the cell to read the leptin signal, even if leptin is circulating and trying to post its message. The leptin signal goes unread.[8] Then the hypothalamus perceives fat reserves to be excessively low (though enormous) and builds appetite while cutting metabolic rate and caloric expenditure, just like the dysfunctional fuel gauge in your motor vehicle displaying an empty tank when it is filled to the brim. Conclusion: elevated insulin levels promote leptin resistance, and more leptin resistance indicates an elevated set weight point, thus a higher weight. I'll discuss insulin in detail in Chapter 9.

If an individual gains 0.5 to 1 kg per year, it means that there is a slow upward setting of the body's weight lipostat. Understanding why this happens, what regulates the set weight, and how to reset it lower is vital. Research shows that the insulin response differs tremendously between lean and obese individuals.[9] Obese individuals tend to have elevated fasting insulin levels and amplified insulin response to food.

It is plausible that these hormonal abnormalities result in weight gain. So the question is: does insulin cause obesity? Understanding the answer to that question is vital to your weight management goals. For now, let's understand how TNF-alpha influences insulin's signal to the brain.

TNF-alpha

Immune system cells that function as the police against injury or infection in the body release TNF-alpha.[10] These cells are macrophages that patrol our body, watching out for potentially invading viruses, bacteria or damaged cells, and any other trouble in the body. When the problem is identified, TNF-alpha triggers inflammation akin to the disposal and arrest of the threat and repair of the damage. When our adipose (fat) tissue attains a specific critical size, an investigation is called in by the cellular police, TNF-alpha. All my clients who were battling obesity showed a high concentration of the inflammatory marker C-reactive protein in their blood test. Evidence suggests that eating ultra-processed food directly affects our TNF-alpha levels.[11] This inflammation[12] negatively affects the hypothalamus and wreaks havoc on leptin levels and our set weight point. It makes sense from an evolutionary perspective that when we are seriously injured or sick, the inflammatory response that is triggered also causes leptin resistance. Factoring in our current fat reserves, any damage repair efforts will consume energy. So an adequate response would consume more energy. This is accomplished by blocking the influence of leptin, causing elevated hunger levels.

In short,

Obesity → swollen fat cells → elevated TNF-alpha → inflammation

Ultra-processed food → increased TNF-alpha → chronic inflammation

Obesity-induced inflammation → hypothalamic inflammation → leptin resistance

You may ask: how is the cellular police connected to insulin?

Obesity-induced inflammation elevates TNF-alpha levels, which in turn block insulin sensitivity. Insulin becomes ineffective at doing its job of chaperoning glucose into the organs and muscles. Interestingly, nine out of ten type 2 diabetic patients are also insulin resistant and are overweight or obese.

Obesity-induced inflammation → elevated TNF-alpha → elevated insulin resistance → elevated insulin → leptin resistance

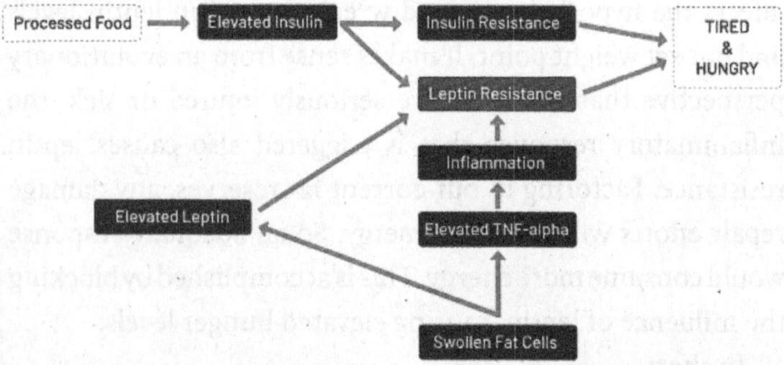

The vicious cycle of leptin resistance and obesity

You may think, now that we have ghrelin, PYY, leptin, insulin and TNF-alpha linked to our obesity, are there any other hormones that we should know about? Yes. Cortisol.

Stress and obesity

When you are under chronic stress, your body releases a stress hormone known as cortisol, which enables the flight-or-fight response and other physiological reactions to potential threats. But did you know that your insulin and cortisol levels are linked? On face value, insulin and cortisol seem to have opposite effects. Cortisol prepares our body for action, removing energy from storage and making it instantly available as blood glucose for fight or flight. In contrast, insulin is a glucose storage hormone. It's remarkable that both insulin and cortisol have similar weight gaining effects. In short-lived physical stress, cortisol and insulin assume the opposite role. However, when we are under prolonged psychological stress, something quite different occurs. Research shows that healthy subjects administered with a high dose of cortisol[13] had a 36 per cent elevation in insulin levels above their baseline, whereas prednisone,[14] a synthetic form of cortisol, elevated insulin levels by 20 per cent and glucose by 6.5 per cent. Chronically high insulin levels also impair the body's ability to respond to insulin, developing insulin resistance in the liver[15] and skeletal muscles.[16] There is a direct dose-response association between insulin and cortisol.[17] Long-term exposure to prednisone[18] results in insulin resistance and even full-blown diabetes. A study on individuals with Cushing's syndrome[19] (long-term elevated cortisol levels) revealed that irrespective of how few calories they consumed and how much they exercised, patients gained weight. This cortisol-induced weight gain was seen even in people without Cushing's syndrome.

All this establishes that there is a direct causal relationship between cortisol and obesity. Stress is neither a calorie nor processed food, yet it can prompt fat accumulation. Chronically high stress levels result in a chronic elevation in cortisol levels, which results in extra pounds of fat. Reducing stress may be challenging but it is critically important. Contrary to popular notions, a sedentary lifestyle and getting glued to our seats binge-watching television or being on our phones and laptops is a poor way to deal with stress. Long hours of screen-viewing affects panoramic vision, leading to cortisol release.[20] Rather, relieve your stress with various time-tested methods: yoga, exercise, mindful meditation and massage therapy. Studies on such mindfulness interventions[21] reveal that subjects could use group discussion, guided meditation, yoga, and exercise to reduce abdominal fat and decrease cortisol.

One fundamental factor in managing your cortisol levels is to get sufficient sleep. In 1910, individuals on average slept nine hours per night.[22] In today's day and age, more than 30 per cent of adults aged between thirty and sixty-four years report sleeping for fewer than six hours per night. One of the potentially adverse effects of this is big changes in the body's endocrine (hormone) system. A week of less sleep can make the body approximately 30 per cent more insulin resistant as compared to a week of normal sleep.[23] Recent research showed that sleeping for half the normal sleep time for just two days makes otherwise healthy men insulin resistant.[24] A single night of sleep deprivation enhanced cortisol levels by more than 100 per cent.[25] The cortisol levels were still elevated between 37 and 45 per cent by the following evening.[26] In a different study, insufficient sleep duration enhanced the risk of diabetes.[27] The critical hormones involved in controlling appetite and body fat, ghrelin and leptin, display a regular rhythm and are disturbed by sleep disruption. The Quebec Family Study[28] and Wisconsin Sleep Cohort study[29] showed that sleep deprivation is linked to weight gain, increased ghrelin and decreased leptin. Insufficient sleep clearly challenges weight loss efforts.[30] So getting sufficient sleep is essential to any weight loss plan.

How does insufficient sleep actually cause an increase in our set point weight?

Melatonin is responsible for our sleepiness or wakefulness and regulates our metabolism. It is a hormone secreted by the pineal gland located right behind our eyes. When there is no ambient light, it prepares our body for sleep. Research shows that melatonin decreases cortisol levels and enhances leptin sensitivity (also stabilizes our set point weight). But if we are working night shifts, melatonin levels drop. This causes a decrease in our leptin sensitivity[31] and our body shifts to a higher set point weight.

Reduced melatonin → leptin resistance + higher cortisol → elevated set point weight

Stress eating

The food we crave when we are stressed is high in calories and provides energy to our body quickly[32] (e.g., chocolates, candy, cake, ice cream, and other processed foods high in refined starch, sugars, and vegetable oils). Sugary foods elevate dopamine and serotonin levels that stimulate the reward centre in the brain and make us feel good. But chronically elevated cortisol encourages fat deposition directly into our fat tissue and indirectly through elevated insulin levels and insulin resistance. Basically, your stress will cause you to gravitate towards high sugar foods and then promptly store them as fat.[33] This an evolutionary reaction to stress.

Alcohol and cortisol

Cortisol is directly linked to beer belly. Studies[34] have documented that alcohol consumption promotes cortisol production. The alcohol calories are poorly used as energy by the body. Alcohol elevates our appetite, compelling us to munch on foods such as starch, sugar and vegetable oil (processed foods), which also raises our set point weight. Roughly 80 per cent of the calories from a shot of tequila goes directly to the liver to be converted to a tiny amount of energy and a copious amount of a chemical called citrate.[35] This citrate enables the conversion of glucose to body fat. So alcohol promotes the generation of fat in the liver, which perhaps explains the alcoholic fatty liver disease. It might also lead to fat deposition elsewhere in the body depending on the quality and quantity of carbohydrates we consume. We typically consume a lot of carbohydrates while drinking. For instance, in a beer, approximately one-third of the calories come from a refined carbohydrate maltose as opposed to two-thirds coming from alcohol itself. This leads to a conspicuous outcome – a beer belly! So when individuals quit alcohol or cease their alcohol consumption, their appetite returns to normal, and their food intake patterns improve. Reducing alcohol consumption also plummets their cortisol levels, decreasing their set weight point and leading to fat loss.

But what explains the countries that have the highest alcohol consumption and do not have high obesity levels? We can find the answer in the type and quality of food they consume. Populations in South Korea, France, Russia, Eastern

Europe and the Baltics have not yet completely embraced the hedonic, ultra-processed foods. So despite their high alcohol consumption, even when they over-consume foods, their set weight point is not elevated and thus they do not suffer from weight issues.

Through this chapter, I wanted you to have the scientific knowledge to understand what causes your weight gain. To keep your body healthy, you must first understand it. I bet that none of the nutritionists or doctors that you have approached in your life explained to you the science behind your weight gain. Blindly following a diet plan and exercise routine will only take you so far. In the next chapter, we will move on to understanding the food we eat and the food that we should be eating. What are the carbohydrate and fat contents that are critical for your weight loss? What are good and bad fats? How do they affect our appetite and satiety centres in the brain and influence our energy expenditure and how much is too much? Does eating fat actually cause a heart attack? Let's find answers to all our burning questions.

8

Fats at the Heart of It All

> 'Men who have excessive faith in their theories or ideas are not only ill prepared for making discoveries; they also make very poor observations.'
>
> Claude Bernard, *An Introduction to the Study of Experimental Medicine*

Does fat in the diet cause cardiovascular disease?

The popular notion is that eating fats raises our cholesterol and raises our chances of having a heart attack. Since the 1950s, government bodies, experts in the field and big businesses have peddled the food pyramid to us, prescribing a low-fat, high-carbohydrate diet as the best option for us to be healthy. There was a study conducted by Dr Ancel Keys in the 1950s where he showed an association between fat consumption and heart disease-related death in test subjects from seven countries. In fact, what was left out was that Keys conducted the study in twenty-two countries. Only seven countries were included in the report because the correlation between dietary fat intake and heart disease was not found in the other fifteen countries.[1] A fundamental truth that we have internalized in our homes and kitchen was, in fact, a lie! There may be many personal, professional and financial reasons for such biased research to be published and such biased research is everywhere in science, including nutrition. On top of it, most dietary research is epidemiological in nature. That means these studies are based on observing a particular population to try to find correlations between the factors that we want to study. There is speculation but no proof of causality. Sadly, these associations don't necessarily translate into establishing authentic causes, and if they are assumed as causative without control experiments, then it's weak science. Epidemiological studies[2] may also associate false positive trends[3] such as a correlation between cigarette smoking and divorce rates. As per the graph below, if one does not want to get divorced in Country X, one must drop one's cigarette smoking.

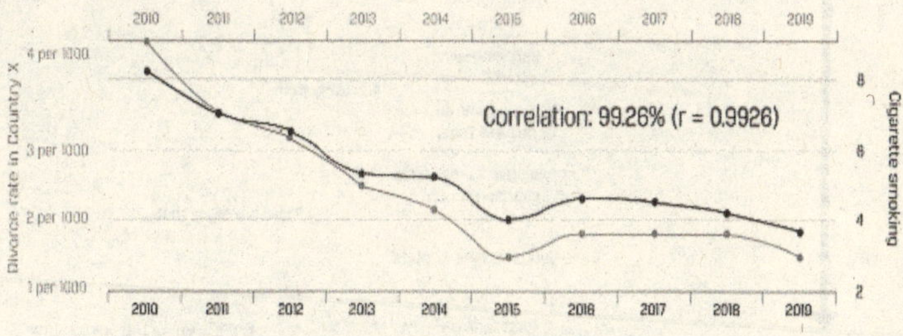

Divorce rate correlated with smoking trend per capita

Epidemiologists had used such observational association studies to link smoking to heart disease post-World War II in the 1960s. And it served as solid proof to conclude smoking caused heart disease due to a strong co-efficient associated with this variable to the development of cardiovascular disease in every study. On the other hand, dietary epidemiological research, which forms the basis of our fundamental beliefs about good diet and dietary advice, has several weaknesses. Infamously unreliable recall questionnaires estimate food consumption, and disease reporting is frequently based not on actual diagnosis but on symptoms. If one pushes this 'loose data' through selective statistical analysis and discards unfavourable results, virtually anything can be proven and become the truth or fact. And the 'facts' will be ascertained by the most prominent industry backers.

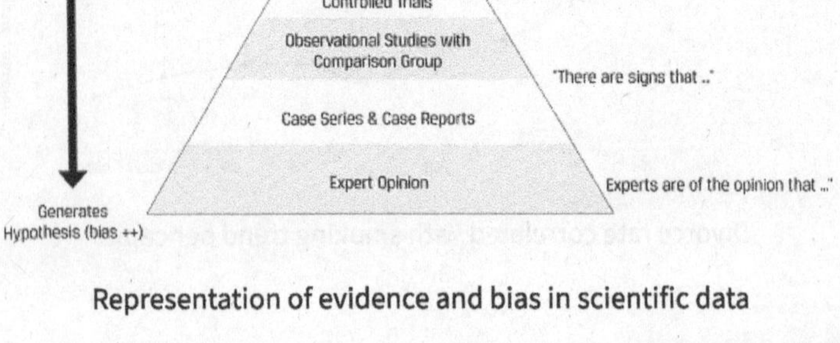

Representation of evidence and bias in scientific data

For five decades, media articles and public health campaigns[4] told us that saturated fats promote heart disease. Even today, we see advertisements on TV telling us the same thing while selling cooking oil and breakfast cereal! Now, when we see fat-rich food such as egg omelettes, bacon, fatty steak or sausage, we tend to recall this picture of the greasy fat in the food clogging our arteries.

Here is the truth about fats in our body

Cholesterol is only one of the many fat-like matters circulating through the blood, collectively known as blood lipids (fats). The other types of lipids are triglycerides and free fatty acids. The combination of three free fatty acids with a glycerol molecule (produced from glucose) that forms the backbone produces triglycerides, the form in which we find fat in our diet and is carried in our body for storage. These substances are not water-soluble and need the help of carriers made up of proteins and fats called lipoproteins to shuttle them around in the blood.

You must have heard of bad cholesterol, otherwise known as low-density lipoproteins (LDL). Its high-density counterpart HDL is called good cholesterol. But this is an oversimplification of the actual science. There is a third class of these called very low-density lipoproteins (VLDL) and these play a vital role in heart disease. What we are generally told is – 'Don't eat saturated fats, they increase cholesterol aka LDL in your blood.' But a 1961 study[5] showed that a high-carbohydrate diet raised the VLDL levels rich in triglycerides, which are not even factored into the total cholesterol test. Because of the popularly peddled low-fat, high-carbohydrate diets, the LDL cholesterol levels of the global population dropped, but the VLDL levels increased disproportionately. A high-carbohydrate diet increases the risk of heart disease in the patient. This is the exact opposite of what we have been told. By the early 1970s, even Nobel laureate Joseph Goldstein and his collaborators from the University of Washington had confirmed this theory.[6] Nevertheless, the idea that a 'negative relation' exists between cholesterol and heart disease simply worked against the grain and the fact that high HDL cholesterol means a lower risk of heart disease was ignored by researchers because it was convenient to believe that too much 'cholesterol' in the circulation 'overloads' the circulatory system, thus enhancing the risk of heart disease.

Consider this: whole eggs contain 70 per cent unsaturated fats, out of which 45 per cent are monounsaturated fats and remaining 25 per cent are polyunsaturated, and 30 per cent are saturated fats. The saturated fats will increase both HDL and LDL cholesterol, monounsaturated fats will increase HDL cholesterol while decreasing LDL cholesterol, and finally the polyunsaturated fats will lower LDL cholesterol but have no meaningful effect on HDL cholesterol (reducing overall cholesterol). Therefore, around 70 per cent of fat in whole eggs will improve the comparative profile of LDL and HDL cholesterol when compared with the effect of consuming carbohydrates such as sugar, wheat, rice and potatoes on the overall cholesterol profile. The remaining 30 per cent will raise LDL and HDL cholesterol and will have an insignificant influence, if any, on the proportion of the overall cholesterol to HDL cholesterol, which is a global risk marker for cardiovascular disease[7]. All of this shows that consuming a whole egg instead of pulao would reduce the risk of heart disease, although virtually no dietary authority would publicly admit it. The same is true for butter and red meat.

After numerous studies, all fats were divided into animal and plant fats, which branched out into saturated, monounsaturated, and polyunsaturated fat and then finally polyunsaturated fats branching into omega-3 and omega-6 polyunsaturated fats. Despite this new classification, we are still hearing from expert governmental and medical organizations that high-carbohydrate, low-fat diets are effective for both weight loss and avoiding heart disease.[8]

What's more, it's believed that LDL cholesterol is a bad cholesterol – but it's not as simple as that and is a little nuanced! There are many subclasses of LDL molecules. Smaller and denser types of LDL molecules stay in the bloodstream for a more extended period and are not disposed of easily as compared to buoyant and larger LDL particles. These smaller LDL molecules have more opportunities and more time to damage the arteries. This is an important distinction. The formation of smaller or larger LDL molecules depends on the quality of the food we eat! Interestingly, LDL or no LDL, HDL is the single most important candidate in our body that provides the highest protection against heart disease. Because HDL actually helps chaperone all the excess cholesterol in the body back to the liver!

A 1988 study revealed that a high-carbohydrate, low-fat diet resulted in more small and dense LDL molecules, suggesting a higher risk of heart disease. A low-fat, low-calorie diet (total fat = 10 per cent of the total calories) leads to a high concentration of small and dense LDL particles among 67 per cent of the population. This translates to three times higher risk of heart disease. What is surprising is that all that I've explained here is in medical textbooks. But it is not common knowledge. Are you convinced yet?

But you must be wondering how this information help you lose weight and be healthy?

Cardiovascular deaths in the USA, UK and France

Year	*Country*	*Cardiovascular Deaths*	*Distribution Base*
2015	USA	60	100,000
2015	UK	46	100,000
2014	France	20	100,000

Consider France, where the average individual eats saturated fats regularly and records a low death rate from heart disease, as shown in the table above. How? The emphasis is on carefully picking fresh ingredients and cooking locally grown foods. They do not often consume packaged and preserved foods. They do not shun saturated fat in their food as it's an integral element of their traditional diet, and they also do not have a culture of snacking between meals. As I have mentioned in the previous chapters, when fat is consumed, the satiety hormones GLP-1 and PYY[9] are released, and we feel full and stop eating. When one has savoured a hearty breakfast, lunch and dinner with fats that produce prolonged satiation and no empty carbohydrate calories, one does not feel compelled to snack. This explains how the French stay slimmer than other populations in Europe and the USA simply by consuming unprocessed, fresh foods, more fat and fewer carbohydrates. This helps them have better and measured insulin levels rather than the yo-yo of a blood sugar spike followed by a crash, which ends in excessive fat storage. A no snacking culture also promotes a healthy insulin response. Additionally, the French government has imposed a cap of 35 working hours in the week[10] to boost the quality of life, lower cortisol and increase melatonin for better sleep, less stress, and lower set point weight. When we eat the correct foods, free ourselves from snacking and have low levels of stress in life, we don't need to count calories, our metabolism will work well and our set weight point will be within a healthy range. The French have not paid heed to the nutritional advice to cut cholesterol from their diet. They continue to savour their steak, cheese and cream while the rest of the world, which has adopted the American way of eating, has switched to refined wheat, sugar and vegetable oils, a switch that has invariably caused the obesity epidemic. The Inuit in Greenland consume copious amounts of pure fat foods such as whale meat, blubber and seal and remain lean and healthy. The Maasai tribe in Kenya, who consume milk, meat and blood, have also avoided heart disease and obesity.

Food culture assumes a crucial role in the health of a population. From the noodles and vegetables of Vietnam to the red rice and meat of Bhutan, from the subzi and spicy curries of India, the wild tubers and meat of the Tanzanian Hadza to the salad, olive oil and salad of southern Italy, food cultures are immensely diverse, not just in what is consumed but also how it is consumed (with chopsticks, hands, knives, forks and spoons). Every food culture is characterized by two common and crucial aspects that are slowly getting lost in this packaged food-first modern world.

1) Food cultures grow over several generations. They are entangled with local traditions and promote social interaction through preparation, cooking and collective consumption of food. When nutritional researchers embraced the sugar versus fat debate, generations of amalgamated food wisdom was discarded. Food culture is much more vital to health than the distinct components of the consumed foods. It leads to a more active, more content and happier population. Food reductionists shun all these elements and only emphasize the benefits and dangers of specific nutrients (fats, carbohydrates, proteins, vitamins, and minerals) and market fortified, highly processed, refined foods to the masses.
2) Traditional food cultures emphasize cooking seasonal, locally sourced fresh ingredients. The kind of food available depends on the time of the year – summer, autumn, winter or spring. Seasonal foods grant us a great variety of healthy local foods throughout the year. As soon as we start getting bored of mangoes by the fag end of summer, the warming *sarson ka saag* will be particularly mouth-watering in the winters. Seasonal foods are woven into our culture by the specialities we prepare for festivals such as Holi and

Diwali. We have begun to ignore these age-old traditions and dishes in favour of nutritional ideology and factory-manufactured foods. Superfood is a novel concept that has cropped up in nutrition discussions, and I'm certain that none of our great-grandmothers would know the word. But your grandmother would have taught you how to make *palak paneer* in the same manner that her mother had taught her.

The Indian government[II] recommends that replacing saturated fats with vegetable seed oils (plant seeds) and grains (plant seed) is better for our health, and our media helped the government promote this message. Food companies also followed suit and invariably added more sugar and refined wheat flour to concoct the low-saturated fat, processed foods that were more palatable and commercially viable. A diet high in refined ingredients promotes a snacking culture to help us cope with the high variability in blood sugar levels between meals. The elevated insulin levels from snacking and sugar consumption and high levels of added omega-6 polyunsaturated fats in vegetable oils metabolically alter our cells, resulting in unhealthy levels of insulin and leptin, insulin and leptin resistance, and weight gain. These changes in our bodies would not have occurred if saturated fats and cholesterol had not been villainized. Now that we've separated the lies from the truth, in the next chapter we will see how this switch in the fat composition of our diet to a diet high in vegetable oils and low in saturated fats leads to obesity.

9

Obesity – A Nutrient Deficiency Disease

'Not that starches and sugars are harmful, but they are low in the essentials we must have for good health. If the proportion of carbohydrates is high, then the amount of something else of greater importance is low. Nutrition is a six-way teeter-totter. Have you ever tried to balance such a device?'

C.C. Furnas and S.M. Furnas,
Man, Bread & Destiny: The Story of Man and his Food

Once upon a time, a lot of saturated fats accounted for a significant nutritional percentage in processed foods. Palmitic acid was one of them. WHO actually linked saturated fat intake to a higher risk of heart disease. Palmitic acid is naturally found in dairy products and meats in minuscule quantities and this is not a problem. The pure form of palmitic acid is produced by heating palm oil at an enormously high temperature, which can also be achieved on an open fire, and it's a staple oil used for cooking food in African villages.

Years later, another dietary report came out. The advice was to replace the 'unhealthy' saturated fats with 'healthy' polyunsaturated oils. Luckily for the food processing industry, seed oils that are rich in polyunsaturated fats were widely and cheaply available. In Canada, advancements in the genetic engineering of rapeseed[1] allowed for large-scale and cost-effective manufacturing of canola oil and it became a novel staple ingredient alongside soya bean oil. Even today, most dieticians will have a zealous glimmer when defining the health benefits of consuming polyunsaturated fats from vegetable seed oils that are low in saturated fats (hail the mighty diet-heart hypothesis) and high in LDL cholesterol-reducing good fats. Currently, we are consuming a copious quantity of these oils when just a century ago, they were used as lantern fuel and to make candles. These oils are laden with trans fats. Most convenience foods available in the supermarket are processed with fat, sugar, and salt. Quite frequently, immensely refined white flour would also be added, finished with preservatives, emulsifiers, colours and flavouring to resemble the taste of the whole, unprocessed foods and mask their offensive characteristics. Distinct consistencies of the manufactured foods such as chewy, soft or crunchy added palatability and pleasure when consuming them. Processed foods are tested on volunteers and designed in labs to screen the concoction that hits the bullseye. The higher the pleasure and addictive nature of the food, the more it will sell. This is fundamental market economics because a food manufacturer must try to have a better product than their competition.

A 2020 online poll[2] of the eating habits of over 2,400

Indian adult citizens revealed that a massive 73 per cent responded they would consume unhealthy options because they are convenient, tasty and part of their everyday lifestyle, despite heightened awareness of the ill effects of unhealthy options rich in added sugar or fats. Therefore, the taste factor reigns supreme in their decision to purchase food. Processed food is a huge, huge business. For instance, the annual revenue of PepsiCo in 2020 was reported to be $70.3 billion. Sadly, the long-term health ramifications of the consumption of highly addictive foods rich in added sugar and fat skew the consumers, diet composition towards more refined ingredients such as refined carbohydrates, sugars and polyunsaturated fats. The food processing industry is not required to have considerations for these unhealthy choices made by consumers. They manufacture the products, and it is left to the consumers discretion to try and not consume too much of it. With claims of 'no added sugar' in high-fat products and 'low cholesterol' in products with high amounts of added sugar, it's all going downhill for our health. Needless to mention that the ingredients on the nutrition label are specifically written in a confusing and deceitful way so that the products sound and look healthy. Thus, we have enticingly tasty foods at our convenience and reasonably low cost with labels claiming them to be healthy and a consumer group of immensely gullible individuals.

This brings us to the novel fat ingredient integrated into our daily diet based on dietary recommendations given by experts in the field – vegetable oil. If you believe that vegetable oils are extracted from compressing plant seeds such as sunflower, soya, and rapeseed, then get ready to take the red pill and enter the matrix. On one hand, olive oil contains healthy and natural monounsaturated fats and is extracted by slowly and gently moving stone or steel cold roller presses,[3] which preserves the integrity of the fats and its natural preservatives. This method goes back to the times of the ancient Greek civilization. On the other hand, vegetable oil manufacturing is slightly more industrial. You may require a background in petroleum engineering or a degree in chemistry to understand its manufacturing process. These oils are extracted from vegetable seeds and processed in large factories and obtained by crushing and heating the seeds at extremely high temperatures of 110°C. The oil is then squeezed out at high pressures ranging from 10 to 20 tonnes per inch, producing more heat. In this process, the oils are exposed to oxygen and light, which are damaging to its nutrient composition. In order to juice out the remaining 10 per cent of the oil from the crushed seeds, the pulp is treated with a chemical called hexane (it is the same one that glue sniffers are addicted to!). Even though this chemical is then boiled off, 0.01 per cent of it may still be traced in the oil. On top of it, this chemical will help retain the toxic pesticides clung to the grains and seeds and the high-temperature processing creates dangerous and unhealthy cell-damaging free radicals in the oil, which break down its vitamin E content. To replace vitamin E and other natural preservatives demolished by heat, their synthetic forms, butylated hydroxyanisole (BHA) and butylated hydroxytoluene (BHT), are frequently added to these oils. Both are implicated in the development of brain damage and cancer. The manufacturing of our healthy vegetable fats is just like any crude oil manufacturing. It is wishful thinking to believe that these novel oils actually are healthy alternatives. Yet, since the 1970s, vegetable oil intake has rapidly increased, fuelled by cholesterol phobia. Indeed, the rise in vegetable oil consumption has offset the drop in consumption of animal fats and is also behind the increase in our total fat intake since 2000.[4]

The same type of processing demolished the healthy polyunsaturated fats – omega-3 and omega-6 – found in vegetable oils. In 2012, the US government has urged food manufacturers to reduce or eliminate the quantity present in vegetable oils.[5] However, the production process of extracting vegetable oils turn them rancid unless a different process called hydrogenation is performed, which loads them up with trans fats. Even cooking methods such as heating the vegetable oil at high temperatures for frying or baking can generate these undesired toxins. Many eastern and western civilizations have traditionally used butter, ghee and coconut oil, which are relatively higher in saturated fats and highly stable under high heat cooking conditions. But in the modern world, due to these dietary guidelines, these traditional fats have been replaced by cost-effective solid forms of vegetable oil known as shortening and vanaspati ghee. The only way to solidify vegetable oil is to hydrogenate it, and this is used in processed foods such as crackers, pies and doughnuts.

> How much trans fats is too much? The latest American Food and Drug Administration (FDA) guidelines recommend no more than 1 per cent of total daily calories translating to 2 g or 20 kcal. Sadly, this quantity can be found in a single serving of biscuits, pastry or crackers.

Ambush of healthy vegetable oils

In India, the vegetable oil intake rapidly grew from 4 kg per individual per annum in 1950 to over 19 kg per individual per annum in 2019, an increase of nearly 400 per cent.[6] Vanaspati ghee, a semi-solid mix of vegetable oils, was introduced as a healthier alternative to butter. Cargill Foods, which manufactures such vegetable oils, has become the symbol of health foods and even promoted its brand by sponsoring teams in IPL in 2016.[7]

The alterations in the type of fats we consume today (less saturated fats and more vegetable oils, margarine and shortening) harmed our appetite and satiety signals (which will be discussed in the next chapter). These changes in turn led to a rise in the total amount of fat intake from 3,350 million pounds in 1970 to 4,600 million pounds in 2010, a 37 per cent increase.[8]

The US government's dietary guidelines recommended an increased intake of purportedly heart-healthy whole grains with no cholesterol, and high in polyunsaturated fats and carbohydrates in the form of starch. The increase in grain consumption profited the government and suited the US Department of Agriculture, which had large stores of corn and wheat to sell and who actually published these guidelines. Intermediary businesses such as food processing plants and fast food restaurants grew, generating more employment and furthering the economy. Soon the public all over the globe, including India, duly adhered to this recommendation. Wheat consumption in whole and refined forms grew from 25 kg to 70 kg per capita per annum from 1950 to 2020.[9]

The dietary guidelines did not encourage public interest in home cooking but increased the confusion in the population on the subject of healthy eating. Consequently, more and more processed food in breakfast cereals and snacks is being consumed frequently. These processed foods have reassuring food labels claiming to be 'heart healthy' or 'low cholesterol'. Most of the food consumption patterns of Indians involve whole grains and processed foods with added fats and not enough from fruits, vegetables and protein-rich sources of food. By 2019, Indians have been consuming high quantities of grains and polyunsaturated fats mixed with other ingredients such as cheap oils, preservatives, flavouring and edible additives, which are required to produce unhealthy instant soups, noodles, gravies, biscuits, cakes and crackers.[10]

This pattern of low protein intake has been documented since the 1980s in India, with the average daily consumption reducing from 61 g to 56 g in 2005.[11] In contrast, significant calories come from carbohydrates in the diet.

In the US, a similar situation was observed before the obesity epidemic in the 1970s. The daily consumption of food grain and vegetable oil increased by a massive 170 kcal and 240 kcal.[12] A parallel decline in consumption of vegetables, eggs and dairy products skewed the caloric intake towards high carbohydrates and processed oils. But the increase in sugar intake was minuscule.

How has this change in consumption pattern affected our bodies? Has this caused micronutrient deficiencies in us? Recent research[13] into fat intake indicates that this may be the case. These alterations may not have caused only obesity but also other lifestyle diseases such as autoimmune conditions, cancer and heart disease. Our scientific understanding of the role of fats within our body is rudimentary compared to our knowledge of micronutrients in our diets, such as vitamins and minerals. It's vital to note that the type of nutrients we consume through food (dietary composition) dictates how the fat reserves regulate themselves, behave, store and release the energy to maintain a constant supply of energy to the body in between meals and at night while we sleep. This energy supply from our fat stores also influences our body's metabolism, drive to exercise, energy expenditure and eating behaviours mediated through potent appetite and satiety signals.

I had come across a case at my fitness centre, which drove home this point for me. On a dark, cloudy, rainy morning in Mumbai, I was approached by a staff member with a case of a personal training client. He told me she was a dedicated and enthusiastic client who worked out regularly and was strong and fit. But in recent weeks, she constantly complained of joint pain, swelling, and lack of energy and didn't train as much as she used to. Though she had taken some sessions with her physiotherapist and was on painkillers for a couple of weeks, she was not getting better and could not identify the source of her problem. I met the client, Samantha the following day. She mentioned that she had returned a couple of months ago from a year-and-a-half long trip in the UAE and ever since, she was suffering from joint aches and her ankles would swell during the day. I first took stock of her nutrition and lifestyle before and after she developed pain in her joints. I could not pinpoint the reason for a problem that persisted even after she had physiotherapy. I ordered basic blood tests to check her kidney and vitamin profiles to rule out irregularities to help me come up with a solution or to see whether to refer her to an orthopaedic doctor. Her blood test indicated a vitamin D (also known as the sunshine vitamin) deficiency. I told her that she needed to get some sun every morning. This was when she mentioned that due to the extreme heat in the UAE, she spent more time indoors and rarely went out in the sun. I recommended her to consult her family physician and get a vitamin D prescription. After that episode, she ensured that she had adequate sunlight exposure every day. In just a couple of days, her joint pain and swelling subsided and she restarted her fitness routine. Had the deficiency not been detected and treated, she would have developed other severe symptoms like muscle twitching, muscle cramps and tingling sensation in the limbs. Incorrect diagnosis would have worsened her condition to osteomalacia (softening of the bones).

Her weakness and lack of enthusiasm to workout were not because she was inherently lazy. In a similar way, nutrition profile and disrupted body fat regulation could be the root cause of inactivity in obese individuals. Correcting that will help the obese feel more energetic and expend more energy.

History, disaster and discoveries of vitamin deficiency diseases

Exhibit A

A couple of centuries ago, vitamin B1 (thiamine) deficiency led to a disease called beriberi that affected the white-rice-consuming tropical belt of the globe. Beriberi has been dormant ever since the correct treatment has been identified. Any disease related to vitamin B complex deficiency such as beriberi, pellagra (caused by diets rich in corn and maize) and anaemia can catch up very fast because vitamin B is water-soluble. We always have approximately two weeks' worth of vitamin B reserves in our body. It tends to affect hunger strikers, famine sufferers and refugees. It had a minor resurgence with the consumption of diets high in corn, white flour (starch) and soft drinks. In their complete form, foods containing starch and sugars also have fat, protein, enzymes, fibre, vitamins and minerals, which help in the digestion and metabolism of those sugars. But sugar-added processed foods lack vitamins and minerals. In fact, the body has to use up its stores of vitamins and minerals to metabolize the carbohydrates in these foods.[14] For instance, when vitamin B is absent in food, carbohydrates cannot be broken down.

Exhibit B

In 1914, Carl Voegtlin demonstrated that consuming a diet rich in cabbage, bread, corn syrup, cornmeal, sugar, turnips and potato causes a disease called pellagra, and this disease could be cured by consuming eggs, milk and fresh meat.[15] Legumes and vegetables such as potatoes, corn and soy have been a relatively recent addition to our diet since the growth of the agriculture industry that began only 12,000 years ago.[16] Before that, for more than two and a half million years of our evolution, archaeological records document that 99 per cent of our evolutionary history was the palaeolithic era, when our ancestors were hunters and gatherers. Any alteration to the behaviours of the palaeolithic era could be categorized as 'unnatural factors'[17]. For instance, potatoes and corn had been brought to Europe and Asia by Columbus and are regarded as the New World vegetables.[18]

Exhibit C

Scurvy is another example of a deficiency disease misunderstood for centuries and has resulted in endless suffering and countless deaths. This condition was believed to be a result of homesickness, filth and poor morals, sedentary lifestyle, and a miasma of foul-smelling air. The disease could result in extreme tiredness, personality alterations, and increased craving for food, exactly like symptoms on a low-calorie diet. It delays the healing of wounds, skin rashes, rotting, and swollen gums. The victims could subsequently succumb to internal bleeding with lethal bouts of vomiting and passing of foul-smelling blood, psychosis and blindness. Vitamin C, just like the B complex vitamins, is water-soluble and its deficiency disease is called scurvy. It was a well-known disease even before the era of long seafaring journeys.[19] A young naval surgeon, James Lind conducted the first-ever controlled trials to test a cure for scurvy in 1747[20] after he acquired extensive first-hand experience whilst on voyages to the Caribbean. Twelve sailors who had developed the disease were split into a random pair of two, each given specific treatments:

1. the elixir of vitriol (standard treatment at the time)
2. a daily intake of 1,100 ml of cider
3. two spoonfuls of vinegar (three times a day)
4. a paste made of horseradish, balsam, garlic, and mustard seeds
5. half a pint of saltwater (daily)
6. one lemon and two oranges (daily)

As you would have guessed by now, the two sailors who were consuming citrus foods rapidly recovered and were able to reassume their duties.

In 1997, nutritionists Tim Byers and Julie Will at the University of Colorado and the Centers for Disease Control and Prevention (CDC) respectively provided a biologically plausible explanation for the relationship between diabetes and vitamin C deficiency.[21] The high consumption of refined and processed foods tremendously increases insulin levels, which not only chaperone blood sugar into our tissues for use and storage but also enhance the vitamin C requirements in the body. This is because the chemical structure of the vitamin C is similar to that of glucose and other sugars in the body,[22] and is transported to the cells in the same insulin-dependent shuttle system used by glucose. Vitamin C and glucose contest each other in the cellular uptake process, just like two strangers simultaneously trying to wave down the same taxi cab.[23] In this scenario, our body greatly prefers the valuable fuel, glucose in the competition and the vitamin C is excreted in the urine.[24] If a high quantity of refined and processed foods are consumed, blood sugar levels will invariably increase and the cellular uptake of vitamin C drops in proportion to it.[25] Glucose also inhibits the reabsorption of vitamin C by the kidney.[26] High insulin levels and low glucose tolerance in the body cause a notable fall in vitamin C levels.[27]

We become unhealthy and get scurvy, beriberi or pellagra not because we don't consume enough fruits and vegetables or our diet doesn't include the food groups containing the corresponding vitamin but because we consume too much of the foods that deplete the levels of vitamins in our body.

Now, the most important question to ask ourselves is - given the modern-day food environment rich in carbohydrates of all kinds, could a dietary deficiency be an indicator to our body to notch up our set point weight and increase our appetite so that we seek for food to acquire those nutrients and overcome deficiencies? Could a dietary defect be misinterpreted by our bodies as a signal of an imminent long hard winter or a famine and thus it gains surplus fat as insurance? If this is indeed the case, if a deficiency could have induced obesity in some individuals, obesity would be equivalent to deficiency diseases such as beriberi, pellagra, and scurvy, which were historically misunderstood by doctors and physicians. Nutrient deficiency as a promoter of obesity would fit in nicely with the set point weight that we discussed earlier.

To recap, the set point weight is adjusted by our hypothalamus (the subconscious brain) by estimating the weight point best for us and our survival. It receives data from our genes and environment to decide our individualized set point weight. Typically, a deficiency of an essential nutrient is due to an alteration in the environment that could notch up the set point weight. When the set point weight is increased above the current weight of an individual, the subconscious brain leads the weight towards the new set point through a drop in metabolism (reducing energy burning and hoarding energy into fat reserves) and through powerful hunger signals (voracious appetite). Before we know it, we are always hungry, can't restrict food, and we gain weight. This is an entirely unconventional approach to obesity. The ravenous hunger, lack of energy and interest in physical activity would no longer be responsible for the dysregulation of fat stores (growing size of fat) in our body but as compensation and a symptom of obesity or weight gain. Most of my clients who have tried a low-calorie diet increased their set point weight because their energy regulation system is abnormal.[28] The release of energy from fat is impeded but fat deposition remains intact. The organs in the body start to feel semi-starved and thus increase hunger in the individual. When we consciously reduce our calorie intake, the previously available fuel to the body is further depleted. The fuel burning in the body further plummets to compensate for a lack of energy, fuel conservation mode is ratcheted up and set point weight is adjusted in the body (energy expenditure is dependent on energy intake and availability to the body). The result is a vicious cycle of weight gain, lethargy and hunger.

Calorie deficit diets on a disrupted energy regulation system resulting in a higher set point weight

This is not a trivial difference. Just as in the case of Samantha where laziness was not the cause but a symptom of low vitamin D, overeating (a mismatch between energy consumed and energy used) is not the cause but a symptom of obesity. Hunger is just an autonomic drive of the brain to increase body weight to acquire essential fuel and nutrients that it is not getting because of an abnormal fat regulation system. As far as the relationship between appetite and nutrient concentration of food is concerned, Curt Richter[29] from Johns Hopkins University and Edward Adolph[30] from the University of Rochester have repeatedly shown that laboratory animals modulate their food consumption in reciprocation to the nutrients available to their body.

Depositing nutrients through a tube straight into the animal's stomachs or slipping them into their drinking water leads to the animal compensating by consuming less food. However, diluting their food with ingestible fibre or water results in the body not getting sufficient nutrients leading it to compensate by consuming a high volume of food to get the requisite and essential nutrients.

Recent research has indicated that saturated fats from natural foods are not a significant risk factor for heart disease. We already know exercise is cardio-protective. In the next chapter, I'll discuss how modifying the fat content in our diet has positively influenced the obesity rates.

10

Obesity and Omega Fats

'If we knew what it was we were doing, it would not be called research, would it?'

Albert Einstein

Before we understand what omega fats have to do with obesity, let's understand what omega-3 and omega-6 fats are.

Plants convert light energy from sunlight into chemical energy. Using this energy, they synthesize carbohydrates (sugar, starch, fibre aka indigestible carbohydrates), proteins and fats. Plants produce all the essential fats that we require. Chlorophyll, which gives plants their green colour, generates omega-3 fats. A single serving of iceberg lettuce, fenugreek leaves, lettuce or spinach possesses essential fats in abundance. Any fish or animal consuming green plants would also have omega-3-rich cells. Fish don't have many food options besides plankton and so possess a considerable quantity of omega-3. Cows, goats and chickens, which graze on grass, contain high amounts of omega-3 fats in their body and in their by-products such as milk and eggs. Similarly, larger predators that prey on animals and birds that consume grass or green leaves will also have omega-3 fats in their tissue. Finally, at the apex of the food chain, humans who consume a diet rich in vegetables or cattle, poultry and fish would also have abundant omega-3 fats. The other essential fats found in plants, especially in their seeds are omega-6 fats. These are not found in green leaves. Just as omega-3 is distributed through the food chain, so is omega-6, which is found in copious quantities in animals and birds consuming a diet rich in seeds.

Both plant and animal food groups provide unique nutrients that help us stay healthy.

Plant sources such as green leafy salads are rich in indigestible carbohydrates (fibre) and low in digestible carbohydrates (starch). A fruit salad is rich in sugar, water and fibre. Grains, legumes, nuts and seeds are great sources of fibre, starch, fats and proteins, however these proteins are not rich in essential amino acids and our bodies lack the enzymes to break down plant protein as opposed to animal protein.

Animal sources lack fibre and carbohydrates but are rich in proteins, fats, vitamins, and minerals. For instance, all animal products are rich in the most actively usable form of vitamin A known as retinol. Animal source foods are the only group that contain vitamin B12. Animal sources of omega-3 fats, namely eicosapentaenoic acid (EPA) and docosahexaenoic acid (DHA), constitute almost 30 per cent of the grey matter in the human brain and support its function, development, and our behaviour and mood. Essential amino acids such as methionine, tryptophan and lysine are not found in considerable quantities in plant foods but are copiously present in animal sources.

The important part is not whether the fat is from an animal or plant source but the degree of its 'saturation' (how many hydrogen atoms are present on each carbon) and length of the carbon chain in the fat. A full quotient of hydrogen atoms makes a saturated fat. Both animal and plant fats are diverse, each with various degrees of saturation and chain lengths, and have distinct effects on our health and longevity. So the popularly promoted idea that all fats found in animal foods are 'harmful' saturated fats and that all 'healthy' unsaturated fats are found in plants and fish is an erroneous idea, to say the least.

The fats in the body not only act as energy buffering stores but also are involved in various other critical functions. The predominant composition of our nervous system (the brain and the nerves) is made up of fats. Roughly 50 per cent of the brain constitutes cholesterol. Therefore, dietary fat is necessary for normal brain and nerve function. Hormones, which are potent drivers of our behaviour, are also formed from fats we consume. Dietary fat also helps us store and transport vital fat-soluble vitamins such as vitamins A, D, E and K, and minerals. When we are physically injured and require 'inflammation and repair' work, the inflammatory responses that facilitate the repair of tissues and battle against infections are driven and mediated by messengers derived from fats. Finally, and perhaps most crucially, fat constitutes the outermost protective cell walls in every organism on Earth. The cell walls function as the final obstacle to blocking unwanted toxins and bacteria from entering the cell. They protect the critical structure that makes us who we are, our genes (DNA), from being attacked or corrupted. This cell wall also has channels to communicate with its outside world and the brain through hormones to understand the body's needs for good health and survival.

There are three types of fatty acids – saturated fatty acids, monounsaturated fatty acids and polyunsaturated fatty acids.

- Saturated fats are solids at room temperature, e.g., butter, ghee, cheese, any other animal fat, palm oil, and coconut oil.
- Monounsaturated fats are liquids at room temperature but will quickly solidify when refrigerated, e.g., peanut, avocado and olive oils.
- Polyunsaturated fats[1] are liquids at room temperature and in the refrigerator, e.g., cooking oils made from seeds. Omega-3 and omega-6 fatty acids[2] are two subclasses of polyunsaturated acids.

Our bodies can synthesize saturated and monounsaturated fats. We are not dependent on our diet to provide us with these fats. I've previously discussed cholesterol, which is a saturated fat and an indispensable component of our protective cell walls and our brain and thus fundamental to our health. In fact, the cholesterol we find in our blood is produced mainly in the liver, to the tune of four parts of five and the remaining one part is supplied from our diet. It is so fundamental to our health that each cell in our body except the brain can synthesize it. Even if we stop eating saturated fats, our liver will take up the slack, make it from scratch, and supply it to the body. The problem is that omega fats can't be synthesized in our body.

Hence, these are called 'essential' fats, which means we need to add them in our diet, just like vitamins and minerals, for our health. We need both omega-3 and omega-6 in our diet but their properties are completely different. Omega-3 instantly gets oxidized, that is, rotten and spoilt compared to omega-6. Fresh foods with a higher quantity of omega-3 such as fish go rancid immediately when left out. Grains, nuts, and seeds and their oils are rich in omega-6 fats, whereas ghee, fish, and fish oil supplements are traditionally rich in saturated fats and omega-3 polyunsaturated fats.

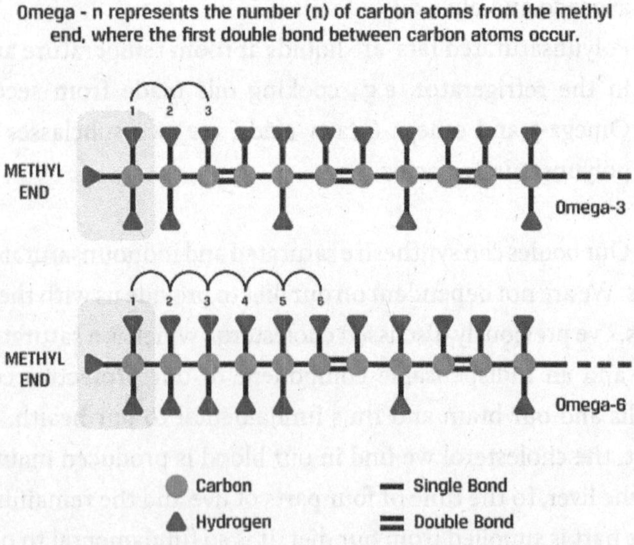

Structure of omega-3 and omega-6 fatty acids

Processed foods contain a colossal quantity of refined white flour from wheat and vegetable oils, and therefore are very high in omega-6.[3] Over the past five decades, an unprecedented rise (by 136 per cent) in omega-6 fat content in our bodies has been observed.[4] India is now the second-largest consumer and the apex importer of vegetable oil.[5] With growing urbanization and swift changes in dietary habits, highly processed foods with a high content of vegetable oils and omega-6 fats are being commonly consumed. Over the last five years, the per capita consumption has stayed in the range of 19–19.8 kg per annum.[6] In recent years, consumption of oils such as vanaspati, soyabean oil and sunflower oil has been rising.[7] These oils are poor in omega-3 and rich in omega-6 polyunsaturated fats.

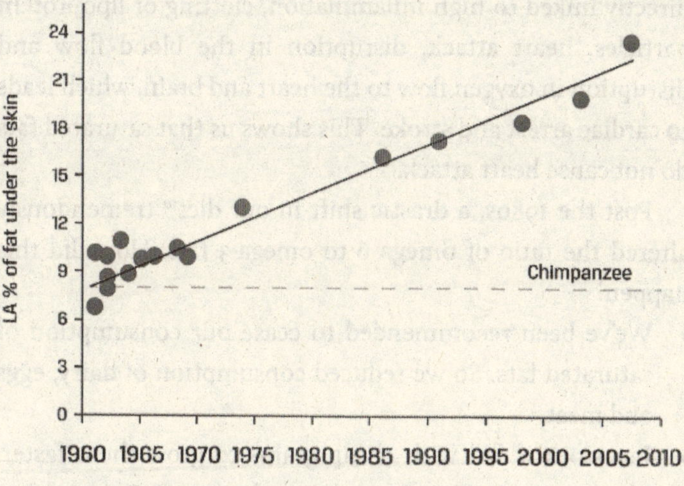

Source: S. Guyenet (2011), Seed oils and body fatness – A problematic revisit. Whole Health Source, 21 August.

Levels of omega-6 found in our bodies versus other primates

In fact, a study compared the current levels of omega-6 fats found in our tissues with chimpanzees.[8] The omega-6 levels in our bodies have increased from 8 per cent in 1961, matching the other primates, to 23 per cent in 2008, corresponding to the large amount of grains and vegetable oils we are consuming.

In 2013, a study[9] tested the health outcomes of replacing saturated fats with omega-6 fats. Men who recently had heart problems were selected as the experimental group and were given a diet with polyunsaturated fat-rich margarine (omega-6) and a type of seed oil, safflower. The control group were allowed to consume their regular diet containing saturated fats. More deaths were recorded in the omega-6 group. Omega-6, which is a polyunsaturated fat, has been directly linked to high inflammation, clotting of lipoprotein particles, heart attack, disruption in the blood flow and disruption in oxygen flow to the heart and brain, which leads to cardiac arrest and stroke. This shows us that saturated fats do not cause heart attack.

Post the 1980s, a drastic shift in our diet[10] tremendously altered the ratio of omega-6 to omega-3 fats. How did this happen?

- We've been recommended to cease our consumption of saturated fats. So we reduced consumption of dairy, eggs and meat.
- Livestock is fed with cheap grains to grow them faster. These grains contain large doses of omega-6. They eat less grass, which is a good source of omega-3. This affects the overall quality of the produce, be it dairy or meat, which leads to more omega-6 and less omega-3 in our diet.

- When we cook our food in animal fats or coconut oil instead of seed oil, the levels of omega-6 fats will not be as high.
- Commercial farming techniques involve feeding grains and legumes to animals because they contain dense energy compared to that of grass. The storage of this commercial feed also lasts longer due to the lack of omega-3 in them, making input costs more economical, convenient and feasible for profitable farming businesses.
- Fish get bigger if they are given a diet rich in grains rather than plankton, which is their natural food. This would mean that these naturally rich sources of omega-3 have less omega-3 and more omega-6 fats.
- Fresh food, when kept out for long, gets oxidized and goes brown due to its omega-3 content. Processed food concocted in factories requires to be relatively less perishable and has a longer shelf life. Any food that is rich in omega-3 fats will spoil very quickly, so omega-3 fats are removed in processed foods.
- Seed oils are required to be low on omega-3. If not, they go rancid. These oils are chemically treated at high temperatures to destroy the omega-3 fats. The hydrogenation process used to eliminate these omega-3 fats lead to the generation of cardio-toxic trans fats,[11] all to make food taste fresher for longer.

In a perfect world, across our evolutionary history, the ratio of omega-6 to omega-3 should lie between 4:1 and 1:1,[12] that is, the omega-6 levels in the diet should be no more than four times the omega-3 levels. Back in the days of hunting and gathering, when farming and industrialization were largely absent from human societies, the time when humans only consumed fresh foods, the omega-6 to omega-3 ratio had been normal. Even today, individuals and populations subsiding on their traditional indigenous diets in remote locations of the world would have similar ratios. However, when the consumption pattern of the population shifts to commercially produced and processed foods, the ratio is skewed with too much omega-6 and too little omega-3. In some urbanized cities, the omega-6 to omega-3 ratio was observed to be an astonishing 16:1.

Population	Omega-6/Omega-3
Paleolithic	≈ 4/5
Current Rural India	5/1 to 6.1/1
Current Urban India	38/1 to 50/1

Alteration of essential fat consumption and omega-3 deficiency

How does this omega-6 to omega-3 ratio influence fat gain?

These omega fats play three important roles in the cell walls of all thirty trillion cells in our body:

1. Cell inflammation and repair
2. Permeability and sensitivity of the cell wall
3. Mood and appetite signalling

Cell inflammation and repair[13]

Omega-3 and omega-6 fats have opposite actions in cell repair in the case of injury or infection. Omega-6 fats release signals to initiate cellular inflammation and blood clotting, whereas omega-3 fats reduce inflammation and decrease blood clotting.[14] A large per cent of omega-6 fats in your body will cause constant low-grade inflammation. The immune system will become extra sensitive and will lose the ability to see the difference between a healthy and an unhealthy cell and starts killing any cell. This might lead to autoimmune disorders such as diabetes, arteriosclerosis, allergies, arthritis, asthma and inflammatory bowel diseases. This also increases the risk of developing cancer[15] and heart disease[16] because your body will develop clots quickly, especially when the polyunsaturated cooking oil is repeatedly heated. Here's the clincher: this low-grade inflammation releases the inflammatory cytokine TNF-alpha. This in turn blocks the detection of leptin levels in the hypothalamus, causing a higher set point weight, dysregulation of the fat energy system. Cue fat gain.

Not only that. Higher omega-6 levels on the cell wall also impair the insulin signalling of the cell. This means that the ability of cells to bring blood sugar into metabolically active organs is impaired. In other words, higher omega-6 levels cause insulin resistance, which I will discuss in the next chapter. The body's knee-jerk reaction is to produce more insulin to push the nutrients down into these cells. Failure to clear the sugar from the blood due to unresponsive cells leads to high blood sugar levels and as a last resort, the body clears this blood sugar by converting it into triglycerides (fats) in the liver for storage in adipose (fat) tissues. When the adipose tissues reach a critical swollen size, inflammation and production of TNF-alpha occurs. This further reduces the effectiveness of the cell membrane to respond, causing even higher insulin and leptin resistance in the brain. Overall, the omega-6-rich vegetable oils and ultra-processed food generate the need for more insulin and increase our body's set point weight.

Permeability and sensitivity of cell wall

The flexible tail of the omega-3 fats enhances the permeability of the cell wall making it more adaptable and fluid in responding to hormones and nutrients in the environment. For instance, essential minerals such as calcium required for muscle function pass through the muscle cell wall more effortlessly when the wall is rich in omega-3 fats. Even our metabolic adaptation and fuel requirements of the body are effortlessly conducted by the fat cells in an omega-3-rich environment. In other words, our fat cells will be more adaptive, sensitive, and responsive to hormonal signalling from the body.

Suppose omega-6 fat content dominates the cell wall. The cell wall becomes rigid and stiff, which makes it difficult for the hormone signals to get into the cell. The cell is disconnected from the requirements of the body and does not conform to the intricately regulated system orchestrated by the brain.

This results in dysregulation of the stored fat energy in the body[17], energy deficit in metabolically charged organs and insensitivity to hormonal signalling. This crucial alteration in the cellular defence layer owing to a higher ratio of omega-6 to omega-3 results in reduced sensitivity of the cell walls of muscles, liver and brain to critical hormones such as insulin and leptin among others. This leads to higher insulin levels and leptin resistance, increasing the body's set point weight and risk of obesity.[18]

Mood and appetite signalling[19]

Do you know how weed or cannabis works on the brain after it is smoked? The endocannabinoids in them act as messaging molecules to activate cannabinoid receptors in the brain. Interestingly, omega-6 fats are precursors to endocannabinoids. When the cannabinoid receptor is activated, you feel happy and have an almost euphoric feeling. This is also called a dopamine hit! An hour or so after this activation, there is a spontaneous increase in appetite and hunger. When you finally eat, the sweet taste in your food becomes enhanced and pleasurable. The same thing happens when you eat omega-6-rich processed foods. The endocannabinoid system gets hijacked by omega-6 fats, leading to increased appetite and hunger. Remember that familiar addiction to Haldiram's, Lay's chips, Cadbury chocolate, and McDonald's fries? The blood sugar and omega-6 fats coming from the refined flour, potato and sugar hijack the endocannabinoid system and make you addicted to these foods.

Not just that. Altering the omega ratios and consuming insufficient omega-3 fats also has a profound impact on the development of a growing child's brain and the maintenance of our neural functions as adults because of the following reasons:

1. Omega-3 fats,[20] especially DHA, form the structural components of neurological tissues (the brain and nerves) and any alterations in our omega-6 to omega-3 dietary intake will affect the ratio in the brain.
2. High levels of omega-3 (1 out of 4) are typically present in the brain cell membranes.
3. Low omega-3 fat levels cause neurological disorders such as Huntington's disease, multiple sclerosis and macular degeneration.
4. High omega-6 to omega-3 ratio has been implicated in depression, suicide, anxiety, mood disorders, dementia and Alzheimer's disease.[21]
5. Severe omega-3 deficiency can result in weakness, blurred vision and numbness.

John Stein, emeritus professor of neuroscience at Oxford University, cautioned that a high intake of omega-6 inhibits the conversion of omega-3 fats (from plant foods) to a more bioactive and usable form of omega-3.[22] Simply put, if the diet is rich in omega-6, it will not matter how many green vegetables we consume; their conversion to a usable form of omega-3 will be inhibited. This is why my patients who are trying to lose weight and consuming a typical low-calorie, low-saturated fat and omega-6-rich diet constantly crave food with sugars, starch and omega-6-rich oils. In my experience, hardly any patient tells me that they crave and want to consume fish, salad or eggs in the middle of the night or after dinner. They typically crave instant noodles, pastries, candies, ice creams, cheesecakes, cookies, chocolates and other sugary foods rich in omega-6 fats.

Here is another interesting study that proves fat is important in our diet. Dr Walter Willett, professor of epidemiology and nutrition at Harvard University, who is one of the world's foremost thoughtful authorities in nutrition, published an article called 'Dietary Fat Plays a Major Role in Obesity: No'[23]. He wrote that reduction in fat energy will not have significant benefits and could further perpetuate the obesity problem. He also said that the obsession with the reduction in fat calories has been a grave distraction in our pursuit of good health and controlling obesity.

Dietary fat actually slows down blood sugar release in the body, which lowers insulin levels, helps us store less fat and burn it quickly. In fact, breastmilk provides more cholesterol than virtually any other food. Over half of its calories are fats, most of which are saturated fats.[24] This is because both saturated fats and cholesterol are essential for the brain development of growing babies and children. Here is an interesting fact: North Indians consume 19 times more animal fats that are rich in saturated fats[25] and have a seven times lower incidence of heart disease than those among South Indians.[26]

You might have a burning question at this point: why doesn't a calorie deficit diet work when we have a skewed omega-6 to omega-3 ratio?

Consider this. Say that an adult weighing 70 kg with 25 per cent body fat requires 1,000 kcal per day. Out of this, 500 kcal is used for daily energy expenditure for bodily functions and 500 kcal is stored as fats for future use and survival. A dramatic shift in this adult's dietary habits may skew his omega-6 to omega-3 levels. Then the way that these calories are distributed will change, causing hormonal imbalance and dysregulation of hormonal signalling to the brain from the fat tissue. Now in the 1,000 kcal, 550 kcal of energy is hoarded in the fat tissue, unavailable for the body to use, while the remaining 450 kcal is available and put into the circulation for the body as energy. The body still needs that extra 50 kcal to fulfil its energy expenditure needs for survival. What will it do? In the acute stage, it will drive hunger to compensate for the loss of those 50 kcal. In the long run, if we are on a calorie deficit diet, the body will reduce its energy expenditure to 450 kcal to match the available energy. Over time, this mixture of natural and unnatural foods that our biology does not understand and has not had adequate time to adapt to will start to dysregulate sugar and fat levels, leading to obesity through lower expenditure of energy and hunger. The sugary foods that we crave will hijack the pleasure centres in the brain, making the individual crave more of it. Thus, a diet of a mixture of whole and processed foods will lead to hunger for ultra-processed foods. This pattern will continue as follows:

Year	Expenditure	Storage	Total
1	500	500	1,000
2	450	550	1,000
3	500	550	1,050
4	450	600	1,050
5	500	600	1,100

Ingredients in processed foods (diet high in omega-6 fats) will continue to wreak havoc in the energy balance system, creating resistance in the hormone signalling to the brain, causing neural inflammation (swelling), and raising the set point weight of the body higher and higher.[27] This causes obesity, hunger and indolence. This phenomenon of an omega-6-rich diet inducing appetite is documented in a study that compared the effect of cooking food in saturated fat-rich oils versus polyunsaturated fat-rich canola oil. Two randomized control trials[28] were conducted, and interestingly the subjects in each trial were used as their own controls and were encouraged to eat to satiation. The researchers found that when boiled potatoes were mashed with butter and milk, the subjects attained their satiation at 701 kcal and 708 kcal, respectively. But when butter and milk were replaced with potatoes fried in canola oil, their satiation was achieved at 1,100 kcal and 1,136 kcal, respectively. So this is a tremendous difference in caloric intake because the only difference in the two instances is the cooking medium. The adipose tissue was able to easily release the stored saturated fatty acids into the circulation[29] than the stored polyunsaturated omega-6 fatty acids[30]. This is why saturated fats elicit higher satiety levels and increase the body's energy expenditure because a lot of fuel is accessible for the body's needs owing to the easy release of fats. This ceaseless and uninterrupted stream of fat energy provided by our adipose tissue, guards us against obesity, keeps us at a stable set point weight and increases the body's metabolic rate. In contrast, omega-6 fats promote obesity by inhibiting the release of energy from adipose tissue, which leads to increased appetite, reduced satiety and plummeting body energy expenditure. Recollect from the previous chapter that the lion's share of our daily calorie expenditure (almost 70 per cent) is used up by our autonomic nervous system to keep the body alive. So tuning in our appetite to this expenditure without energy deprivation and with correct nutrition is the way to sustainable and effortless weight loss, which is promoted by saturated fat intake and inhibited by an omega-6 fat-rich diet.

As the adipose tissue is relatively restricted in releasing the stored omega-6 fats into circulation, chronic consumption of processed foods rich in omega-6 fats will result in a lot of omega-6 fats stored in our fat tissue. As seen earlier, the adipose cells get very large, reach a critical point of size, become insensitive to insulin and start releasing omega-6 fatty acids and inflammatory molecules into the blood.[31] They get deposited into the viscera[32] (organs), where we don't want fat to be deposited, leading to organ malfunction (especially in the liver) and hormone resistance, leading to the breakdown of the body's homeostasis of fat regulation. Ectopic fat[33] (excess fat stored in tissues other than adipose tissue) is like having a giant splinter. This leads to inflammation signals because the body doesn't recognize organs rich in ectopic fat as itself but as a foreign object. The immune system is triggered and macrophages (specialized cells that detect and destroy bacteria and other harmful organisms) arrive at the scene. These macrophages occupy fifty to sixty per cent of mass, resulting in more inflammation and the development of degenerative diseases. This is why, most tragically, disorders such as obesity, diabetes, osteoporosis, multiple sclerosis, arthritis, digestive disorders, diabetes, Alzheimer's, cancer and heart disease, which were rare a century ago, have become common. Diseases that afflicted elderly individuals before are now striking even our children and those in the prime of their life.

The trick to deal with the obesity problem is to correct the dysregulation of fat stores induced by the new foods in our diet by reducing or eliminating them rather than reducing all calories. Our set point weight is a programmed reciprocation to data from our former and current environment, epigenetics and genes. These data points are used by our bodies to distribute energy to our brain, muscles, liver, etc. and choose an adequate size of our stored energy reserves for survival. When we think of the obesity problem in this manner, it is well-known that omega fats function as messenger molecules, like a proxy from nature educating our bodies about our future environment. Instances from nature may give us clues on how the omega fats in our diets evolved as messaging tools and why these messages can modify our immune (inflammatory) response and weight regulation.

Seasonal changes in the omega-6 to omega-3 ratio

The ratio of these omega fats in our diet alters in response to the seasons and the nature of food availability across that season. In temperate regions, there are seasonal variations in omega-6 and omega-3 fat intake owing to the types of food available during different seasons.[34] Typically during the spring season, omega-3 fats are abundant in the diet because the plants begin to grow leaves. However, when the leaves dry up and shed in the autumn, the intake of omega-6-rich nuts and seeds rises as they are found in abundance during this time of the year. This increases the ratio of omega-6 to omega-3. The amount of omega fats in the cell wall of animals and humans change, mirroring their food environment. The omega-6 to omega-3 ratio is typically higher in autumn and winter and lower during the spring and summer, balancing it all out (1:1) annually. These seasonal cellular alterations affect our biology, behaviour and reproduction cycle to prepare us for that imminent season.

As the sunlight begins to dissipate in autumn and winters, the quantity of food plummets. Animals are mandated by this environment to begin adjusting and adapting to use the available energy and calories efficiently for survival. Their equilibrium of energy metabolism is stressed as the environmental messages estimate more 'energy out' than 'energy in'. Unlike birds that adjust by migrating and flying off to tropical countries where the sun is brighter and food is abundant, land animals cannot migrate long distances and are stuck on land. For instance, brown bears will develop extreme hunger as the winter season approaches. They will put on weight (particularly fat; almost one-third of their current weight) to use it gradually during hibernation in the winter months. In preparation for winter, the brown bears gorge until their fat tank is saturated to the required set weight point best for their survival. During hibernation, the metabolic requirement for survival is less because their body temperature is lowered and movement is reduced to conserve their fat stores. Research shows that high omega-6 to omega-3 ratios are essential to induce torpor, lower body temperature and lower energy expenditure during this period.[35] Some researchers have proposed that the insulin resistance observed with a higher ratio of omega-6 to omega-3, leading to dysregulation of blood sugar and its elevation, is indeed a survival strategy ingrained in living beings from the time of primordial living beings.[36] This is to guard themselves against freezing during cold winters because when sugar is added to water, its freezing point decreases. All these biological responses to the type of food and its quality (or a lack thereof) are elements of our primordial evolutionary adaptation to assist survival and reproduction.

The omega-6-rich cooking oils in our diet signal our bodies that we are ravenously hungry. So the significant cause of obesity has less to do with morality, lack of willpower or laziness and more to do with the dynamically responsive homeostatic system in our bodies that adapts to any environmental change. Sadly, processed food intake has changed our nutrient composition throughout the seasons. This research – discovering the influence of nutrients on fat regulation fits in with all that I've read, researched and experienced about obesity.

11

Insulin Resistance – The Hidden Player in Obesity

'The three most harmful addictions are heroin, carbohydrates, and a monthly salary.'

Nassim Nicholas Taleb

I have called insulin the blood sugar chaperone before. Insulin signals to the fat cells to not use its energy until the food energy has been cleared from circulation and the insulin levels are back to normal. Many individuals only think of insulin as a medication to treat diabetes patients. Insulin,[1] in reality, is a hormone that we naturally produce in our bodies except for individuals with type 1 diabetes. Like most hormones, insulin is a protein produced in a single part of the body. It moves through our blood and influences various systems of the body. Insulin is manufactured in the pancreas, a tiny organ found underneath the stomach. Its most famous role is to normalize blood sugar levels. When we consume food that raises blood glucose, the pancreas releases insulin, which 'opens the gates' to usher glucose from the blood to several organs of the body such as muscles, fat tissues, heart and brain.

But what many people don't know is that insulin influences every cell in each body tissue and has a large audience to cater to! This is uncommon among hormones. Typically, they influence only a single or perhaps a few organs in the body. The particular influence of insulin on cells depends on the type of cell. For instance, when insulin binds to the liver cells, the liver does two things - stores glucose within itself as glycogen and makes fat from it. When insulin binds to a muscle cell, it triggers the production of new proteins and stores glucose energy as glycogen, among other things. From the hair on our heads to our toenails, insulin influences how cells use energy and alter their size, impacts the generation of other hormones and even dictates if a cell lives or dies. Its ability to function well is the difference between good health and awful chronic disease. The results of insulin increase and weight gain are very consistent and invariable.

Did you know that many elite athletes use insulin to perform better? Have you ever wondered apart from training hard, getting good nutrition and getting good sleep and rest, how elite athletes develop a competitive edge? Despite ageing, athletes maintain top physical condition. Their muscles appear to defy fatigue and look healthy. An important but lesser-known ability of insulin is to make cells bigger through a process called 'anabolism'. For this reason, it is very popular in the competitive bodybuilding community as athletes need freakishly big muscles. About 10 per cent of recreational and professional bodybuilders in Iran, some recreational weightlifters in the UK, and 25 per cent of recreational bodybuilders in the US reportedly use insulin.[2] It is a performance-enhancing drug (ergogenic agent) used to promote glucose uptake in the muscle from the bloodstream. This helps the muscle store more energy and work harder for longer. It also inhibits muscle breakdown, thus preserving lean tissue size and strength. Posing their big, buffed, symmetric bodies on the bodybuilding stage wins bodybuilders their medals, and greater power output helps athletes win strength sports such as weightlifting, powerlifting and sprinting. All these superhuman feats are achieved by carrying a lot of energy in the muscles aided by insulin.

Insulin infusion protocol is usually used after the athletes have finished training. Usually, the sugar stored in the body known as glycogen is used up entirely during their intense training. Like a squeezed-out, dry sponge, their muscles are ready to pounce on the next dose of energy they get. After training, these athletes drink a solution of around 80 g of glucose and 40 g of whey protein diluted in water along with multiple vitamin supplements. Then they get injected with an appropriate dose of insulin. The blood is flooded with nutrients, and the insulin injected facilitates the muscles to store more glucose and nutrients for a more muscular body. Insulin is eliminated from the body within minutes, leaving no trace. Hence, the testers cannot catch these athletes.

Another lesser-known fact is that insulin is also produced after protein consumption. However, protein consumption also stimulates the energy-releasing hormone known as glucagon, which has the opposite effect of insulin (i.e., storing energy). This is why the hormonal effect of protein on fat regulation is neutral. Taking extra insulin along with extra quick-releasing carbohydrates and quick-releasing protein when the muscles are depleted leads to maximum recovery from the session. This process is known as the hyper-insulin clamp[3] or the post-exercise window of anabolic opportunity[4]. Through this strategy, muscles store more water, carbohydrates and proteins to rebuild and grow, which makes them look fuller and the body lean, shredded, sharp and sculpted. But there is a big risk! If the glucose intake is not timed well with an insulin injection, the extra insulin will clear all the available blood glucose into the cells, leading to an episode of hypoglycaemia. In this case, nothing is left in the body to provide energy to the brain. The athlete will rapidly fall into a coma and ultimately die. This protocol should only be followed under the supervision of a trained physician. If you are a well-trained individual, then following this post-exercise protocol of carbohydrate intake is a great way to get glucose into muscle cells and improve body composition.

In contrast, consuming large quantities of fast-acting glucose while leading a sedentary lifestyle could have a different effect on insulin, which will force glucose into fat cells. Instead of your muscles appearing full and ripped, your belly will appear fuller instead of ripped. When insulin levels are elevated in your bloodstream, the sugar energy goes only one way, that is into the fat cells. The energy is not let out until the insulin levels plummet, which happens when the blood sugar levels are normalized. Only then do the fat cells open to release their energy into circulation. When insulin stops working, we develop a condition known as insulin resistance, a peculiar characteristic of obesity.

Do you know that a 35 ml sugar-sweetened beverage and 305 g of broccoli have the same quantity of sugar in them as found in our entire body (in 5,000 ml blood) at a resting/fasting level? Foods containing complex carbohydrates such as vegetables, grains, beans and legumes take a lot more time to digest and break down into glucose. So the infusion of glucose into the blood will be slow and gradual. If we consume a can of soft drink, sugar is infused into our blood within minutes, which causes a massive surge in blood sugar, maybe even doubling the levels, and leads to abnormally high insulin levels. However, if we consume 300 g of broccoli, our digestive system will require up to two hours to completely break down the complex chain of carbohydrates into simple sugar glucose. The blood sugar levels and consequently insulin levels will rise slowly. The amount of insulin produced by the pancreas is proportional to the quantity of glucose in circulation and the rate at which the sugar is released into the bloodstream from our meal. Therefore, your insulin levels post a meal are directly impacted by the quality and type of food consumed.

Interestingly, the body never secretes a precisely calculated quantity of insulin. It depends on a rough estimate based on the initial magnitude and rate of blood sugar entering the circulatory system. If we start our meal with a sugary food or drink (processed carbohydrates), high levels of insulin are released at once. Even if you eat high protein foods after this first sugary food, your body has already estimated how much insulin is needed and dumped a massive amount into the bloodstream. This means that too much sugar leaves the bloodstream and goes into the cells because insulin's job is to chaperone sugar into cells. This rings emergency bells in the brain that depends on glucose for energy. This alarm is translated to a feeling of anxiety and a very potent hunger for high sugar foods to get the energy back quickly. The brain is now in survival mode. You become hungrier and look for more sugary food. The brain requires only around half a teaspoon of sugar. However, what it gets is undoubtedly a sugar-filled pastry. The sugar floods the circulation again, insulin is called up into action again, initiating a massive roller coaster ride of not just emotions but also energy in the body.

This classic bumpy ride typically starts with breakfast, where you might have eaten cereal or toast with jam and downed it with orange juice (processed food rich in sugars) and experience a sugar spike. By late morning, your blood sugar levels drop because of an enormous reactive spike in insulin. All the sugar is removed from circulation and goes into storage. We get the most terrible craving for more sugar now. You have a mid-morning snack of sugar-rich tea or coffee, biscuits and toast. We feel good now! The blood sugar and insulin is up again. You experience another blood sugar crash right before lunch. Then you have a lunch of a sandwich, crisps and a coke. This bumpy ride[5] continues all day every day. This process of the sugar roller coaster brings back the idea of homeostasis we discussed earlier. Abnormally high blood sugar levels are a significant deviation from the body's norm. Thus, any external influence (a bad diet) will quickly be compensated to reduce blood sugar. In this case, the adjustment that the body makes is to convert more sugar into fat and increase fat stores to bring down the level to the normal homeostatic range of 80–100 mg/dl (4–5 g of sugar in circulation) and not above 200 mg/dl (10 g of sugar in circulation) postprandial.

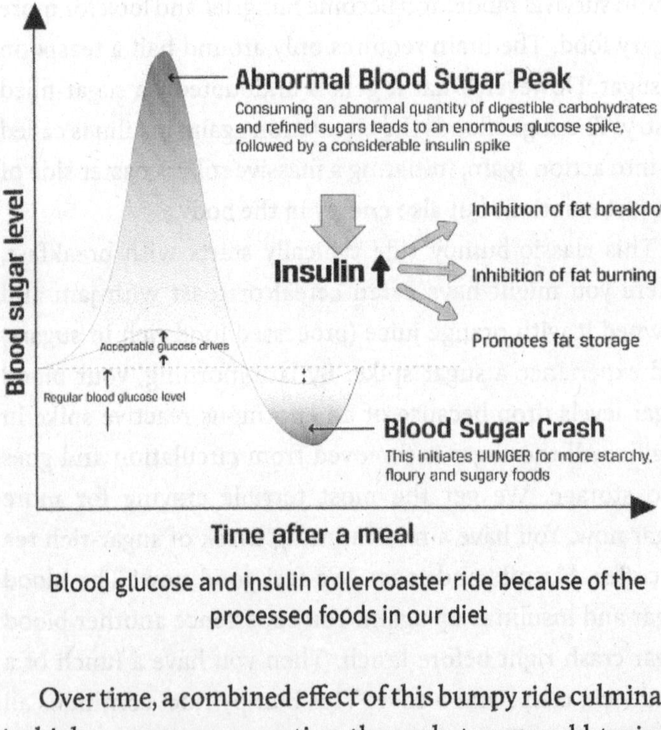

Blood glucose and insulin rollercoaster ride because of the processed foods in our diet

Over time, a combined effect of this bumpy ride culminates in higher sugar consumption than what we would typically crave when we eat a whole food diet. Higher insulin levels undermine the leptin signals (weight controller) to the hypothalamus. If leptin is not detected, our set point weight is increased, and our body will programme itself to gain weight to reach that higher set point weight. If we can manage to decrease our average insulin levels, our set point weight point and our weight will automatically drop. In part two of this book, we will look at ways to do this by adjusting our eating habits and weaning ourselves off of sugar addiction. So, in short:

Higher insulin → higher set point weight
Lower insulin → lower set point weight

Ultimately, it is not the number of calories that counts. Had that been the case, all of us would be weighing over 100 kg. Whenever we eat too many calories, our body burns the surplus calories to avoid weight gain beyond our set point. This is our regular metabolic adaptation to overfeeding. This means that the true reason behind our weight gain is insulin resistance.

Insulin resistance

I'm sure you think that insulin resistance occurs only in diabetes patients. This is far from the truth. Insulin resistance can set in long before an individual develops type 2 diabetes. Insulin is always discussed in tandem with glucose, which isn't fair given the hundreds and maybe thousands of actions that insulin performs in our body. Nonetheless, if blood sugar levels are within the normal range in a healthy body, insulin is usually normal.

What is insulin resistance?

When a cell ceases to respond properly to insulin, which can be caused by sedentary, dietary or stress factors, it becomes insulin resistant. As different body parts become insulin resistant, the body is deemed insulin resistant. In this case, cells require more than the normal quantity of insulin to get a normal response. Our hormones (e.g., growth hormone, insulin, parathyroid hormone, cortisol) are naturally secreted according to our circadian rhythms[6] in quick and short bursts to prevent any future resistance to their effects. They are released at high levels at a particular time of the daily cycle to generate their unique effect. After its effects are noticed by the body, the levels dramatically drop and remain very low. Accordingly, in case of insulin resistance, the body produces more insulin to overcome this resistance.

What happens in the cell because of this insulin resistance?

Like a key that perfectly fits into a door's lock to open it, all hormones function similarly on the surface of cells in our body. So when a hormone such as insulin, in this case, no longer fits into the insulin receptor of the cell that it acts on, such as the muscle, organ or liver cells in our body, the cell door does not open completely to allow the sugar to enter. Consequently, less sugar (glucose) energy enters the cell. Too much glucose is outside the cell in the bloodstream. Starved for energy, the cell demands more. As a response to this demand and to open the door to let glucose into the cell (be it brain, liver, or muscle cells), the body releases extra insulin (keys). The fit is still poor and the doors don't open completely even now.

Let's understand this with an example. In an ideal situation, when cells normally respond to insulin, one insulin allows one glucose energy into the cell. Currently, in a fasting state, 80 units of glucose are in the blood, and the body is doing fine. As we eat, we raise the glucose in the blood to 90 units. In response, the body will produce 10 units of insulin to put the 10 extra units of glucose into the cells to revert to its homeostatic state of 80 units of sugar in the blood. In case of insulin resistance, the hinges of the cell doors are jammed and the doors don't completely open. Only five glucose units are pushed into the cells when 10 insulin keys were produced. We still have five more units of glucose to be removed from the blood. What will the body do? To compensate, it will produce 10 more keys and a total of 20 to do the same job. The key has become less effective at doing its job. Though ultimately we manage to maintain the same blood glucose levels, we were able to do so by putting more pressure on our metabolic system (i.e., by producing more keys).

Does insulin resistance occur in the body in all the cells at once?

The parts on which insulin acts in the body are the brain, muscles, liver and fat cells. Not all cells in the body become equally resistant to insulin. Thus, insulin resistance is compartmentalized. Change in the insulin resistance in one part of the body does not alter insulin resistance in the other parts. For example, insulin resistance in the liver (hepatic) tissue does not make other metabolically active tissues such as the brain or muscles resistant to insulin. When we eat a higher quantity of easily digestible refined carbohydrates, we develop insulin resistance in the liver. But a tremendous dietary intervention will progressively take our liver back to being insulin sensitive and reverse the localized resistance. However, this will not affect the resistance developed in the muscles or brain. Similarly, lack of physical activity promotes insulin resistance in muscles, and exercising the muscles will enhance their insulin sensitivity. But this will have a minuscule effect on improving liver or brain insulin sensitivity. The generalized insulin levels elevate if insulin resistance occurs in muscles and the liver. In this case, if the brain is not insulin resistant, then the impact of insulin on the appetite centres within the hypothalamus is unaltered, and they continue to be responsive to insulin. Sedentary lifestyle is often considered as the primary culprit[7] in causing insulin resistance with age. But the actual reason is that exercising (and using your muscles) maintains insulin sensitivity. Even if healthy individuals are inactive for a couple of days, a noticeable insulin resistance develops,[8] and this problem is exacerbated with age.[9] It is not exactly a subtle effect either. A week of sedentary behaviour can enhance insulin resistance sevenfold![10]

Intriguingly, insulin resistance materializes with unbelievable consistency in the muscles that are not used. For instance, if one leg is made immobile with a cast, it becomes half[11] as insulin sensitive as the other mobile leg within a few days. Thus, when we neglect our muscles and our body,[12] insulin resistance is driven up. Even something as evidently innocent as sitting frequently for extended periods[13] is correlated with higher insulin resistance.

> **Did you know?**
> If we continuously sit for 120 minutes before a meal, the blood sugar response to the meal is driven up approximately by 45 per cent. An easy solution to mitigate the effects of extended sitting on insulin resistance is to simply get moving every 2 minutes for every 20 minutes of sitting. It could also be done by merely flexing your muscles 30 times for a couple of seconds each and contracting them from time to time to help buffer the risk adequately.

Insulin resistance is not exclusive to diabetes

One of insulin's primary functions is to normalize blood sugar. Chronically elevated blood sugar levels are fatal, and so our bodies require insulin to escort the glucose from the blood and bring down the blood sugar levels back to normal.

However, what about blood glucose control in the case of insulin resistance?

In this case, the blood sugar lowering effect of insulin is compromised, resulting in abnormally high blood glucose levels or 'hyperglycemia', a common symptom of diabetes. Because of insulin resistance, our body produces abnormally high levels of insulin. Sadly, the only treatment done for insulin resistance is to treat the elevated blood sugar. But high blood sugar is just a symptom and not the cause.

In ancient India, physicians noted that specific people produced honey-like urine that attracted insects, which they called *madhumeha.*[14] *Madhu* means honey and the term *madhumeha* literally means sweet urine. These patients also lost a lot of weight. This condition is actually what we know today as type 1 diabetes. Only much later did the Indian physicians observe that there were two distinct states of diabetes, one correlated with children and weight loss (type 1) and the other with adult and excessive body weight (type 2). Both conditions are characterized by frequent and excessive glucose-loaded urine, technically known as polyuria. The absence of modern technology to see any other difference between the two types of diabetes resulted in the disease being defined as a glucose-related condition. Therefore, injecting both types of diabetic patients with insulin had become the gold standard of treatment. This treatment is not effective in the long run because type 1 diabetes results from too little or no insulin, while type 2 diabetes is caused by excessive insulin secretion. This is counterintuitive in the second case because we are injecting the patient who has high insulin levels with even more insulin which worsens type 2 diabetes and causes obesity.

Type 1 diabetes	*Type 2 diabetes*
Too little or no insulin.	Too much insulin.
Insulin-generating cells in the pancreas get affected.	The cells in the body become insulin resistant, resulting in elevated insulin levels.
Less insulin implies that blood glucose after a meal cannot be chaperoned properly to each cell in the body. Blood sugar remains high and elevated, and glucose is excreted through urine.	Too much insulin causes leptin resistance, resulting in a raised set point weight and obesity.

Is insulin resistance the reason you are not able to lose weight?

Elevated insulin levels have long been strongly correlated with crucial biomarkers of ill health and weight gains, such as increased waist size and elevated waist-to-hip ratio.[15] Obese individuals have higher insulin levels than non-obese individuals. In lean individuals, insulin levels immediately return to baseline after a meal, whereas in obese individuals, insulin levels remain raised – these are almost 20 per cent more elevated.[16] However, this strong correlation between insulin and weight gain does not confirm its causal nature. Indeed, it may be challenging to accurately assess insulin levels due to their high variability throughout the day in reciprocation to our variety in food intake. However, considering an 'average' level is possible by measuring the levels multiple times in the day. Yet, measuring fasting levels of insulin after an overnight fast is an effortless, single-step technique.

In 1993, the landmark Diabetes Control and Complications Trial[17] compared the effects of standard-dose versus high-dose insulin injections on type 1 diabetics. At the end of the study, after six years, it was confirmed that, on average, the subjects in the regular-dose group gained roughly 4.5 kg fewer than subjects in the high-dose group. In the intensive therapy group, 1 out of 3 patients had tremendous weight gain! Subjects from both groups were slightly obese with more or less the same weight before the start of the trial. The quantity of insulin given to each group was the sole difference. Despite no sudden lack of willpower, indolence or gluttony, simply higher insulin levels resulted in weight gain.

The Prospective Diabetes Study Group[18] was a long-term study on people with type 2 diabetes organized in the 1970s in the UK. It demonstrated a similar weight-gaining effect of insulin. Subjects within the intensive group were given one of the two treatments – a drug that stimulated the body's production of insulin known as sulfonylurea or insulin injections. Insulin levels rose in both treatments but by distinct pathways. However, insulin injections elevated blood insulin levels higher than the sulfonylurea group. The average weight gain in the intensive group was approximately 3 kg, and the subjects who were given insulin injections gained even more weight, an average of 4 kg. Either way, increasing insulin levels caused notable weight gain.

Could it be possible that a calorie deficit diet would counteract the weight gain caused by insulin medication?

In a compelling study conducted on a group of type 2 diabetic patients in 1993,[19] the dose of insulin administered to the subjects started from zero and gradually increased day by day to 100 units over six months. At the same time, the subjects reduced their daily caloric consumption by more than 300 calories. The patients had well-controlled blood sugar. The average weight gain was around 9 kg. Patients put on a lot of weight despite reducing their daily caloric intake. Clearly, it's not the calories but the hormone insulin that results in weight gain.

If you think this effect is seen only in diabetics, you would be wrong. Insulin causes weight gain in non-diabetics too. Tumour insulinoma (tumour in the pancreas) is a condition typically found in only four people per million per annum. In these patients, the pancreas continuously releases a very high amount of insulin, resulting in frequent episodes of low blood sugar (hypoglycaemia). A prospective case study[20] showed that 72 per cent[21] of patients reported weight gain. Removal of the malignant insulinoma resulted in speedy and long-term weight loss.[22]

Increased caloric consumption did not cause weight gain, and decreased caloric consumption does not cause weight loss. The defining characteristic of fat accumulation or its loss is insulin.

So, if weight gain results from elevated insulin levels, would lowering it cause weight loss?

Another fascinating study conducted by a research group from Tennessee led by Dr Robert Lustig[23] observed the effect of decreasing the insulin levels in obese subjects. They administered a series of injections of octreotide, a drug that reduces insulin secretion from the pancreas. After the experiment, the subjects lost an average of 3.5 kg. Moreover, the insulin sensitivity of their body improved, and the group reported a reduced appetite after the treatment. Indeed, we can expect considerable and significant weight loss when insulin levels decrease to shallow levels.

A few years ago, a type 1 diabetes patient consulted me. He developed type 1 diabetes in childhood, started his treatment and fought obesity for several years. He was only thirty-three when he came to me for consultation and was already on insulin therapy. He told me that after he started insulin therapy to control his blood sugar, he put on a lot of weight and was at 90 kg with reasonable blood sugar control. Then he intentionally started to underdose insulin. As a result his weight reduced to 70 kg but he had poor blood sugar control. He showed symptoms of developing retinopathy (damage to the retina owing to low glucose uptake by the cells), which could result in blindness.

I explained to him that stopping insulin is not a healthy solution as it may result in more complications, such as retinopathy and limb amputation, and he was too young and had a long life to be dealing with such degenerative diseases at this early age. The trade-off wasn't beneficial at all and would do more harm than good. The healthiest approach for him to lose weight sustainably was to reduce the need to use higher doses of insulin to manage blood sugar. This could be easily achieved by regular physical activity, such as strength training to increase the stores of sugar energy in the body through a process known as hypertrophy (increase in the size of muscle tissue) where the body super compensates as a result of subjecting the muscles to picking heavier resistance. Additionally, increasing his total number of daily steps to 10,000 would assist glucose into his body independent of insulin, that is through increased muscle contraction, which initiates glucose transporter type 4 (GLUT4) transport and passive diffusion of glucose into the cell without insulin. Finally, minimizing sugar consumption to less than 5 g and starch to less than 45 g a day divided in three meals, and lastly, encouraging him to have a regularized sleep schedule of 7–8 hours daily. Within two weeks, his insulin dose started to reduce, and eventually within ten months he was able to maintain his weight between 73–75 kg with well-managed blood sugar, hence requiring a lower daily insulin dose.

Insulin influences fat mobilization and storage

At the beginning of the 1990s, a team of scientists at the University of Texas in San Antonio methodically tested this notion of why fat cells are so sensitive to elevated insulin levels.

Their results demonstrate how insulin is released from the pancreas in response to blood sugar levels and reduces the flow of fat from the fat tissue. At low insulin levels, the body uses free fatty acids from the fat tissue for energy expenditure. However, as soon as insulin is produced, the use of body fat is instantly stopped. When the insulin levels in the blood are at their low basal level, fatty acids are slowly released from cells and the use of body fat is at its peak. As soon as the insulin level rises from 10 to >15 μU per ml, the fat is locked in the fat cells until insulin levels drop below 15. Another important thing to remember is that insulin rises faster after consuming fast-digesting and easily absorbable starches and sugar, i.e., a diet high in carbohydrates and low in fats and protein. Above a certain insulin level, the fat cells hold on to fat; below it, they release the stored fat into the blood to be taken up as fuel for energy expenditure. If we eat food high in carbohydrates, our body concentrates on releasing more insulin to use these carbohydrates for energy expenditure instead of the body fat in storage. If this continues indefinitely, the stored fat keeps accumulating in our body.

How much daily carbohydrates are too much?

Every individual has varied tolerance to carbohydrate metabolism. Some are more sensitive to the fat-storing effect of insulin than others based on age, gender, ethnicity and body composition. This is similar to how different individuals have different tolerances for lactose in milk or gluten in wheat. The same carbohydrate levels in a diet will affect different individuals based on their state of insulin resistance. Some individuals stay lean, whereas others gain fat. Carbohydrate tolerance can change in the same individual at distinct phases of life. Unfortunately, the threshold of glucose metabolism for insulin-resistant individuals, such as type 2 diabetics or those at high risk of diabetes, is shallow.

I have previously discussed about how leptin resistance occurs. To recap, due to perpetually high insulin levels, the brain becomes leptin resistant. Leptin acts to reduce stored fat by releasing it, whereas insulin promotes fat storage. Obese individuals typically suffer from hormonal resistance, namely insulin and leptin, because both the fasting insulin and fasting leptin levels are perpetually elevated. Food intake in different individuals leads to different leptin responses. Leptin levels typically increase after food intake in lean individuals, which is an expected response to food intake as leptin is a satiety hormone. In contrast, the leptin levels in obese individuals decrease after food intake due to their brain's inability to detect higher leptin levels and leptin resistance which would signal satiety and cessation of food intake.[24]

Not only this, but any hormone can develop resistance in the wrong circumstances. To understand this more clearly, let's take a step back and observe other biological mechanisms as a guide. Various instances of biological resistance can be considered, which may not particularly concern insulin resistance. Still, they shed meaningful light on how the body adapts and restores homeostasis by developing resistance. When we consume coffee for the first time, there is an intense 'high'. With every subsequent cup of coffee, the high becomes less intense. So the individual must start taking more coffee to experience the same 'high'. The body develops a tolerance or resistance to the effects of coffee through persistent exposure to the caffeine in it. Similarly, individuals can build a tolerance to viruses and other drugs such as antibiotics, nicotine, alcohol, marijuana, narcotics, morphine, nitro-glycerine and benzodiazepines. This development of drug resistance is well known and well acknowledged in medical science. Even in the sub-disciplines of economics such as microeconomics and organizational economics, the law of diminishing marginal utility is a well-known, established law that proposes that the marginal utility decreases as every additional unit is consumed or employed.

If too much insulin causes obesity as we have seen, the clear line of treatment is to lower the levels. Now, the most important question: How to balance insulin?

Snacking – The perpetuator of insulin resistance

What should we eat? When should we eat? A recent survey[25] noted that over 70 per cent of Indians[26] agreed that they snack more throughout the day than they did a year ago. In the future, they plan to snack more often, increasing their eating frequency from three square meals a day to over five meals including snacking. Around 70 per cent[27] of these calories come from carbohydrates and not necessarily healthy sources but from refined flour and high sugar-based products. As one would expect, snack foods[28] are typically processed foods.

Our ancestors at the turn of the twentieth century would eat breakfast at around 9 a.m., lunch in the afternoon and dinner at 8 p.m. They balanced 11 hours of feasting with 13 hours of fasting. Elevated insulin pulses occur right after mealtimes followed by extended periods of low insulin levels during fasting and sleep. However, snacking and continuous insulin exposure changes the situation completely.

You may ask – what about the thermogenic effect of food? Shouldn't we eat food every two and half hours? Six meals a day drives up the metabolic rate six times a day! If the body's metabolic rate is elevated throughout the day, don't we burn more calories because of this constant digestion? The answer is no. The total thermogenic effect of food over a day would be the same even if we ate frequently or ate strategically three meals a day. Consuming smaller meals more frequently during the day did not benefit weight loss.[29] In contrast, adding snacks to your diet, getting restaurant food delivered home even in the wee hours of the morning, and 24/7 flexibility in consuming meals have totally destroyed the equilibrium between the fed and insulin-dominant state and fasted and insulin-deficient state. Most of our time today is spent in an insulin-dominant state as we constantly expose our bodies to elevated insulin levels and consequently develop insulin resistance. And then, when we want to lose weight and reduce our calorie intake, we wonder why we are not losing weight. Typically fasting insulin levels are shallow. But because of snacking, insulin levels remain high even in the fasting windows between meals and during sleep. After an overnight fast, we begin our day at higher insulin levels rather than lower ones. By consuming frequent high-carbohydrate meals, we have now checked both the criteria for developing insulin resistance: high levels and persistent exposure. The popular advice to follow is a low-fat diet, which inevitably results in a diet rich in refined, ultra-processed foods, triggering elevated insulin levels and eventual weight gain. As per the experts, the frequency of meals is almost twice as critical as an alteration in the diet,[30] and matters significantly in the progression of obesity.[31] To lose weight, we wholeheartedly research the next novel foods, such as chia seeds, quinoa, and açaí berries but give no time, energy or thought to how frequently we should be consuming food.

Myth: Consuming food often controls hunger.

Another myth: Frequent eating helps keep the blood sugar steady and stops it from dropping too low.

Fact: Unless one has a poorly regulated blood sugar system or diabetes, one's blood sugar will remain stable irrespective of whether we consume six meals a day or six meals a week.

In today's world, the cultural norm is to eat food anywhere and everywhere. We eat while working, thinking, in front of the TV, in the library, in theatres, in theme parks and in our car while driving. Our bodies remain in an insulin-dominant state for up to eighteen hours a day, with only the remainder time of six hours spent in an insulin-deficient state. To sum up:

> Frequent snacking → elevated insulin levels → insulin resistance → higher insulin levels → leptin resistance → higher set point weight → lower energy expenditure and satiety

Dietary carbohydrates and blood glucose – Influence on insulin

Nutritionists are typically apprehensive about reducing carbohydrates in the diet and favour prescribing a higher carbohydrate diet for weight loss. They are frequently indifferent to the quality of carbohydrates consumed as long as at least 130 g of carbohydrates are consumed. This is because the brain generally burns up to 130 g of glucose per day. They are under the assumption that glucose only comes from carbohydrates and remain sceptical of the idea that body fat plays any role in glucose buffering other than as a long-term reserve of energy for emergencies such as a famine.

Though glucose is a primary source of energy for the brain, it is not the only source of fuel. Furthermore, dietary carbohydrates are not the only source of glucose for the body. When carbohydrates in the diet are low or when an individual fasts for a prolonged period, the fatty acids in the liver breakdown to produce ketones. These ketone bodies provide the necessary fuel for our brain and central nervous system. This phenomenon is called fat metabolism. However, some of the cells in the body cannot use any other fuel but glucose, such as red blood cells. In this case, glucose is produced from other molecules in the body. For example, red blood cells get the glucose produced from glycerol, which in turn comes from the breakdown of triglycerides in the fat tissue. In cases of extreme starvation, glucose comes from the amino acids originating from the dietary protein or from muscles. In such a case, the body is technically in a state known as ketosis. Such a diet is frequently referred to as a ketogenic or keto diet. Whether the diet is ketogenic or not depends on the exact amount of carbohydrates in the diet because even a difference of a few tens of grams of carbohydrates determines if the body uses glucose or ketone bodies as the primary source. Ideally, exceeding 50 g of daily carbohydrate intake will put an individual out of the ketosis state. This ketosis is known as nutritional ketosis and is very different from ketoacidosis of untreated diabetes. The former is a common condition of carbohydrate restriction and prolonged fasting, whereas the latter is not.

There is a direct association between consuming refined carbohydrates and increased hunger and another direct association between increased satiety and consuming a meal rich in protein and fats and restricted in refined carbohydrates. When our body is adapted to using fat as the primary fuel for energy, we will experience less hunger, even when we are consuming nothing at all, because our cells will be fuelled by the fat from fat tissue 24/7.[32] However, if processed foods[33] are

The key differences between ketone and glucose as fuel source

Attributes	*Ketone*	*Glucose*
Definition	Ketone is an alternative to glucose as an energy source for the brain.	Glucose is the primary source of fuel in the blood. It supplies our organs with instant energy.
Classification	Acetone, Acetoacetate, Beta-hydroxybutyrate	Glycogen, starch, dextrose
Benefits	Ketone is a cognitive performance enhancer. A planned diet consisting of Ketone helps in fat-burning and weight loss.	It allows the body to perform high-energy tasks.
Downside	In the initial stages of fat-adaptation from glucose to ketone, side-effects may be observed.	Stimulates addiction to sugary, floury, and starchy foods.
Which is a more efficient energy source?	An efficient supplier of energy to the brain with minimum waste production.	Produces instant energy but is waste-producing relative to Ketone.
Source in diet	Supplied by dietary fat	Contained in carbohydrates

added back to the diet, the sugar rollercoaster will begin. We will be frequently dependent on glucose as the primary fuel for our body and thus overwhelmingly hungry. Therefore, if we break our fasting windows with whole foods rich in proteins and fats,[34] we stay satiated for a more extended period.

Thus, the question is not whether to go on a keto diet or not. The question should be how to lower our set point weight and our average insulin levels.

Will the keto diet also do that? Yes.

Is it practical? No, because adhering to a ketogenic lifestyle can be really challenging as it is restrictive, especially for vegetarians who do not have many food choices to remain in a state of ketosis.

Are there other approaches? Definitely yes! Without being in ketosis 24/7, you can still dramatically lower your insulin levels, insulin resistance and set point weight.

The point of this book is to offer a sustainable dietary and lifestyle approach to lose weight and improve your health. The trick here is to understand how to lower insulin levels and encourage a hormonal environment in the body that lowers the set point weight without drastically altering the body's homeostasis. In other words, you shouldn't feel restricted from enjoying that piece of cake on your birthday or that hearty meal during the holidays.

12

Carbohydrates and the Glycaemic Index Mania

> 'Is a persistent [high blood sugar] a cause of arteriosclerosis in diabetes? It very likely is a cause because it is an abnormal condition and any abnormal state would tend to wear out the machine.'
>
> Elliott Joslin, *Arteriosclerosis and Diabetes*

Are all carbohydrates fattening? Plants take energy from sunlight and make carbohydrates. These carbohydrates come in digestible forms such as sugar and starch and indigestible forms such as dietary fibre. Dietary fibre is made up of glucose, but the human digestive system lacks the enzymes to break down the fibre to extract energy. That is why fibre does not count in the calories added to the energy balance in the body. However, fibre makes the digestive system work hard to breakdown the starch and sugars that are consumed with it, increasing the thermogenic value of food and delaying the release of sugar into the blood. It is the opposite of the metabolic chaos created by processed foods, which lead to instantaneously high blood sugar levels and high insulin swings.

When biochemists speak about sugar, they're referring to a whole host of elementary carbohydrate structures, all of which are marked, among many other things, by their sweet taste and ability to dissolve in water. Their chemical names all terminate in '-ose' – sucrose, fructose, glucose, lactose, galactose, among others. All the carbohydrates we consume through our diet are broken down and converted to glucose.

When doctors and physicians speak about blood sugar, they mostly talk about glucose. However, relatively low concentrations of other sugars can be found in the circulatory system.

Then there's the layperson's usage of 'sugar', referring to the white, sweet and powdered variety added to confectionary items, coffee and tea. This is table sugar (sucrose), which is composed of equal parts of fructose and glucose. In this chapter, whenever I am talking about 'sugar', I'm referring to sucrose, and whenever I say 'blood sugar', I'm referring to glucose.

Our bodies use glucose to accomplish many cellular processes that give us energy for daily activities such as thinking and walking. Since glucose is required by the body to perform all its operations, it can be considered essential to life. The body prefers to maintain a healthy level of blood sugar throughout the day and functions best with 80 mg/dl of glucose.

Carbohydrates are categorized as simple and complex carbohydrates.

Simple carbohydrates	*Complex carbohydrates*
• a single molecule of sugar known as monosaccharides (mono = one and saccharide = sugar) • two sugars bonded together known as disaccharides (di = two and saccharide = sugar)	• tens of thousands of long glucose chains • contain fibre and starches and have to be broken down into simple sugars during a long-drawn digestion process

Starches found in vegetables, nuts and legumes have diverse, complex structures. Each type of starch breaks down and raises blood sugar at a different rate in our body. For example, vegetables such as potatoes and sweet potatoes[1] are rich in starches known as amylose and amylopectin. Amylose has a thick structure of glucose chains and takes more time to break down than amylopectin, which has branched glucose chains and is relatively easier to break down. If a food item floods our circulation with glucose quickly, it is categorized as a high glycaemic index food, and if it releases glucose slowly, it is a low glycaemic index food. The rise in blood sugar among different individuals varies tremendously based on consumption patterns. For instance, after carbohydrate depletion due to diets such as the ketogenic diet and also exercising, the first bowl of rice will not cause as much blood sugar rise (the depleted muscles and liver readily take up glucose like how a dry sponge sucks water in) as would the same bowl of rice repeated after 2 hours because now the muscles and liver glycogen are fuller (the sponge has already some water in it) thus a higher blood sugar levels. The second time, the blood sugar goes higher with the same food and quantity in the same person due to the body not having readily available space to store the sugar nor the parts of the body such as the brain desperately asking for it because they have sufficient glucose coming from the previous bowl of rice. So the glycemic index is relative. It's not a fixed number for a particular food but a range. Potatoes and sweet potatoes have different glycaemic indices because potatoes are richer in amylopectin, and sweet potatoes are richer in amylose starch. Because amylose raises blood sugar at a slower rate, it is a relatively lower glycaemic index food than amylopectin.

However, this is not an accurate assessment of how healthy the carbohydrate is for us. This classification of simple versus complex carbohydrates has been rendered less meaningful years ago as it only categorized carbohydrates based on their chain length. For instance, even though white rice has complex carbohydrates and long glucose chains, it still causes an instantaneous spike in our blood sugar, almost equivalent to a spike caused by sugar-sweetened beverage containing simple sugar (sucrose, a disaccharide). In another example, fructose is a monosaccharide and still does not raise blood glucose levels instantaneously, which is why it has a tremendously low glycaemic index.

The invisible killer – Fructose

Glucose can be used by each cell in our body and be stored in muscle tissues and the liver quickly as glycogen because it has the molecular shape of a six-sided ring. Fructose has the fundamental molecular structure of a five-sided ring and is found naturally in honey and fruits. Fructose in the body is exclusively metabolized in the liver, and most of it does not enter our circulatory system. It cannot be directly used as energy by the organs of our body, such as the brain, heart and muscles. Our blood glucose levels are not remarkably altered when pure fructose is consumed. There is only a little elevation of insulin as compared to glucose. Due to this, public health authorities deemed it a healthier and more benign sweetener, especially for people with diabetes. It is also the predominant sugar in fruit, is frequently referred to as 'fruit sugar' and seems somehow healthier simply under that association. For example, a pear[2] contains approximately 4.5 per cent fructose, 4.2 per cent glucose and 2.5 per cent sucrose by weight. Table sugar is a dehydrated form of sugar containing nearly 100 per cent sucrose, which is made up of 50 per cent glucose and 50 per cent fructose.

But fructose is an invisible killer! And I'll tell you why.

These days, fructose is in everything. Only four centuries ago, fructose was present in our diet in smaller and extremely diluted amounts, no more than 20 g in our daily intake of seasonal fruits and honey. However, after the widespread use of fructose in soft drinks and other processed foods, its consumption in the US[3] gradually increased until the year 2000, when it peaked at per capita daily consumption of 110 g.

The sugar used in the processed foods on the supermarket shelves,[4] increasingly being consumed by Indians,[5] is extracted and refined from corn. It is called HFCS (High-fructose corn syrup, or technically HFCS-55)[6] and is composed of 55 per cent fructose and 45 per cent glucose. It is indistinguishable from the taste of table sugar. Developed in the late 1950s, high fructose corn syrup[7] was the liquid equivalent of table sugar. Very soon, the sugar found its way into almost every manufactured food under the sun, be it tomato ketchup, instant soup, noodles, loaves of bread, pizza sauce, cookies, cakes, you name it. The big food manufacturers didn't care what it would do to the health of the global population. They keep adding it because it's cheap, highly palatable, rewarding and profitable. In 1985, the per capita sugar consumption in India was 11 kg per annum, which more than doubled and rose to 23 kg per annum in 2019.[8] Per capita consumption of sugar-sweetened beverages increased eleven-fold[9] between 1998 and 2013. Due to the current level of sugar consumption, obesity is on the rise in India[10] and is estimated to be at almost 50 per cent of the total population[11] by 2023. Although HFCS-55 is fundamentally identical to table sugar upon digestion, the public has perceived it and the industry has treated it as a healthy additive as opposed to table sugar, which has carried the taint of controversy for decades.[12]

Many of the diet books on obesity treatment and recommendations of public health officials for diabetes management are based on the glycaemic index of food. The greater the glycaemic index, the faster the breakdown of the carbohydrates and the higher the subsequent blood sugar. The more refined the carbohydrates, the higher the blood sugar and insulin responses. Any food processing method that enhances the speed of breakdown of carbohydrates in our body, such as cooking, juicing the fruit into liquid form, adding sugar to flavoured water as is the case with calorically sweetened sodas and other beverages, mashing potatoes, polishing rice, or refining wheat will increase the food's glycaemic index and the speed with which our blood sugar levels are elevated after consumption. Therefore, adding refined carbohydrates in the traditional diets rich in fibrous vegetables, whole fruits, eggs, meat, fish, milk, and coconut would elevate the blood sugar and insulin levels in the body. On the other hand, consuming fats, protein, and fibre in the meal will reduce the food's glycaemic index.

The glycaemic index is a helpful measure but very misleading on many levels:

1. The presence of fructose in the food does not reflect in the glycaemic index owing to fructose's inability to raise blood sugar. But fructose still raises blood insulin levels.
2. The presence of protein and fat in the meal reduces the blood sugar response, reducing its glycaemic index. This may mask the deleterious effect of omega-6 fats, trans fats and sugar, the true culprits that negatively influence our fat tissue regulation and set point weight. For instance, the glycaemic index of ice cream and sponge cake is low at 51 and 46 majorly due to their fructose, fats and protein content. It however should be noted that when the goods and bads within these foods were to be considered overall, consuming these foods on a regular basis on the pretext of being low the glycaemic foods would do more harm than good due to their concentrated fructose, glucose and trans fats content. Yet if we were to simply observe it through the lens of the glycaemic index, consuming cake or ice-cream is a completely benign and justified indulgence.

Both cornflakes and watermelon have a glycaemic index of 80. If we make our food choices based on this index, we could mistake both to be equally healthy, and this would be wrong. For one, the sugar in watermelon is diluted in lots of water. A better measure to compare the blood sugar-raising effect of the two foods is to consider the glycaemic load[13] of the meal, which factors in the concentration of sugars and starch in the food. A glycaemic load of a specific food is a number that shows by how much an individual's blood sugar level will be raised after eating it. This number is calculated by multiplying the glycaemic index value with the carbohydrate content in the food and dividing it by 100. This measure, though more accurate in its prediction, has limitations and is misleading in determining whether the meal is healthy or harmful to our fat loss goals. Though these two indices could be found on the internet in many databases, they have minimum practical meaning. Knowing its source is the best way to assess whether a food controls your blood sugar and improves your health. If the food is found naturally, then it will improve your health. However, if it is artificially processed from a factory, whether it has a low or a high glycaemic index, it will cause more harm to your health than good.

By categorizing the carbohydrate foods as good or bad for fat loss based on their glycaemic index, we as health experts and enthusiasts have effectively misdiagnosed the influence of fructose on weight regulation. Glucose goes straight into the bloodstream and is used by the muscles and organs as energy, only some of it[14] passes through the liver. None of the cells in our body have the faculty to use fructose as energy, while glucose can practically be used as energy by all of them. For maximal absorption, glucose needs insulin, while fructose needs none. Fructose can only be metabolized in the liver, whereas glucose enters the blood circulation to be channelled throughout the body as energy. Like a guided missile, fructose is targeted at the liver. As no other organ can help in using fructose, excessive fructose in the body exerts tremendous pressure on the liver. It is like pricking something down with a hammer versus a needlepoint. If all the pressing is focused on a single point, much less pressure is required to do the damage. High fructose intake contributes to non-alcoholic fatty liver syndrome because excessive fructose is easily converted into fat in the liver. Developing a fatty liver is critical to developing hepatic insulin resistance. There, that dreaded term – insulin resistance – again!

The more processed foods that you consume, the more fructose there is, which increases the body's triglycerides and fat deposition levels. Our bodies slowly adapt to long-term chronic consumption of processed foods such as sugar and fructose. As the consumption increases, the pattern of fructose metabolism will alter over time. The longer the consumption period and the more fructose[15] there is in the diet, the higher its conversion into fat by the liver. Additionally, fructose inhibits both glucose metabolism in the liver and the conversion of glucose into its storage form glycogen. Consequently, the pancreas releases more insulin to deal with this glucose traffic jam at the liver. The muscles try to compensate and become less responsive to insulin.

Even though, in the short run, fructose has little effect on either insulin or blood sugar, in the long run, it takes us to the same point of insulin resistance and higher set point weight. Imagine what would happen if more carbohydrates were consumed when the liver is already saturated with them? Insulin then attempts to force the issue and crams more sugar and fat into the liver, even though the stores are already saturated with them. Just as it is more challenging to get more contents into your luggage when it is filled to the brim, it is more difficult for insulin to thrust more energy and fat into a fatty liver. In a fatty liver, more and more insulin is required to usher an equivalent quantity of food energy. Gradually, the body starts to resist insulin's attempts to bring sugar into the cells and reduce blood sugar since normal insulin levels are inadequate. As a result, the liver becomes insulin resistant. Like an overfilled luggage, the liver tries to displace the sugar back into the circulation. This means that perpetually elevated insulin levels are required to keep the sugar inside the liver, which causes more insulin resistance and a classic vicious cycle.

Table sugar (sucrose) = 50% glucose + 50% fructose

The glucose in refined sugar and processed foods directly triggers insulin secretion, while excess consumption of fructose results in a fatty liver which directly promotes insulin resistance. Thus, table sugar promotes insulin levels in the short and long run. That is why, when compared to pure glucose, sucrose is at least twice as bad. The glycemic index reflects glucose's effect but fructose's impact is silent. Sugar is specifically fattening and causes type-2 diabetes compared to other refined carbohydrates. The risk for weight gain and diabetes is considerably increased with regular consumption of sugared drinks. Setting higher taxes on sugar[16] has not discouraged Indians from consuming sugar. However, by far, fructose is the worst offender and is found in cold beverages, fruit juices and sweetened teas. Did you know? The consumption of processed food increased almost threefold between 2005 and 2019 in India.[17]

How to find the sugars in food labels?

Manufacturers fool their consumers into thinking that a particular food doesn't have added sugar by using various alias terms in the ingredients list. This ploy averts 'sugar' from getting labelled as the primary constituent in packaged food.

- Names to watch out for: sugar, dextrose, sucrose, fructose, glucose, maltose, honey, hydrolysed starch, molasses, cane sugar, corn sweeteners, high fructose corn syrup, brown sugar, agave nectar and cane/malt/palm/maple/corn/rice/golden syrup.
- These added sugars intensify the flavour of ready-made soup, noodles and sauces such as plum, barbeque, sweet and sour, hoisin, honey garlic and other dipping and flavouring sauces.
- Tomato ketchup may contain as much as 15 g (3-4 teaspoons) of sugar.
- Commercial salad dressings and relish frequently contain lots of sugar.

The bottom line is that foods that come in a package are most likely rich in added sugar.

No added sugar at all would be ideal. But it might not be possible in practice. I'll give you some practical recommendations on how to avoid sugar in Part II of this book.

Blood glucose orchestrates fat use

What happens after a meal? Immediately after a meal, the free fatty acid levels are surprisingly low, while the blood sugar and insulin are at their highest. After a few hours, the fatty acids rise again steadily as the blood glucose ebbs. Our body possesses the flexibility to use either glucose or fatty acids for energy. Injecting insulin or glucose into the circulation almost instantly reduces the fatty acid level. When excess glucose is available to the body for burning, as indicated by elevated insulin levels, the circuiting fatty acids in the blood are swept into the fat cells for future use.

Here is what you should know about the relationship between fat and carbohydrate metabolism:

1. As long as the blood sugar is elevated and the reserves of carbohydrates stored in the liver and muscles as glycogen are not depleted, the body will burn carbohydrates for fuel and restrict the use of fatty acids.
2. During fasting, the reduced intake of refined carbohydrates and sugar or an abrupt increase in the demand for energy due to exercise or mental stress lets our body know that

our carbohydrate reserves are depleted. Then the fatty acids are released into circulation to pick up the slack.

3. Usually, the energy that we get from our meals is stored instantly and gradually released once the meal is digested.
4. Between meals and during the overnight fast when we are asleep, this stored fat from the food we consume during the day is released as fatty acids to provide 50 to 70 per cent of our energy expenditure at those times.
5. Fat tissue is not static but is an important site of active modulation of energy mobilization and storage, one of the essential control mechanisms responsible for an organism's survival.

I keep saying if we have too much blood glucose, it gets stored as fat. How does this happen? It is actually quite simple and direct.

Remember the triglycerides that I have talked about before. These triglycerides are put together in the liver by the addition of the glycerol 'part' (derived from the breakdown of carbohydrates in the liver) and the fatty acids. Glucose is burned as energy to ensure the breakdown of carbohydrates. So, literally, the more glucose there is available, the more energy there is in fat cells to produce the glycerol part. And the more glycerol molecules are produced, the more fatty acids are assembled into triglycerides. High consumption of ultra-processed foods elevate blood sugar and more glucose is transported into the liver, resulting in conversion of more fatty acids into triglycerides for storage as fat. These triglycerides are then carried to the fat cells to be locked up. But their size is too big to pass through the fat cell's cell membrane (the fencing wall). So these triglycerides are broken into fatty acids and re-joined as triglycerides inside the cells. Any fatty acids that are not instantly repackaged into triglycerides will escape the fat cell and come back into circulation as a readily transportable fuel source for the body. If any rogue free fatty acid is still circulating in the blood, these are taken back as triglycerides into the liver and stored in fat tissue.

Suppose it has been a long time since our last meal has been digested or we are in a prolonged fast when we are sleeping, the amount of glucose transported into cells is at a normal level and the insulin drops to its basal level. No glucose is lying around in our blood to be burned as fuel. Insulin is scarcely available. There is no production of glycerol phosphate. Fewer fatty acids are assembled into triglycerides, and more of them have the freedom to enter the blood circulation. Consequently, the fatty acid concentration in the circulatory system rises, but insulin levels must drop for that to happen. The bottom line is that normal blood sugar levels have a compensatory effect of increasing the release and use of stored body fat as energy, thereby promoting the rate of fat breakdown and a reduction in the size of the fat cells. This is known as the glucose-fatty acids cycle or the Randle cycle.[18] But when the blood sugar and insulin levels rise, and the release of fatty acids in the blood diminishes, the cells compensate by burning glucose to reduce its levels.

In conclusion, when glucose is being used for energy, fat is not being used for energy. It is being stored. When we have normal blood sugar (glucose) levels, fat is being used as energy.

This has been a well-known scientific fact for the last five decades.

> **Interesting fact**: Fructose converts to glycerol phosphate very efficiently, even more so than glucose. So more triglycerides lead to more fat storage. Fructose cannot induce insulin production, but when it is in combination with glucose, for example, in table sugar and high fructose corn syrup, insulin is produced courtesy glucose, fats are produced courtesy fructose and glucose, and fats are stored because there are high blood sugar levels. It is a deadly duo!

What insulin starts, LPL finishes

Lipoprotein lipase (LPL) is called the 'gatekeeper'[19] for fat accumulation. Researchers[20] have reported that obese individuals have elevated LPL activity in their fat tissue.

What does LPL do?

Insulin is the primary modulator of LPL activity, although not the only one. When blood sugar and insulin levels rise, muscles are forced to burn glucose instead of fatty acids and LPL activity increases in the fat tissue to deposit the fat. When insulin levels plummet, the LPL activity increases in the muscle cells and decreases in the fat cells. Then the fat cells release fatty acids for use in muscle cells and other organs of the body where LPL activity increases.

Interestingly, during a calorie-restricted weight-loss diet, LPL activity increases in the fat tissue and decreases in the muscle tissues, both of which contribute to sustaining fat levels in the fat tissues. Any negative energy balance that may be attempted by a semistarvation diet doesn't work. When we exercise, LPL activity in the muscles increases resulting in enhanced absorption of fatty acids into the muscles to be burned as fuel for energy. However, once the workout is done, the sensitivity of the fat cells to insulin is adequately improved, and the LPL activity in the fat tissue elevates to restock the fat lost and surrendered during exercise.

LPL activity affects people in different ways:

1. We gain weight and then regain the weight once we have lost it because LPL activities increases in the fat cells and decreases in the skeletal muscles.
2. We accumulate more fat in some areas of the body first before other areas.
3. Women have greater LPL activity in their fat tissues than men, which may be one reason why obesity is more frequent in women than in men.
4. Fat distribution is different in men and women. LPL activity in men is higher in the abdominal fat tissue than in the fat tissue below the waist, which is known as obesity of the android type (a beer belly!). Women have more LPL activity in the fat tissues of their hips and thighs and less in the abdomen, which is known as gynoid distribution. However, post menopause, the LPL activity in their abdominal region catches up with that of men. This means that the LPL activity is also regulated by the altering flux of

sex hormones in the body that determine fat distribution over time in men and women. Testosterone, the dominant male sex hormone inhibits LPL activity in the abdominal region but has little effect on LPL activity below this region. That explains why ageing men increasingly accumulate fat around the abdominal area as testosterone levels fall. In contrast, progesterone, the dominant female hormone, increases LPL activity explicitly in the hips and buttocks, but estrogen, another female hormone, reduces this LPL activity. Menopause causes reduction in estrogen levels and thus an increase in LPL activity, which explains why women frequently gain weight post menopause or after hysterectomy (removal of the uterus).

This explains:

- why all the subjects in the overfeeding studies did not gain the estimated weight
- how obesity and malnutrition can coexist
- why women, on an average, accumulate more fat than men
- why low-calorie high-carbohydrate diets don't give sustainable results
- why even though exercise burns fat, it doesn't help in losing weight
- why exercising more does not necessarily lead to sustainable weight loss due to its appetite-stimulating effect

Glucagon – The other side of the coin to insulin

How does the body ensure a steady supply of fuel in the absence of food? In the course of the day – during the times that we have fasted – after the food energy is digested, another homeostatic mechanism operates to ensure that the energy that we restocked during mealtime is released into circulation. It starts with the stabilization of blood sugar and insulin levels reduced to normal. Then the pancreas will release a hormone known as glucagon.[21] This hormone does the opposite of what insulin does. Where insulin stores energy in the body, glucagon wants to use it. Insulin clears blood glucose by pushing glucose and fat into the body's tissues, while glucagon raises blood sugar and pulls out nutrients from their storage depots. Glucagon does this by triggering the liver and fat cells to share their stored energy in the form of glucose and free fatty acids. As insulin and glucagon operate against each other to promote and restrict metabolic processes, the balance between these two hormones determines which of the processes occur. Glucagon helps break down the triglycerides within the fat cells and release them for use. This leads[22] to an increase in body energy expenditure, metabolic rate, satiety and appetite suppression. Then LPL helps pull the free fatty acids, ensuring a constant supply of energy to the body. This is how the body's energy regulation system works to supply fuel to the body throughout the day.

But when we regularly consume ultra-processed food and a diet high in refined sugar and white flour, our set point weight is raised. Our insulin is abnormally high all the time. No fat breakdown occurs. As a result, we feel full and there is an energy imbalance in the body.

In fact, a study[23] at Harvard University and the National Institutes of Health revealed that when insulin levels

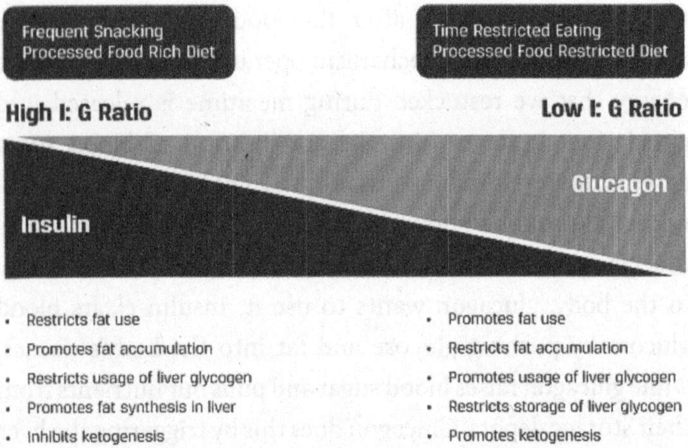

Low insulin to glucagon ratio promotes fat burning while high insulin to glucagon ratio promotes fat storage

dropped drastically, and the body started to use ketone bodies, which come from using fat as the primary fuel source, the daily metabolic rate increased by approximately 100 to 300 calories. Another study showed that subjects were hungrier when fat and protein calories were substituted with high carbohydrates in their diet than when fat and protein calories were included in the diet. The implication is that when high quantity of glucose is not available to the body from the breakdown of easily digestible carbohydrates of processed foods, our stored fat will fuel the body. Whenever individuals follow a low-calorie diet and lose weight, this association is often attributed to low-calorie intake. However, this is a confusing association with cause and effect. Even if individuals following a low-calorie diet lose weight, it does not imply that the decrease in calories caused the weight-loss. It simply means that the diet was a weight loss diet and low in calories. The diet could have been entirely successful by some other mechanism, such as reducing the set point weight. This results in both a decrease in appetite and weight loss, which are the consequences of the autonomic response of the improved functioning of the energy regulating system in the body, brain and fat stores.

Some people critique the diets that restrict processed foods and refined sugar and point out that the diet naturally works because removing muffins, white bread, cakes, refined sugars, etc., makes food less palatable and brings repulsion, distaste and boredom to food consumption and thus automatically generates a calorie cutback. But that is not necessarily true. For instance, Dr Ancel Keys[24] severely restricted the food choices of his experimental subjects. Recall that he wanted to emulate the low-calorie, high-carbohydrate food available to the population in Eastern Europe during the second world war and so only allowed the consumption of potatoes, bread, turnip, cabbages, cereals and token portions of dairy products and meat. Yet, his semi-starved subjects didn't hint that they were bored of or would not consume more food had it been available. On the contrary, they were ravenously hungry, depressed and irritable when food was not provided to them on time. So, the notion that appetite can be eliminated or reduced due to a lack of food choices when processed foods are eliminated or limited in the diet is extremely difficult to embrace. When an individual's energy regulating system is not compromised, it provides constant internal fuel to the body. Consequently, they would compensate by consuming less food because their fat tissue is shrinking. This does not mean the shrinkage of their fat tissue is caused by consuming less food. Additionally, it would be naïve to assume that when an individual exercises, they lose weight, implying that physical activity causes weight loss. An association is being mistaken for causation. Instead, correcting the defect in energy regulation will make more fuel available for the body, which could be put to use by exercising.

However we look at it – omega-6 to omega-3 polyunsaturated fats ratio, insulin resistance, leptin resistance, glycaemic index, fructose – carbohydrates, especially the processed ones with added sugar, should be consumed less to lower your body's set point weight. These should be substituted in favour of good calories that support optimal regulation of hunger and satiety hormones in the body and that brings the set point weight down to healthy levels. The consumption of naturally occurring saturated, monounsaturated and omega-3 fats, high-quality protein and naturally occurring carbohydrates and sugars bonded with dietary fibre found in fruits and vegetables improves the calorie composition of the meal and lowers insulin levels and set point weight point. Doing so would profoundly and positively influence our satiety and increase our non-exercise activity thermogenesis.

Despite all the anguish of the obesity crisis, I'm honestly very confident that we will turn the corner with the application of this knowledge. The data is amalgamating, and awareness is rising. The unabated rise of obesity, at least in developed countries, has lately begun to slow, and some regions have also started to see a decline in obesity for the first time. Eliminating added sugar from the diet assumes no insignificant role in the triumph of maintaining a healthy weight.

So, with that we have finished part one of the book which is to understand why we get fat and how eating less and moving more fails to give long term results. If our weight set point is elevated above our current lost weight the body will compensate to regain that weight by making you spend less energy by reducing your metabolic rate, making you lethargic and keeping you of from exercising and increasing your food seeking behaviour. The only sustainable treatment to the problem of weight gain is to lower your set weight point so that your metabolic rate is always optimal, you are energetic and the thought of food does not flood your brain in odd hours and the throughout the day even when you are at your desired weight. Thus, if eating less and moving more is not a solution then what empirically can we do to lower our set weight point, lose weight and maintain it without starving? This crucial question brings us to the part two of the book which gives you all the answers and it will translate the science of weight management we discussed in part one of the book into actionable points to lose weight and maintain it sustainably without starving.

PART TWO

HOW TO LOSE WEIGHT AND MAINTAIN IT

How to Lose Weight and Maintain it

There are two significant findings from every dietary study conducted over the years.

1. All diets work
2. All diets fail

When it comes to sustaining a healthy weight range, what does it imply? Losing weight traces the same fundamental pattern that dieters are well acquainted with. They certainly differ in the magnitude of weight loss, but the issue comes up six or seven months into the diet. You face a weight loss plateau,[1] possibly regain some weight, despite strictly adhering to your diet. For instance, in the decade-long Diabetes Prevention Program, the participants, on average, lost 7 kg of weight after a year. However, the dreaded plateau hit them, followed by weight regain.

Remember the human health tripod? Indefinite weight loss depends on it.

1. performing the right exercises
2. consuming nutritious food
3. managing cortisol levels through rest and sleep

From all that we've learnt in this book, obesity is not because of just one thing. It is a multidimensional disease.

- Does lack of muscle mass cause obesity? Partially true.
- Do calories cause obesity? Partially true.
- Does sugar cause obesity? Partially true.
- Do dietary carbohydrates cause obesity? Partially true.
- Does stress cause obesity? Partially true.
- Does insulin resistance cause obesity? Partially true.
- Does dietary fibre guard us against obesity? Partially true.

Every aspect mentioned above intersects at various hormonal routes that result in weight gain, and the most critical component in this is insulin. Typically, we consume a diet rich in carbohydrates (greater than 50 per cent) and poor in protein and fat calories. So, when we cut all calories equally and go on a low-calorie diet to lose weight, we also cut a lot of carbohydrates, thus reducing insulin release. When we follow a low-carbohydrate diet, we increase the number of fat- and protein-based energy in the diet and reduce carbohydrates, thus reducing insulin. We reduce insulin when we follow other versions of a low-carbohydrate diet such as the paleo and carnivore diets. When we follow 'only a soup and salad' diet, we reduce insulin.

A constant debate on a single cause for obesity persists – too little exercise, too much eating out, too much added sugar, too many carbohydrates, too many saturated fats, too much red meat, too much lactose, too much gluten, too much highly palatable processed food with added fats, too much stress and the list goes on. The 'excess calorie' lobby and 'keto' lobby ridicule one another. The vegans deride the keto devotees. The 'keto' lobby mocks the 'high-carbohydrate, low-calorie diet' lobby. All diets work because they are focused on addressing the distinct component of the disease. However, none of them result in sustained success because none focus on the comprehensive nature of obesity. If we don't understand the science of obesity, we are condemned to a never-ending cycle of blame without achieving our objective.

The familiar, connecting element in weight gain is hyperinsulinemia, which wreaks havoc in regulating our fat tissue and thus our appetite, satiety and food intake. For some individuals dealing with their weight problem, the primary concern may be due to chronically elevated stress levels. For others, it could be low lean tissue mass, while for someone else, it could be the high consumption of refined and easily digestible carbohydrates. Controlling stress levels, increasing lean tissue through strength training and exercise, and following a diet that eliminates processed foods will do just one thing - improve your metabolic health by reducing elevated insulin levels and enhancing insulin sensitivity.

It is crucial to customize one's weight loss programme to deal with the underlying cause of elevated insulin levels. So if, for instance, late-night exposure to artificial blue light emitted from mobile phones or TV screens is disturbing your sleep and causing sleep deprivation and high cortisol levels, then that is the primary reason for your weight gain. Decreasing carbohydrates or increasing exercise is unlikely to address that issue. If excessive sugar consumption is the issue, then exercising more will not be specifically helpful. Weight gain is a result of a hormonal abnormality of energy regulation. It is characterized by elevated insulin levels that stimulate weight gain, so the logical treatment for this problem is to reduce insulin levels.

The all-important question is: how can *you* balance *your* human health tripod?

1

Eat Well, Not Less

When we restrict fats in the diet, we invariably also restrict protein because all the food sources of protein contain fats too. So, what exactly does a high-carbohydrate, low-calorie diet do?

- With reduced protein intake, we lose the lean tissue in the muscles and bones needed for a strong and healthy body and have no control over where the weight is lost in the body.
- With the loss of lean mass, we'll have less glucose storage area in the body, and our body becomes insulin resistant because we lack the tissue to clear the glucose from circulation and quickly re-establish the baseline insulin levels.
- A very low-calorie[I] diet also elicits stress on the body, which is evident in notable alterations in hormonal levels such as a marked increase in the quintessential cortisol, the stress hormone. Recollect that one of cortisol's primary hormonal actions is to kickstart a flight-or-fight response. It counters insulin's actions and increases blood sugar levels and makes the muscle tissues insulin resistant, as would naturally be the case as glucose would be reserved for the brain under high-stress conditions.

- Our thyroid levels[2] also drop. Thyroid is a hormone that tells the body to increase energy expenditure and burn more calories. This also ultimately diminishes our metabolic health.

With physical activity, it's just a choice between 'doing' or 'not doing'. When it comes to your diet, it is way more complex because the food that we consume can either improve our health or break our health. No food is health-neutral. Making the right choice of what to eat and when to eat is profoundly influential in attaining and sustaining your weight goals.

I have designed a nutritional protocol based on twelve years of experience. This protocol will help your body adapt to eliminating fat out of your fat stores and controlling your weight. Thousands of my clients successfully reversed their lifestyle-related diseases – unexplained weight gain, diabetes, autoimmune conditions, thyroid, depression, anxiety psoriasis and rheumatoid arthritis, by following this **FRFP protocol**:

1. **F** – Fast first
2. **R** – Restrict refined carbohydrates
3. **F** – Fuel with fats
4. **P** – Proceed with protein

F – Fast first

The most vital and straightforward step in correcting the metabolic derailment and moving in the right direction of reversing the metabolic forces that cause obesity is to maintain minimal blood sugar and insulin levels for an extended period of time. Even if we adopt the dietary weight loss strategy of improving the composition of our diet and consuming all the correct foods, every food raises our insulin levels. Our body's immediate response to food intake under insulin resistance is to elevate insulin levels, producing even more resistance. We must create reoccurring periods of low insulin levels to halt this state of insulin resistance. Recall that the development of resistance means having both relentless and high levels of insulin. All foods at the end of the day promote insulin release. The only manner to reduce elevated insulin levels is not to consume food.

The solution we are seeking is, in a word, fasting.[3]

Timing of your meals

Step 1: Don't eat any food for one hour after an overnight fast, that is, one hour after we wake up.

This will lead to around nine to ten hours in 24 hours when we would have fasted.

Step 2: If you complete your dinner by 8.30-9.00 p.m., don't eat any food until 7.00 a.m. the following day.

This will help you maintain a 12-hour overnight fast. The sweet spot for balanced insulin levels is to aim for 12 to 16 hours overnight fast.

Step 3: After you get used to the 12-hour fast, try extending this to a 16- to 18-hour fast two to three days a week. Eat dinner at 7.00 p.m. and then another meal at 1.00 p.m. the following day.

Pro tip: If you want a beverage other than plain water during your fast, try having black coffee or tea.

Provided that your meals comprise fat-rich foods and no refined carbohydrates, you'll be amazed at how effortless this becomes as your body adapts to being fuelled by your body fat and the fat from your meals. This scenario will only transpire when your insulin levels are at a bare minimum for a prolonged period. It is also safe to go all the way and fast for a single twenty-four hours every two to four weeks.

As far back as the 1980s,[4] most of us consumed meals separated by five hours, but now we eat every three and a half hours. Many believe that fasting is unhealthy for the body, but research demonstrates that it is beneficial. Fasting involves consuming food regularly for a certain period, with intentional periods of food avoidance without the need to count calories. Rather than seeking some 'never-seen-before exotic diet' miracle to facilitate and assist us in breaking the insulin-resistant state, let's focus on one of the most ancient remedies in the history of humanity, one that has been an essential component of practically every religion and culture on our planet – fasting.

Fasting is not the same as starvation. Starvation is termed as an involuntary food consumption pattern. It's neither intentional, deliberate, nor controlled. When an individual starves, they don't know when, where and how their subsequent food will come. In contrast, fasting is an intentional control over food intake for health, spiritual or other purposes. It can range from any period, from a couple of hours to a couple of days. If you think about it for a moment, we all fast every day. In a sense, it is a component of our daily life. The term 'breakfast' means any meal of the day that breaks our overnight fast when we were sleeping, which is done every day. Fasting for spiritual reasons is practised widely and is a component of practically every prominent religion worldwide. Islam, Christianity, Buddhism, Hinduism, Jainism, Judaism and Taoism, you name it. All of these significant religions share a common belief in the power of fasting. In philosophical expression, it is frequently termed purification or cleansing. Empirically, it quantifies the same practice. Fasting as a religious and cultural practice has independently developed among different geographic regions, not as something detrimental but as something that was profoundly, inherently healing to the human spirit and body.

The transition from fed state to fasted state occurs in various stages:[5]

1. **Feeding:** During meals, the insulin levels rise. Glucose is chaperoned into the tissues such as the muscles and brain for use. Surplus glucose is stored in the liver as glycogen.
2. **Post-absorptive phase:** This phase ranges from six to 24 hours after the beginning of a fast. Insulin levels start to drop,[6] and simultaneously glucagon hormone levels rise. The liver glycogen stores are broken down to increase blood sugar levels for approximately 24 hours.
3. **Gluconeogenesis:** This phase ranges from 24 to 48 hours from the time of the fast initiation. The liver converts glycerol (from the fat stores) and amino acids (from dietary protein and the breakdown of muscle tissue) to glucose. This ensures that blood sugar stays in a healthy range.
4. **Nutritional ketosis:** This stage occurs 24 to 36 hours

after the beginning of a fast. The stored fat (triglycerides) is broken down into free fatty acids and glycerol components and released into circulation. The liver converts glycerol into glucose to stabilize the blood sugar levels and breaks down the free fatty acids into ketone bodies. This increases metabolic expenditure even though there is no physical activity involved. Think of running on a treadmill. One uses energy and burns more calories but does not cover any physical distance. These ketone bodies[7] can supply up to three-fifth of the brain's energy requirements, while the remaining comes from glucose from the glycerol breakdown. The two primary ketone bodies generated during fasting are acetoacetate and beta-hydroxybutyrate, whose concentration can rise up seventy-fold.[8]

5. **Protein preservation phase:** After 120 hours of fasting, the growth hormone levels almost double to support and preserve bone density, lean tissue and muscle mass. The use and availability of body fat as a significant energy source in the body are promoted by elevated growth hormone levels. Though the secretion of growth hormone reduces steadily as we age, fasting[9] is one of the most powerful stimulus for growth hormone secretion. The body's energy requirements can be completely met by ketones and free fatty acids. Elevated adrenaline (norepinephrine) levels after 48 hours of the beginning of a fast increase the metabolic rate by 3.6 per cent.[10]

You can take two approaches:

1. Compress your eating windows to two to three meals daily, with considerable gaps in between. With more frequent meals, insulin levels would also rise every couple of hours irrespective of how much is consumed throughout the day. This logic also applies to intermittent fasting schedules that help in consuming less than three meals daily. Or you could consume just breakfast[11] and lunch or just lunch and dinner[12].
2. Consume foods normally for a few days, then restrict it completely for a day or two.

Individuals who fast for 24 hours once a month[13] are roughly half as likely to be insulin resistant compared to those who don't.

In a study on type 2 diabetes patients,[14] it was identified that regular 24-hour fasts were so powerful at improving insulin sensitivity that subjects had to be deprescribed insulin. For one patient, it happened in just five days! But to ensure that the body doesn't feel the symptoms of food deprivation and feels satieted even throughout the fasting period, the nutrient quality of the food you eat in your eating windows is key. How an individual begins and ends their fast matters tremendously.

Myths about fasting

1. It's an unhealthy and extreme weight loss method.
2. It causes dangerously low blood sugar.
3. It puts the body into starvation mode and reduces the BMR and energy expenditure.
4. It can cause glucose deficiency, leading to coma and death.

5. It causes muscle breakdown, catabolism of muscle tissue, muscle atrophy and physical weakness.
6. It will increase one's appetite and overwhelm them with hunger.
7. It leads to nutrient deprivation.
8. It causes overeating when feeding is initiated.

When abstaining from food, our body does not immediately reach out to our muscle proteins to break them down for energy. To put it logically, our stored fat is a preferred fuel reserve for our body, and muscles are functional structures retained for movement. Fat available in our body is the first place the body reaches out to to get energy in a situation of food abstinence. It is like collecting wood logs from the forest to build a fire versus burning the wooden furniture at home to keep warm.

A study[15] on this alternate day fasting approach for over seventy days showed that body weight of the subject reduced by 6 per cent, with lean mass unchanged and a 11.4 per cent reduction in fat mass.

Another associated myth related to fasting is that it activates the body's starvation mode, which severely reduces basal metabolism and causes the body to shut down. There was no discernible drop in overall energy output as per a study that employed an alternate-day fasting regimen for twenty-two days.[16] Neither was there any activation of the starvation mode nor a reduction in metabolism. The use of carbohydrates as energy was reduced by 53 per cent, while fat as an energy source increased by 58 per cent. The body migrated to burning fat from burning sugar. Continuous fasting for four days, in fact, elevated total energy expenditure by 12 per cent.[17] Adrenaline (norepinephrine) levels increased 117 per cent from the baseline to sustain energy output. Free fatty acids skyrocketed over 370 per cent from baseline as the body adapted to the lack of dietary glucose and switched to using fat for energy. Blood sugar levels decreased marginally but stayed in the healthy range, and insulin reduced by 17 per cent.

People worry that fasting may lead to excess food intake. The average energy consumption after a one-day fast was observed to have elevated from 2,436 to 2,914 kcal.[18] Yet, over a period of two days, the net food intake was at a deficit of 1,958 kcal. The deficiency of calories on the fasting day overcrowded the increased caloric intake on the subsequent day after fasting.

Research has confirmed that fasting endows tremendous health benefits – your energy levels increase, blood sugar and insulin normalize and metabolism increases. While we are on this point, I would like to dispel another common myth. Many confuse intermittent fasting with calorie deficit and assume intermittent fasting is equal to calorie restriction. They assume that as long as they simply cut calories and eat normally for 14–16 hours a day, they will see all the benefits – improved metabolic health, better insulin sensitivity, lower waist to hip circumference, better weight loss and better cholesterol, blood lipid profile and blood pressure. Caloric restriction may result in some of the above mentioned benefits but not all. The intermittent nature of food intake during intermittent fasting is what acts to improve your hormone regulation, the key to combating obesity. So intermittent fasting works independently of caloric restriction.

The only remaining concern is if you can do it. I'm sure I can get a 100 per cent yes by now.

Breaking the fast

Good breakfast options	*Bad breakfast options*
• soaked chia seeds with apple or orange • boiled, scrambled or half-fried eggs • full-fat milk with whey protein • yoghurt with fresh fruits • buttermilk with soaked chia seeds and condiments • multigrain bread with butter • paneer sandwich with cheese and veggies • chat made with sprouted pulses, nuts and condiments such as turmeric, cucumber, onion, tomato and pepper Check out my favorite healthy breakfast recipes at the end of this chapter.	• banana bread • cakes • muffins • bread with added sugar • Danish pastry • jellies • jam • peanut butter with added sugar • fruit flavoured low-fat yoghurt • cereals • bagels • juice • rice Pro tip: Avoid anything processed and with added sugar.

Did you know?

- A serving of a popular branded strawberry greek yoghurt contains three teaspoons of sugar (14.5 g).
- Instant flavoured oats are highly refined and processed to allow for quick cooking and contain an

enormous quantity of added sugar and flavours. Most of the nutritional content in the whole and steel-cut oats are not present in these instant oats. Packaged instant masala oats have up to 10 per cent sugar per serving and amount to one and a half teaspoons of sugar (7.1 g).

- Commercial breakfast cereals have more than 15 g of sugar per 100 g of cereal. If you want to have breakfast cereal on busy mornings, consume cereals that have less than 4 g of sugar per serving. Some of my favourites are: Bagrry's Crunchy Muesli (No Added Sugar); Gaia Crunchy Diet Muesli Multi-Grain; GoWhey – Breakfast Fuel Muesli – Keto Granola – Dark Chocolate – Hazelnut Crunch.

Stop snacking

Most pre-packaged snack foods possess an enormous quantity of refined sugar and flour.

Avoid biscuits, cookies, chips, sweet and salty mixes, canned fruits, instant noodles, soups, microwave popcorn, cereal bars, granola bars and masala oats.

Pro tip: If you snack habitually, replace this habit with another that is less detrimental to your goals. Perhaps instead of the snack, you can have a cup of black tea, coffee or green tea in the evenings.

Did you know?

- A serving of Maepranom Brand Sweet Chilli sauce contains two and a half teaspoons (12 g).
- Crispy rice crackers are usually advertised as gluten- and cholesterol-free, low-fat snacks, but sugar is added to compensate for their lack of taste.
- Processed and canned fruits have many tablespoons of sugar. For instance, a Del Monte Fruit Cocktail serving has more than four teaspoons of sugar (21 g).

Coffee: Because of its caffeine content, coffee is often regarded as unhealthy. But research shows that coffee may not be as bad as we think. Coffee is a significant source of chlorogenic acid,[19] antioxidants,[20], magnesium and lignans.[21] In different studies, coffee has been proven to reduce the risk of diabetes and shield against neurological disorders such as Parkinson's,[22] Alzheimer's,[23] liver cancer[24] and liver cirrhosis.[25] These studies are certainly not the confirmation of benefit. However, they are indicative of an association. Therefore, to get the maximum benefit from coffee consumption, ensure that the beans are kept away from excessive light, heat, and moisture and are stored in an airtight container. Stored ground beans frequently lose their flavour. Thus, purchasing a coffee bean grinder is often worth every penny. Grind the beans only before brewing. It is very effortless and economical to make iced black coffee on hot summer days for consumption. Just brew a pot of regular or decaffeinated black coffee, keep it in your refrigerator overnight for cooling, and add some ice before consuming. To add different flavours to your coffee, you may use dark chocolate, nutmeg, saffron, cinnamon, vanilla extract, coconut oil and full-fat cream that will enhance your experience without altering the healthy characteristics of your coffee.

Tea: You can have unlimited variations of tea – black, oolong, green, or herbal – as cold or hot beverages. Black tea is fermented and has higher caffeine content compared to other versions. Partially fermented teas such as Oolong tea undergo a shorter fermentation period. It has enormous concentrations of a group of potent antioxidants known as catechins, which are known to impede enzymes that help digest dietary carbohydrates leading to diminished glucose levels[26] and guarding the pancreatic beta cells.[27] The polyphenols in green tea boost metabolism[28], which may aid in burning fat.[29] Various health benefits have been ascribed to the consumption of green tea, including enhanced fat oxidation during physical activity,[30] improved resting energy expenditure[31] and lowered risk of many types of cancer.[32] Even then, the effects of green tea on weight loss are modest. For additional flavours, you may infuse your tea with lemon peel, mint, saffron, black pepper, cardamom, cinnamon, ginger, lemongrass, orange peel and mint. Herbal teas, by design, are infused with spices, herbs or other plant derivatives. So, you can add it to hot water for flavour and consume it without any problem. However, these teas are not authentic as they contain no tea leaves. Some popular varieties include lavender, hibiscus, mint, ginger, chamomile, rose hips and lemon balm tea. Spices such as cinnamon can improve the tea's flavour.

R – Restrict refined carbohydrates

Avoid as much as possible: cold drinks, fruit juices, iced teas, fruit punch, smoothies and shakes with natural or added sugars, vitamin water, lemonade, iced cold coffee, energy drinks, flavoured milk, desserts (puddings, cookies, cakes, mousses, pies, sorbets, candy, milk chocolate and ice cream), alcoholic drinks (Long Island iced tea, cider beers, margaritas, pina coladas, ice wine, dessert wine and other liqueurs).

> **Did you know?**
> When sugars and starches from several food sources are fermented, they produce alcohol. The sugars are digested by yeast and converted into alcohol. The alcoholic beverage tastes sweeter due to the residual sugars. Sweetened dessert wines are, of course, rich in sugar and are not advised. But moderate intake of red wine[33] is not associated with elevation of insulin or impairment of insulin sensitivity and thus may be enjoyed. Daily intake of up to two glasses[34] is not correlated with significant weight gain and may cause an improvement[35] in insulin sensitivity. The alcohol by itself, even beer, appears to have minimal impact on insulin secretion or insulin resistance.

Dessert

Desserts can be enjoyed occasionally in celebrating life and cultural events such as graduations, weddings, birthdays, and festivals such as Diwali, Christmas, and Eid.

There are many healthy dessert options one can try. For instance, any locally grown fresh seasonal fruits, a bowl of seasonal cherries or berries with whole fat whipped cream with no added sugar, a small plate of cheeses and nuts, dark chocolate with more than 85 per cent cocoa, 15-20 g of dry fruits such as dried figs, raisins and nuts (almonds, pistachios, walnuts and cashews).

Dark chocolate also possesses a notable quantity of fibre and antioxidants such as flavanols and polyphenols that decrease blood pressure,[36] heart disease[37] and insulin resistance[38], as indicated by various studies. In contrast, most milk chocolates are high in sugars and these milk chocolates are slightly more than candies, possessing too insignificant a component of cocoa to be deemed beneficial and healthy. The experience of consuming dark chocolate can be made sweeter and crunchier by adding some dry fruits. Most dry fruits contain nutrients along with the natural concentration of sugar in them. Nuts are rich in healthy monounsaturated fats and fibre and contain little or no carbohydrates. Several studies demonstrate a correlation between increased nut intake and better health, including reducing the risk of diabetes[39] and cardiovascular[40] disease. For instance, pistachio nuts are rich in vitamins, gamma-tocopherol, and minerals such as magnesium, calcium, selenium and manganese and are widely consumed in a Mediterranean diet. A Spanish study[41] reported that including pistachios in the regular diet improved insulin, insulin resistance and fasting blood sugar levels.

Pro tips:

1. If your objective is to lose weight, your first and most meaningful step is to curtail your sugar consumption severely. If needed, opt for non-caloric sweeteners such as stevia, erythritol, xylitol and monk fruit extract.
2. If you specifically have cravings for desserts, rice or pasta, then eat them at the end of your meal to lessen their influence on your insulin levels.
3. Begin your day with a healthy intake of omega-3 fatty acids by adding a small quantity of flaxseed to your breakfast. Flaxseed is low in phytic acid and need not be soaked when consumed in small amounts.

Carbohydrates for your meals

Consuming bread made out of whole wheat and whole grain flours are an upgrade over consuming bread made out of refined, white flour such as maida. Whole grain flour has more vitamins, minerals, protein and fibre, while the latter lacks them – the grain's bran fibre guards against abnormal insulin spikes. However, in today's modern flour mills, whole grain flour goes through very high levels of processing and refinement due to the use of electric rollers. Modern milling techniques result in ultrafine particles that ensure instant flour absorption by the intestine, even whole wheat flour, which results in high insulin levels. The preferable processing technique is traditional stone-mill grinding. If you purchase grains that have not been cracked or rolled, they should not be sourced from the big storage bins in kirana stores as the grains tend to go rancid in the bins. The best option would be to purchase biodynamic or organic whole grains and crack or roll them yourself with the help of a grain or roller grinder.

Grains can be made into porridges with the addition of cream or butter, which contain fat-soluble activators that act as catalysts to help absorb minerals. Individuals with lactose intolerance or milk allergies can generally have a little cream with their breakfast cereal or can consume them with some butter. Soya milk is not recommended as it possesses several antinutrients. Do check out my favourite healthy porridge recipe at the end of this chapter.

What causes bloating?

High-carbohydrate diets increase insulin levels. Elevated insulin levels encourage the kidney to retain water and give the body its bloated look. This is why when you switch to a low-carbohydrate diet, much of your initial weight loss will be that of water.

Healthy carbohydrate options

Carbohydrate	*How to consume it*
Quinoa:[42] It is one of the so-called traditional grains and is referred to as the 'mother of all grains'. It is not exactly a grain but the fruit of the Chenopodium family. Originally grown in the Inca province of South America, it comes in three varieties: white, black and red. Quinoa is rich in protein, fibre and vitamins,	We must soak all quinoa products before cooking to neutralize their anti-nutrients. Quinoa can be consumed with pulses, vegetable subzi or as a side dish with meat or eggs.

Carbohydrate	*How to consume it*
has a low glycaemic index and possesses anti-inflammatory antioxidants such as kaempferol and quercetin.	
Amaranth:[43] Another grain from South America, which can be consumed in many ways.	It should be soaked at least overnight (24 hours is better) and can be used to make porridge. Find the recipe at the end of this chapter.
Buckwheat:[44] It is a seed of an herb, a relative of rhubarb and is valuable for its vitamin B17 content.	It should be sprouted before consumption. Soak untoasted whole buckwheat seeds in water and rinse it 2-3 times daily. In two days, tiny sprouts will shoot up. It can be consumed in coleslaw, soups, salads, crepes and noodles or as a side with fish or chicken.
Chia seeds:[45] These have been dated to the Mayans and Aztecs and are native to Australia and South America. The term 'chia' is an ancient Mayan word for 'strength'. Chia seeds are rich in omega-3 fats, protein, fibre, vitamins, minerals and antioxidants. They form an edible gel when soaked in water as they absorb water ten times their weight.	These seeds should be soaked in filtered water for 25 to 30 minutes until a chewy pudding-like texture is observed. Soaked chia seeds can be mixed with salad, smoothies and granola and can be refrigerated for up to five days. When soaked in water, these seeds can absorb almost ten times their original weight to form a layer of edible gel.

Carbohydrate	*How to consume it*
Beans: They are robust, fibre-rich carbohydrates popular in traditional diets. They are an exceptionally good source of protein for vegetarians. Edamame beans are a staple in Japanese cuisine, providing 11 g of protein and 9 g of fibre per serving.	Beans are known to cause digestive problems owing to the two complex sugars stachyose and raffinose. These sugars are not easily broken down by enzymes typically found in our intestines. However, beans and other legumes can be made more digestible by soaking them in filtered water for an extended period before cooking as this process helps breakdown the starches. If prepared in the proper way, beans can be easily digested by most people. To sprout beans, place them in a jar and fill it with water up to a quarter full. Rinse it four or more times daily. Sprouts will be ready in approximately four days. The adzuki bean sprout is ready to use at 1-inch, and mung bean sprouts are ready to use when they are 2 inches long.
Fibre-rich whole fruits and vegetables: These are good carbohydrates rich in dietary fibre that improve[46] insulin sensitivity. A diet rich in natural sources of carbohydrates and no refined carbohydrates has been proven to be effective[47] for individuals	Fruits and vegetables can be consumed in the form of soups, salad, fermented pickles and as a main course with a side of bread or rice.

Carbohydrate	*How to consume it*
with insulin resistance at improving their health and losing weight compared with the typical low-fat diet. This type of a high-fibre diet is valuable for vegans and vegetarians. Typically, most plant food sources are poor in proteins and fats and primarily contain carbohydrates, with notable exceptions of 'fatty fruits' such as olives, coconut, and avocado. Some plant foods are rich sources of dietary fibre that can help regulate glycaemic impact. *Examples*: spinach, carrots, kale, eggplant, brussels sprouts, peas, broccoli, asparagus, bell peppers, tomatoes, avocados, zucchini, cauliflower, watercress, cabbage, beets, lettuce, cucumbers.	
Fermented foods: If you are a vegan or a vegetarian, fermenting your food will greatly improve your gut health, which is closely related to mental health and mood. Consuming fermented grains, pulses, fruits and	Fermented fruits and vegetables: Apple cider vinegar, sauerkraut, pickled beets, pickled cucumber, pickled carrot, pickled ginger, pickled pearl onion, pickled corn relish, pickled lemon.

Carbohydrate	*How to consume it*
vegetables improves the nutritional value of the protein, vitamins and carbohydrates in the food.	Fermented Chutney: Mint, cherry, pineapple, papaya, mango, apples, peaches, raisin and pears.
	Cultured soy products: miso and natto.
	Cultured dairy: yoghurt, curd, dahi, buttermilk, cottage cheese (casein), whey, kefir, koumiss, långfil, kjaeldermelk, laban, crème fraiche, sour butter, cream cheese, cultured sour cream and piima.
	Fermented grains: sourdough bread and rice milk.
	Germinated/sprouted cereals, beans and legumes: lentils, dried chickpeas, bulgar, barley, dried beans and almonds, buckwheat, adzuki, mung, black beans, lima beans, kidney beans, brussels sprout.
	Soaked seeds: sunflower, pumpkin, melon, sesame, onion, chia, fenugreek, radish, cress and poppy.

Food fermentation – The old blessing

Our intestinal microbiome has made us highly vulnerable to the new gamut of human viruses, cancers, autoimmune diseases and hordes of pathogenic microorganisms. Interestingly, it is not drugs, vaccinations or antibiotics that will be a cure for these diseases but a restored, healthy relationship with the varieties of lactobacilli in our system. Fermentation is a process that involves certain beneficial bacteria digesting the sugars in our food such as lactose, glucose, fructose, etc. In this process, they are also generating acids (gives the food a tart taste), carbon dioxide (generates air pockets in foods and bubbles in drinks) or alcohol in trace to high quantities based on the type of the food and type and period of fermentation. The chemical by-products of fermentation are interesting because both what is lost (sugar) and what is gained are important to determine the beneficial effects of that particular food on insulin sensitivity. When bacteria ferment grains, they do not digest the protein or fat but only the glucose in the starches, thereby reducing the food's ability to elevate our blood sugar and insulin levels instantaneously. This means that the benefit of consuming fermented foods is two-fold:

1. We consume less starch and sugar.
2. We improve our gut health and digestion process by ingesting beneficial bacteria that can function as probiotics in our intestines.

Because describing various methods to prepare fermented foods is extensive and beyond the scope of this book, I will provide you with a basic understanding of how you can enhance a vegetarian diet by fermentation. Perhaps, this is the topic of my next book, in which there will be an extensive section dedicated to fermentation techniques and recipes of fermented foods you can make and relish while becoming healthy and losing weight.

(a) Fermentation of fruits and vegetables

Various species of bacteria generate lactic acid when digesting sugar and starches found in fruits and vegetables. These bacteria are called the lactobacilli, and they are omnipresent in the soil and on the body of every organism, especially on the roots and leaves of plants. The health benefits of lacto-fermentation of fruits and vegetables are immense and go beyond the rudimentary function of food preservation. The growth of lactobacilli through this process makes vegetables easier to digest and enhances nutrient levels. These bacterias also generate beneficial enzymes and anti-carcinogenic substances. Moreover, the lactic acid released as a by-product keeps fruits and vegetables in a state of immaculate preservation and, upon consumption, encourages the proliferation of gut flora and improves the health of the digestive system.

The consumption of lacto-fermented foods in various forms around the globe is adequate to confirm its health benefits. Sauerkraut is the principal fermented vegetable consumed in Europe. It is described in the Roman texts as being delicious and having medicinal properties. Turnips, beets and cucumber along with lesser-known pickled sorrel leaves, grape leaves and herbs are also traditional lacto-fermented foods. Pickled green tomatoes, lettuces and peppers are found in Poland and

Russia. The tradition of consuming lacto-fermented foods has been maintained in most Eastern and Asian cultures. The most prominent is a mix of fermented vegetables known as kimchi. The populations of China, Japan and Korea consume pickled turnip, cucumber, cabbage, onion, eggplant, carrot and squash. Korean kimchi is a lacto-fermented condiment of cabbage with other seasoning and vegetables, which is consumed daily. A Japanese meal is incomplete without a portion of pickled vegetables. In the USA, many kinds of relishes (cucumber, corn and watermelon rind) are a part of their tradition. We Indians ferment fruits with spices to make chutneys and the Japanese prize pickled plums of umeboshi. Surely enough, consuming kimchi[48] lowers blood sugar and insulin levels in individuals at high risk of developing insulin resistance. A study compared the impact of fresh kimchi to that of ten-day-old kimchi, indicating that it wasn't the vegetables that were crucial but the effect of the fermentation process on these vegetables. Equivalent benefits may be observed with fermented soya beans[49] and ginseng.[50]

Recipe to make fermented fruits and vegetables at home:

1. Wash the vegetable or fruit and cut them.
2. Mix with salt and spices or herbs and then pound briefly using a wooden pounder or meat hammer to remove juices.
3. Press them into an air-tight, quart-sized, wide-mouth mason jar. The vegetables and their juices grow marginally during the fermentation process, so it is essential to avoid filling the jar to the brim and leave around an inch of space between the top of the jar and the vegetables. Ensure that

the jar is locked and closed very tightly because of the anaerobic (respiration in the absence of oxygen) nature of the lacto-fermentation process. The presence of oxygen will spoil the final product once the fermentation process has begun.

4. Add salt and whey or just whey. Salt prevents bacteria from decomposing for many days until sufficient lactic acid is generated to preserve the vegetables for several months. The quantity of salt can be decreased or even eradicated if whey is added to the pickling mixture. Whey functions as an inoculant and is rich in lactic acid and the bacteria that generate lactic acid, which reduces the time required for the generation of adequate lactic acid for preservation. Dried whey or commercially concentrated whey powder is not recommended. Whey cannot be skipped for pickled fruit preparation.
5. The room temperature should generally be about 22 degrees Celsius to complete the lacto-fermentation in approximately two to four days. However, if the ambient temperature is warmer, it will take less time; if it is cooler, it will require more time. After two to four days, the jar should be shifted to a dark, cool place, typically with a temperature of approximately 4 degrees Celsius. You can opt for a small refrigerator or wine cellar and keep the setting temperature at 'moderately chilled'. If not, the refrigerator's top shelf will also do. Lacto-fermentation of fruit chutneys requires approximately two days at room temperature, after which they should be stored in a refrigerator. According to the experts,[51] the flavour of lacto-

fermented vegetables is enhanced with time. Sauerkraut, for example, may require several months to complete fermentation. However, it's okay if these are consumed instantly after two to four days of fermentation at room temperature.

These fermented vegetables can be used as condiments in a meal and preserved for as long as nine months in cold storage. However, jelly, marmalade and other fruit conserves should only be stored up to two months from the preparation date and should be consumed within that period. The fermented chutneys made of vegetables and fruits, in particular, can get bubbly, but it's okay as it is natural and expected. There is no reason to be perturbed if a white layer is formed on the top. It is totally benign and should be removed with the help of a spoon. You would know that lacto-fermentation has been a success if the fruits and vegetables which have undergone the fermentation process remain conserved for many months in cold storage.

A single tablespoon of raw apple cider vinegar taken after a starchy meal helps reduce blood sugar and the impact on your insulin levels.[52]

Pro tip: Take two[53] tablespoons of raw apple cider vinegar in the evening to control your blood sugar for the following morning when blood sugar levels swing upwards. If it is difficult for you to consume raw apple cider vinegar you can dilute it in 200 to 250 ml of water. I personally use Bragg Raw Unfiltered Apple Cider Vinegar. Another good option is WOW Life

Science Organic Apple Cider Vinegar. Otherwise, consuming probiotic bacteria in powder or capsule supplements[54] can also help lower fasting blood sugar and insulin.

(b) Fermentation of grains and seeds

Traditionally, in India, lentils and rice are fermented for at least two days before preparing dosa and idli. In some African countries, corn is soaked overnight, coarsely ground and added to their stews and soups. They also ferment millet and corn for many days to make *ogi*, a sour porridge. A similar traditional dish is made by the Welsh population from oats. Traditionally, it is required to soak corn or its flour in lime water. This process frees up vitamin B3 (nicotinamide), which is otherwise bound up in the grain. It also enhances the amino acid profile of protein in the germ. Thus, if you are a frequent consumer of corn, the easy precaution of soaking corn flour in lime water can help mitigate the risk of developing pellagra, a vitamin B3 deficiency with severe symptoms of fatigue, sore skin and mental disorders.

In some Latin American and Asian countries, rice is fermented before it is prepared for consumption. Ethiopians ferment a grain known as teff for several days before baking their distinctive injera bread. In Mexico, corn cakes are fermented in banana leaves for many days, even up to two weeks. Europeans, prior to the introduction of commercial brewer's yeast, made bread by adding fermented starters to grains soaked in soured milk or water overnight, and let it ferment for as long as possible before they were cooked, served and consumed as gruel or porridge. The USA pioneered sourdough bread, biscuits and pancakes, in which bacteria facilitate the dough to rise over time in the absence of the 'fast-acting', omnipresent brewer's yeast. Modern nutritional science[55] has discovered that all grains contain phytic acid, an organic acid in which phosphorus is attached to the bran or the outer layer. Untreated phytic acid can combine with magnesium, calcium, zinc, copper and especially iron in the digestive tract and inhibit the absorption of these minerals in food. This is why diets rich in unfermented whole grains[56] may often result in fatal bone loss and mineral deficiencies.

Consumption of copious amounts of unfermented whole grains improves the colon transit time initially, but in the long run it may lead to irritable bowel syndrome and result in various other adverse effects. Soaking the grain lets lactobacilli, enzymes and other beneficial organisms digest and counterbalance phytic acid in grains. As brief as seven hours of soaking in the acidic warm lime water will counterbalance an enormous portion of phytic acid.

Pro tip: Rolled or cracked cereals can be soaked overnight in filtered warm water containing fresh lemon juice or apple cider vinegar, which is an acidic medium, and eaten as breakfast. For every 240 ml of liquid, use one tablespoon of acid medium. This significantly improves their nutritional value.

Must be soaked or fermented	*Do not require soaking*
Grains containing gluten such as wheat, barley, oats and rye.	Grains such as millet, rice and buckwheat, which do not possess gluten.

Soaking seeds in warm water also counterbalances enzyme inhibitors and promotes the generation of many beneficial enzymes. These enzymes also enhance the quantity of many vitamins, particularly B vitamins.	It is not mandatory to soak whole millet and whole rice. They should be gently cooked in a gelatinous, mineral-rich broth for at least two hours. This counterbalances some of the phytates they possess and provides additional minerals to make up for the phytates still attached, while the gelatine in the broth will tremendously help digestion. Cooking grains in a pressure cooker is not recommended because they are cooked instantly.

(c) Fermentation of legumes

Pulses or legumes such as lentils, chickpeas, cashew, peanuts, peas and beans have nourished humans for several centuries. They are considered the poor man's meat across the world. Combining whole grains, pulses, a small quantity of animal protein and excellent quality animal fat is an economically ideal and healthy diet for vegetarians.

Legumes are rich in B vitamins and minerals. Recently, studies have suggested that legumes[57] possess many anticancer agents. They all contain essential fats and omega-3 and omega-6 fatty acids. Pinto and kidney beans[58] are higher in omega-3 fats, and chickpeas[59] are higher in omega-6 fats.

Legume	
Beans	Can be soaked in tepid, slightly acidic or alkaline water for extended periods before cooking. The beans should then be washed and in the case of chickpeas, the skins are peeled off. As the legumes are cooking, all the foam that rises to the top of the cooking water should be skimmed off. Sometimes the water is replaced midway through the cooking process. Such care in cooking is required to ensure that legumes are digestible and all the nutrients they possess can be well assimilated. This preparation breaks down difficult-to-digest complex sugars and counterbalances enzyme inhibitors and phytic acid. Bland-tasting legumes work synergistically with sour foods. Lime juice or liquid from lacto-fermented vegetables or sauerkraut should be added to bean and lentil soups. Beans and lentils in salads are enhanced with a good amount of onions. Canned beans are not recommended because even though the phytate content is removed during the processing with high pressures and temperatures, this processing causes degradation of the protein content and other nutrients in the beans. So canned beans are best consumed sparingly.
Soya beans	Asians use soaked and cooked soya beans to make products such as natto, miso and tempeh. They contain high amounts of potent enzyme inhibitors and are high in phytic acid, which can generate fatal gastric distress, chronic deficiencies and reduced protein digestion, leading to compromised uptake of amino acids. Unfortunately, these enzyme inhibitors and phytates are not neutralized by ordinary cooking. Additionally, phytoestrogens and goitrogens found in soy foods are powerful endocrine disruptors especially impeding thyroid function.[60] Thus cooking them properly or fermenting them is important to mitigate these problems.

Legume	
	Vegans have long championed soy foods as the ideal protein source. However, textured soy protein has many antinutrients.[61] It has copious quantities of phytic acids, which prevent the absorption of essential minerals. It also has trypsin inhibitors (trypsin is a vital enzyme necessary for digestion) and three phytochemicals, genistein, isoflavones and daidzein, which show antithyroid activity. No other dietary staple has such a considerable amount of antinutrients[62] as textured soy protein, and ironically, no other food has such a colossal backing of lobbyists and public relations firms working for it. Consuming commercially available soya milk is also not recommended due to these reasons and because carcinogens are formed during the processing of soy products.
Sprouted grains	These can be used in sandwiches, salads, breakfast cereals, vegetable dishes and as an addition to bread and other baked goods. Sprouting promotes vitamin B content, particularly B2, B5 and B6 and carotene, a precursor to vitamin A. It counterbalances phytic acid and enzyme inhibitors present in all seeds, breaks down complex sugars responsible for internal gas, converts a part of the starch in grain into sugar, inactivates aflatoxins and potent carcinogens found in grains and promotes various enzymes that assist digestion. However, you should be warned against overconsumption of raw sprouted grains as they contain troublesome substances to keep animals from consuming the young shoots. These substances can be counterbalanced through cooking. Sprouted grains should be lightly steamed or added to casseroles and soups.

How to sprout grains?

1. Fill a mason jar with seeds or grains of your choice up to one-third full.
2. Add filtered water to the top and close it with its screen insert.
3. Let the seeds soak for one night and pour out the water.
4. Rinse the seeds properly. This can be done without removing the top by inverting the jar and allowing it to sit at an angle so the water can drain out and let the air circulate.
5. Wash the seeds every couple hours or at least twice daily.
6. Sprouts will be ready in one to four days.
7. Wash them properly, remove surplus moisture, and replace the screen insert with a proper lid.
8. Sprouts can be stored in the refrigerator.

Almost all seeds or grains can be sprouted – dried beans, barley, wheat, almonds, chickpeas, onion seeds, chia seeds and radish seeds. Delicate seeds such as sunflower and pumpkin also germinate well. Hulled seeds should not be bought from open bins in Kirana stores but in tightly sealed packages to minimize oxidation. Seeds such as oat seeds do not sprout easily. After being separated from their outer hulls, they will not germinate. Flaxseeds become viscous after sprouting and can't be washed well. Seeds such as the ones sold as spices and that have been irradiated will not sprout. Nuts such as walnuts and pecans that have been separated from their shells cannot be sprouted. However, an overnight soak in salted, filtered warm water will counterbalance sprout inhibitors.

Skinless peanuts and almonds will frequently sprout, a sign that their skins have been separated by a mechanical method and not by a process involving roasting and boiling.

(d) Fermentation of dairy products

Cultured or fermented dairy products assume an essential role in various traditional cuisines. The western practice of consuming milk only in the natural or unfermented state is relatively new.

Curd	Before the industrial revolution, Europeans consumed milk as clabber, curds, whey and cheese. Without refrigeration or pasteurization, milk sours and immediately disintegrates due to lacto-fermentation. Curd bacteria selectively digest the milk sugar (lactose) and milk protein (casein) from the milk, leaving the fats in the milk intact for us. These beneficial bacteria produce sufficient lactic acid to inactivate all putrefying bacteria and the resultant curd does not spoil for several days or weeks. Cheese is formed after different kinds of fermentation for several years.
Yoghurt or dahi	It is a fermented milk product which is well-known around the globe. It originally comes from Bulgaria. In India, milk from water buffalo or cows is heated and cultured overnight to produce dahi, which we consume almost every day with every meal.
Kefir	Kefir means sour milk or fermented milk and is a popular beverage in Russia. It is an effervescent beverage, sometimes slightly alcoholic, and is made from sheep, goat or cow milk.

Koumiss	A popular drink in the eastern region of Russia, made from mare's milk.
Långfil	In Scandinavian countries, this cultured milk product is produced using wooden barrels for several months. The Norwegians produce a variety of långfil made in caves known as kjaeldermelk (cellar milk).
Crème fraiche	In Europe, fermented or sour cream is used as an indispensable ingredient in sauces and soups. It is produced using a Finnish culture known as piima or with cultured buttermilk. The tasty sour butter from Germany and France is produced from churning fermented cream. Cultured butter is rich in digestive enzyme content, requires no salt and is easily digested.
Cottage and cream cheese	These are traditionally produced by fermentation for many days until the casein or white milk curds in the milk disintegrate from the whey. When this cream cheese is inoculated or weighed down with additional cultures, it undergoes further fermentation, leading to various distinct kinds of cheese.
Whey	In earlier times, whey from cultured milk helped produce a variety of other fermented foods and beverages, but today its benefits are unknown to a layperson, who sees whey as nothing more than a waste product. Homemade cultured whey is a key ingredient for making fermented chutneys, beverages, and vegetable and grain dishes. It can be produced from many kinds of cultured milk, good quality yoghurt or even fresh raw milk, which sour and disintegrate naturally at room temperature for various days.

Casein, commonly found in cow milk, is one of the most challenging proteins to break down and digest. Fermentation breaks this protein down. Culturing restores lactase, which is destroyed during the pasteurization process and which assists the digestion of milk sugar or lactose. Culturing also restores other enzymes that help the body absorb calcium and other minerals. The lactase produced during this process allows lactose-intolerant individuals to tolerate these particular milk products. Fermentation also increases the vitamin B and C content in the dairy product.

Research has revealed that regular consumption of cultured dairy products protects against bone loss and lowers cholesterol. Furthermore, cultured dairy products provide lactic acid and gut-friendly bacteria to the digestive tract. These beneficial organisms and their by-products keep pathogens at bay, shield us against infectious diseases and help in the complete digestion of all the foods that we consume. Perhaps this is why various traditional societies valued fermented dairy products and insisted on giving them to aged or sick individuals and nursing mothers.

Fermented dairy products can be effortlessly created from goat or cow milk. Milk culturing may require tweaking to individual circumstances. The piima culture, for instance, is the most temperature-sensitive, needing a constant ambient temperature of 22 to 24 degrees Celsius. In contrast, the kefir culture produces thicker sour milk, and is not as temperature-sensitive as piima culture. However, for kefir, grains must be added to new milk to keep the culture active. The kefir culture can be stored as a powder but a new packet is required for each new culture. Another relative fool proof culture, which remains active for several weeks without re-culturing and is not temperature sensitive, is the buttermilk culture. Fascinatingly, even these sour milk products carry observable protection against insulin resistance. If you can make milk culturing a dedicated component of your routine and consuming these fermented products a part of your daily diet, it will result in tremendous payoffs. If you want to try your hand at fermenting a milk product at home, check out my easy kefir recipe at the end of this chapter.

Not only do fermented foods reduce[63] the blood sugar and insulin burden of foods such as grains, fruits, vegetables and milk on our body, but they also improve[64] the long-run regulation of blood sugar.

The bottom line is:

- Avoid very sweet foods
- Avoid vegetables rich in starch
- Avoid drinking or mashing your carbohydrates
- Consume fermented carbohydrates

F – Fuel with fats

Dietary fat triggers no insulin effect at all. Pure fat such as coconut oil or ghee neither stimulates glucose nor insulin. A greater quantity of fat does not trigger any higher insulin response. This doesn't mean that all fats are beneficial. The general rule is that if it's a naturally occurring or 'real' fat, then it's healthy for us as opposed to artificial and industrially extracted seed oils found in processed foods.

The more saturated fats the cooking oil contains, the more heat it can take without becoming oxidized and rancid. On the contrary, the lesser saturated fats a particular oil has, the more mono and polyunsaturated fats it contains. Thus, they can tolerate less heat and are more susceptible to oxidation.

I have discussed earlier about the skewed ratio of omega-6 to omega-3. If you've been eating a lot of processed foods, which have pro-inflammatory, obesity-promoting omega-6, your omega-3 to omega-6 ratio is probably as low as 15:1 or maybe even lower.

An omega-3-rich diet indicates to the body that it is summer and that food is plentiful. Our metabolism revs up as a response to the comfort that this message provides. In contrast, an omega-6-rich diet indicates food scarcity. Therefore, the body stores more calories and conserves its energy expenditure. The problem with modern seed oil-rich diet is not an omega-3 deficiency but excess consumption of omega-6.

How to recalibrate this balance?

There is a simple way to balance out our omega-3 to omega-6 ratio. It is better than force-feeding ourselves fish oil capsules. We could switch our cooking oil from omega-6 rich vegetable/seed fats to saturated fat rich medium such as ghee, butter, coconut oil or monounsaturated rich cold pressed virgin olive oil. This will ensure that we don't overdo omega-6 fats and bring the ratio of omega-6 to omega-3 up.

Did you know?

Two tablespoons of sunflower oil contain 18 g of omega-6 and almost no omega-3 fats. If we consume a generous portion of food with the highest omega-3-possessing foods available such as 150 g of Atlantic salmon, we consume 3 g of omega-3 and negligible omega-6. Therefore, every time we use sunflower oil for cooking our food, we would require a humongous portion of omega-3-rich salmon to match the quantity of omega-6 in the sunflower oil. Alternatively, we could consume omega-3 supplements typically containing 1 g per capsule, so we will have to consume eighteen capsules daily to bring up our omega-3 to omega-6 ratio to 1:1. You can start to see why our omega-3 to omega-6 ratio is so low when we consume foods cooked in vegetable oil.

Oils

A brief snapshot of fats in the market:

Oils	*Properties*
Coconut, clarified butter (ghee), butter, meat lard and tallow	These are healthy saturated fats. These saturated and monounsaturated-rich oils have significantly less omega-6 than seed oils and should be used for cooking.
Macadamia nut oil, avocado oil, olive oil	These are healthy monounsaturated fats found in nuts and fruits, contain significantly less omega-6 than seed oils and can be used for cooking. Pro tip: Olive oil should be purchased in a tin, and if it is in a glass bottle, it must be stored in a dark cupboard as sunlight diminishes and destroys the beneficial antioxidants in the oil.

Refined seed oils such as corn oil, soyabean oil, canola oil	These are polyunsaturated fats, contain hundreds and thousands more omega-6 polyunsaturated fats and negligible omega-3 fats. The omega-3 fats[65] found in whole seeds such as flaxseed and chia seeds are beneficial and improves insulin signalling. Low levels of polyunsaturated fats and a mixture of all fats found in chia and flaxseeds, nuts and meats are alright.

Did you know?

Canola oil is a seed oil often marketed as high in omega-3 polyunsaturated fats. If you observe the amount of omegas in a tablespoon of this oil, it has 1.2 g of omega-3 and 2.6 g of omega-6, which is marginally below 1:2 and not really bad, to be honest. This oil definitely does possess a good amount of omega-3. The issue arises when we start to heat the oil for cooking. Most of the omega-3 will be degraded at high cooking temperatures. Thus the omega-3 health claims on such bottles are simply a marketing gimmick to entice us to purchase and use them.

Nuts

Nuts such as pecans, almonds, peanuts (a legume) and cashews make for great healthy snacks, whether plain, as nut butters or in mixes. Nuts are immensely nutritious foods if prepared and consumed properly. Traditional habits of society should act as a guide. We instinctively know that nuts are best consumed after partially sprouting or soaking. The enzyme inhibitors in the nuts cause digestive stress if we eat too many of them. Nuts should be soaked in salt water overnight and dried in a dehydrator or warm oven. This way, their nutrients become more readily available and easier to digest. This method reflects the conventional practice of soaking squash or pumpkin seeds in brine and allowing them to dry in the sun before consuming them as is or grinding them to add to a dish. Soaking the seeds in salt water activates enzymes that counterbalance enzyme inhibitors. Crispy nuts along with raw cheese makes for the perfect snack!

Wondering whether nuts contain carbohydrates? Like dairy, some nuts are rich in fats but are also high in proteins and carbohydrates.

Nuts	*Relative carbohydrate content*
Pecans and macadamia nuts	lowest
Almonds, walnuts and most nuts	moderate
Cashews and pistachios	highest

Bone broths and vegetable stock

In earlier times, when the butcher sold meat on the bone instead of individual filets and boneless breasts, our intelligent and thrifty ancestors utilized every part of the animal by preparing broth, stock or bouillon from the bony parts. Fish and meat stocks are almost ubiquitous in traditional cuisines from around the globe, be it Chinese, Japanese, Russian, Middle Eastern, African, Italian, French or South American. For several cultures, soup is breakfast food. However, in modern times, homemade meat broths made of marrow, cartilage and bones to produce flavourful and nourishing sauces and soups have nearly disappeared from the Indian culinary tradition, an unfortunate result of our modern hurry-up, throwaway lifestyle and meat processing techniques. Cartilage and collagen, another crucial component of broth, have been used with notable results in the treatment of bone disorders,[66] rheumatoid arthritis and other ailments. In folk wisdom, the popular Jewish penicillin, the rich chicken broth, was a prized therapy for the flu. Even in the twelfth century, physician Moses Maimonides[67] famously prescribed chicken broth to treat asthma and cold. Recent research[68] confirms that broth helps mitigate and prevent infectious diseases.

For non-vegetarians

Animal fats and gelatine-rich bone broths[69] aid in the absorption of protein in eggs, milk, meat and fish. Gelatine aids digestion and has been successfully used in treating various intestinal diseases[70] such as colitis, hyperacidity and Crohn's disease. Though gelatine, by no stretch of the imagination, is a complete protein, it is rich in the amino acids – glycine and arginine – and functions as a protein sparer in the body, a substance that ensures that all dietary protein is used for building muscles rather being converted to glucose for energy. Gelatine also helps treat various chronic diseases such as diabetes, anaemia and muscular dystrophy.

Pro tip: If one has budgetary constraints when it comes to daily protein intake, consume eggs, liberal amounts of good quality natural animal fats and bone broths.

Making broths is economical because animal bones can be easily sourced from local butcher shops. They also require minimum cooking skills and are easy to make. One can make them in enormous batches and easily store them in the fridge. In practically every culture, bone broth is a traditional dish that is both delicious and nutritious. Animal bones are gently boiled with vegetables, spices and herbs added for flavouring. The prolonged boiling time releases most gelatine, minerals and nutrients. To separate the stored minerals in the bone during the cooking process, adding a tiny quantity of vinegar really helps. Amino acids such as arginine, glycine and proline are abundantly found in bone broths along with minerals such as magnesium, phosphorus and calcium. Fish stock is particularly rich in minerals, including all-vital iodine. However, most commercially made broths are nothing like the homemade variety. Pre-packaged broths have monosodium glutamate (MSG) and artificial flavours and some don't even have nutrients such as gelatine and minerals. The best indicator of whether your stock contains gelatine is whether it thickens, even to the point of jellying, when chilled and refrigerated.

For vegetarians

Vegetable stock and clear soups are the perfect way to get family members who regularly turn up their noses at green foods or who may have problems digesting raw salads to actually eat vegetables. Bean and lentil soups served with whole-grain bread make for a complete nutritious meal that is easy on the budget and quick to prepare.

To sum up, to improve your metabolic health and reduce your set weight point:

- Eliminate vegetable oil from your kitchen.
- Use only butter, ghee, coconut and olive oil for cooking.
- Avoid fast foods, packaged foods, margarine and other oily spreads and ready-made cooking sauces.
- Avoid foods that have extreme levels of omega-6 polyunsaturated fats.
- Choose meat high in saturated fats and omega-3 polyunsaturated fats.
- Consume fresh vegetables and dairy products.

P – Proceed with protein

Proteins[71] are the building blocks of the animal kingdom and are essential for normal growth. The human body synthesizes approximately 50,000 unique proteins to form enzymes (the catalysts and assistants in every biochemical process in our body), hormones (the leader in every biochemical process), antibodies (the immunity booster), nerves, organs and muscles. All proteins in the body are a combination of 22 amino acids. Think of these amino acids as letters and the protein in the body as words in the English language. Every sequence of letters in the word forms a different word and has a different meaning. Similarly, different combinations of amino acids make different proteins that have unique functions. Nine amino acids are essential for humans due to the body's inability to make them and hence need to be provided in the diet. With the help of these essential amino acids, the body can build the other non-essential amino acids if they have not been supplied through your diet. However, if there is a deficiency or lack of even just one essential amino acid, the body cannot make the corresponding proteins or the other non-essential amino acids required even though the overall protein intake is sufficient.

Just as animal food sources are our only dietary sources of vitamins D and B12, animal proteins are the only complete source of protein. Animal proteins contain all of the essential and non-essential amino acids in optimal quantities for the human body. However, vegetarian sources of proteins possess only incomplete protein, meaning that they have low quantities of amino acids or lack one or more essential amino acids, even though they may be adequate in their overall protein content. For good health, the body must get all the essential amino acids to make all the proteins, especially for growing and ageing populations.

The two best sources of plant-based protein are legumes and grains. However, plant proteins alone cannot sustain healthy life because they do not contain sufficient essential amino acids.

For vegetarians

The best possible protein combination for vegetarians is plant sources, grains and pulses combined with a small quantity of animal protein such as curd or milk. Unfortunately, a diet devoid of animal protein cannot sustain good health. Most grain-based cuisines instinctively have these protein combinations. For instance, dal and rice or roti and lentils in

India, soya beans and rice in southeast Asia, chickpeas and whole wheat in the Gulf and the Middle East and animal sources plus beans and corn in Mexico. Vegetarians must take care to consume both grains and pulses at every meal as each consumed alone cannot supply the complete amino acid profile essential for good health. If you're a vegetarian, you can follow an intelligent, insulin-sensitizing dietary plan. You're required to search harder to identify the minor sugary and starchy foods rich in protein and fats. And if you can consume non-meat sources, eggs and dairy are your best options.

Irrespective of your dietary preference, be it vegetarian, vegan or omnivore, try to source all your dairy, eggs and meat from sources as close to your home as possible. Preferably choose products of pasture-raised animals, who have been allowed to consume their natural diet i.e., grass instead of grains. While there is no compelling evidence to support the notion that free-range eggs, meat or dairy is any better for health than regular produce, it's definitely a more sustainable and ethical approach. Also, be cautious of cured meats including sausages and specifically jerky. These frequently contain a good quantity of sugar. And don't be afraid of fatty fish and meat such as salmon and lamb or organ meat such as the liver.

The same logic applies to those health-conscious individuals who follow a plant-based diet. Purchasing locally grown produce and avoiding produce from farms that employ monocropping ensures that your purchase supports a sustainable method. Consume fermented dairy products such as curds and cheeses and foods such as homemade mayonnaise and cream that have carbohydrates removed and fat retained.

Ideally, a healthy protein intake of 1.5 g per kg[72] of your body weight or up to 30 per cent of your total calories should be consumed in your daily diet. Protein intake higher than this is not sustainable unless whey or casein protein supplements are added. Protein food such as eggs, dairy or meat frequently contains a notable quantity of fat. Plant proteins such as legumes and grains frequently have a notable quantity of carbohydrates too.

As you age beyond 40, your body's ability to convert dietary protein into muscles progressively decreases.[73] Protein-rich foods sourced from animals[74] contain predominantly proteins and fats with low sugar and starch content and are thus ideal for weight management.

Meal replacement and protein shakes

Protein shakes are typically made out of milk which contains two principal types of dairy proteins, whey (20 per cent) and casein (80 per cent). Cheese essentially contains casein. Whey is the by-product of the cheese or curd-making process (the liquid part). Elite sports athletes and bodybuilders often consume whey protein supplements. Whey contains the branched-chain amino acids (BCAAs) – valine, leucine and isoleucine, which are crucial for muscle building. Thus, whey supplements are taken to initiate recovery after strength training workouts.

Many regard calcium as the compelling reason to consume milk, but the main reason milk is good for you is its fat content.

If you wish to lose weight, don't be afraid of dairy fat. Whole milk has been correlated with reduced risk of obesity when compared with low-fat, skim milk. Full-fat cheese, butter, sour milk and whole milk were correlated with less weight gain. Consumption of whole-fat dairy products has been proven to decrease the risk of developing diabetes compared with the consumption of low-fat, skim dairy products.

Many popular meal replacement shakes have high sugar content and thus don't aid sustainable weight loss. These are good examples of nutritional thieves in a crowded marketplace. Most of the fats in these drinks are seed oils such as soya bean oil.

For vegans and vegetarians, several protein concentrate and isolate shakes are available that don't have added sugars and fats. This is your best option for fulfilling your daily protein needs, a minimum of 1.2 g per kg of your body weight. This means that a 70 kg individual should consistently consume 85 g of protein. A good whey protein supplement for vegetarians that I recommend is Ultimate Nutrition ISO Sensation 93. It's a pure isolate with almost 91 per cent protein purity extracted through a physical cold press filtration technique known as crossflow microfiltration. This physical method ensures that the protein is not exposed to chemical treatment or heat that would denature it or destroy its subfractions necessary for building good immunity. In addition, isolates are usually very low in lactose. Ensure that you opt for a product containing little to no fructose or any other sugar and no seed oils. A good protein supplement for vegans is the Mypro Sport Nutrition Plant Protein Powder (Pea & Brown Rice Protein), which has protein sourced from peas and brown rice.

Dietary protein – A potent satiety factor

Protein brings satiety to your meals and ensures long-term adherence to a healthy diet. Research shows that our stomach releases hormones known as incretins that work on food absorption and excretion mechanisms. With the help of nerve cells, hormones and receptors, the gastrointestinal tract almost works like a 'second brain'. Two incretin hormones, glucose-dependent insulinotropic polypeptide (GIP) and GLP-1, are released when any nutrient (glucose, fatty acids and amino acids) is consumed. The incretin effect begins within minutes of thinking, seeing, smelling or tasting of food, known as the 'cephalic phase'.[75] The incretin effect peaks at approximately 60 minutes after a meal. Incretin helps in insulin secretion and delays the transit of food from the stomach into the small intestine, and thus slowing down the absorption of glucose into the bloodstream. Whey protein supplement consumption raises GLP-1[76] by almost 300 per cent. Incretins have a significant role to play in improving satiety levels as it ensures a gradual absorption of nutrients into the body, leading to lower blood glucose and insulin levels.

Studies[77] using the class of drug known as exenatide have shown that selective invigoration of GLP-1 generates weight loss, as the subsequent appetite suppressing effect is powerful. Therefore, we should not forget that animal protein sources have this incretin effect, making us feel full and satiated. This helps us effortlessly match our food intake to our energy expenditure. This effect leads us to either consume less food throughout the day or even completely skip it to allow our bodies to get the 'time to digest'. Infants do not forcefully consume more food when they are not hungry. Animals in the wild also show the same inhibition. But because of our constant snacking on processed foods, our appetite and satiety signals have been hijacked and we've been conditioned to ignore our feelings of hunger and satiety.

An easy tip for weight loss that should be evident but is not is if one is not feeling hungry, it is alright not to eat. Your body will communicate with you through the incretins' protective effect on your satiety when you should consume the next meal. So after consuming a hefty meal, as is usually done when we celebrate any life or cultural event, if we are not feeling hungry, the idea of skipping the next meal should not be a reason for paranoia, and there is no compulsion to schedule it. Mandatory scheduling of three or more meals comes with an obsession that may typically transpire due to an irrational fear that skipping a single meal will ruin our metabolism. So skipping a meal or two is fine under prolonged satiety.

How should you plan your meals to lose weight?

As there is a fundamental difference in one's tolerance to carbohydrates due to metabolic variation based on age, gender, physical activity levels and genetics, there is no one-size-fits-all diet.

Here are some general rules of macronutrient amounts as percentages of total calories that you can use to plan your new diet:

- **Level 1:** Start off by making minor but impactful changes. Consume no greater than 100 g of carbohydrates per day or a ratio per meal as follows: Fat: Protein: Carbohydrates = 55:25:20 or 55:30:15.
- **Level 2:** The next level of this change would be based on your assessment of fat lost in stage one. If it does not reap the desired results, you may reduce the consumption of carbohydrates to no greater than 75 g per day or a ratio of Fats: Proteins: Carbohydrates = 65:25:10.
- **Level 3:** The final level of this change if you want to go very aggressive with your diet and see significant fat loss is to have no more than 50 g of carbohydrates per day or a ratio of Fats: Protein: Carbohydrates = 70:25:5.

Remember that these ranges should be tweaked often based on your daily exercise schedule. Consume more carbohydrates on the day when the workout is very intense and lesser on the days you have an off or a rest day from your training. These numbers are not meant to be final. These are only indicative. Also, consuming less than 30 g of starch and sugars per day is very likely to be a ketogenic diet for most individuals.

If you're still uncomfortable with it and feel strongly that you require more carbohydrates, make every effort to consume it from leafy vegetables and fruits while keeping your intake of carbohydrates to no greater than 30 g per meal, assuming you are planning to consume three meals a day. Another point is that we don't need to be in a continuous ketosis state to enjoy the insulin-sensitizing benefits of a carbohydrate-restriction or careful-carbohydrate approach. Aim to balance carbohydrates and nutrients by choosing plant foods (vegetables and fruits) that are high in nutrients and fibre and low in starch and sugar. Be mindful of overconsuming starchy vegetables such as potatoes and squash and high sugar fruits such as apple, pineapple and bananas.

The most significant hurdle of adopting a low-carbohydrate diet as a vegan or vegetarian is dealing with sugar and other carbohydrates present in large amounts in plant foods. Also, many can initially have an addiction and craving for starchy, floury and sugared foods. Though the debate[78] rages on their addictive nature, I define food addiction in the following easy way:

1. Is it food that you crave?
2. Is controlling the consumption of the food challenging for you?
3. After overindulging, do you feel guilty?

Pro tip: To test if you are genuinely hungry for food, first consume some water infused with salt and lime to assess if you are still feeling hungry because the brain pathway to signal craving for food and thirst for water is the same. We can easily confuse the two signals and end up eating when what actually the brain was seeking was water for hydration. In many cases, that does the trick but if you are still hungry and craving something salty or sweet, try consuming some dark chocolate, dry fruits, cheese, seeds or nuts.

Controlling what you eat and when you eat in a social environment can be really tricky. Friends and family are undoubtedly very caring and outstanding individuals. However, once you commit to consuming sweets at a particular frequency in a week, say only one treat a week, then be warned that they may suddenly be less supportive in helping you achieve that goal. Over the years, I've come across many cases of individuals trying to make crucial dietary changes by cutting down sugars, only for their dear and near ones to zealously oppose the changes by teasing and making fun of the individual's efforts to be healthier. It is perhaps human nature that we don't instinctively accept individuals making alterations that we know we should be making, and it's easier to discourage others when they do that and ignore the issue if everyone is a part of that inertia. Nonetheless, using the dietary framework that I have laid out for you in this chapter has helped many of my clients to lose weight with relative ease, without the daunting feeling of constant hunger, and helped them keep it off sustainably. Not only that, but studies showed that many type 2 diabetes patients have gone off their medication after following this kind of protocol backed by science.[79]

RECIPES

My favorite healthy breakfast recipes

CULTURED-MILK SMOOTHIE

Serving size: 710 ml
Calories: 637 kcals
Ingredients:
150 g berries (fresh or frozen) or one ripe banana
300 ml whole milk, yoghurt, buttermilk or kefir
2 tbsp extra virgin edible coconut oil
Two egg yolks
¼ tsp stevia powder
One tsp vanilla extract (exclude if adding berries)
Pinch of nutmeg (exclude if adding berries)

Smoothies made from high-quality cultured milk are an incredibly healthy and quick breakfast, snack or meal for busy professionals. Unfortunately, most commercially available smoothies contain artificial ingredients, inferior quality protein such as soy protein powder and problematic sweeteners. Fortunately, smoothies are convenient, easy and quick to make at home.

Method:
Blend the berries or banana in the food blender or processor until smooth. Add the remaining ingredients and blend.

BREAKFAST PORRIDGE

Serving size: 4

Calories: 364 kcals

Ingredients:

80 g cracked or rolled oats

240 ml warm filtered water plus two tbsp yoghurt, whey, buttermilk or kefir

½ tsp sea salt

240 ml filtered water

Optional: One tbsp ground flaxseeds

Note: Those with severe milk allergies can use vinegar or lemon juice instead of yoghurt, whey, buttermilk or kefir.

Method:

Oats should ideally be soaked overnight or even longer for maximum benefits and optimal assimilation. Soaked oats cook in less than 5 minutes.

Mix oats with warm water plus two tbsp yoghurt, whey, buttermilk or kefir.. Cover and leave in a warm place for a minimum of 7 hours and as long as 24 hours. Boil 240 ml of water with sea salt. Add the soaked oats to the boiling water, reduce the heat, cover and simmer for 5 minutes. Remove the oats from heat, add the ground flaxseeds (optional) and let stand for a few minutes. Serve with plenty of butter or cream and a natural sweetener like raw honey, stevia or monk fruit extract. You may also wish to add natural peanut or almond butter, chopped almonds or walnuts or dried coconut meat.

Variations:

1. **Spelt or Kamut porridge**: Use 80 g of coarsely ground or rolled spelt or kamut instead of oats.
2. **Rye porridge**: Use 80 g of coarsely ground or rolled rye instead of oats. Rye may require extra soaking time and more water for total hydration.
3. **Teff porridge**: Use 80 g whole teff. It is really delicious as a breakfast cereal, and it may be soaked overnight, but 24 hours is better.
4. **Amaranth porridge**: Use 80 g amaranth and use the same method as that for teff porridge.
5. **Grits**: Use 130 g of coarsely ground corn and 240 ml limewater instead of filtered water.

Note: Traditional corn recipes require soaking corn or corn flour in lime water. Doing so releases nicotinamide (vitamin B3), which otherwise typically remains bound in the grain. Additionally, soaking enhances the amino acid quality of proteins in the germ. If you consume corn products frequently, then the simple precaution of soaking corn or corn flour in lime water will help you mitigate pellagra, the vitamin B3 deficiency disease with its brutal symptoms of fatigue, sore skin and mental disorders.

Method to soak corn: Place about 1-inch pickling lime in a 1.9 litre jar to make lime water. Fill up the jar with filter water, shake well, cover tightly and let stand overnight. The powder will settle, and the resultant clear liquid is lime water. Store the jar in a cool place (it's not mandatory to refrigerate), and use it for soaking cornmeal. You may also use commercial masa flour (cornmeal prepared by soaking corn kernels in lime water before grinding). However, cornmeal quickly goes rancid and develops a bitter taste, like all whole-grain flours, so it's best to grind the corn yourself.

My favourite fermented food recipe

SOURDOUGH BREAD

Serving size: 5-6 smaller loaves

Calories: 6920 kcals

Ingredients:

1 kg sourdough starter

360 ml cold filtered water

2½ tbsp coarse sea salt

1.5 kg freshly ground whole wheat, rye, spelt or einkorn

Method:

Traditional sourdough bread is prepared with a sourdough starter culture rather than with yeast and has a delicious flavour. In grains, spelt gives the most satisfactory loaf.

Begin with your sourdough starter culture at room temperature, having gone through the frothy and bubbling stage. Place the starter, salt and 240 ml water in a large bowl and mix it with a wooden spoon until the salt crystals have dissolved completely. Gradually mix in the flour. Towards the end, you'll find that mixing it with your hands would be easier. If the dough becomes too thick, you may add 120 ml of water. The dough mix should be relatively soft and easy to work. For 10 to 15 minutes, knead the dough mix right in the bowl by pulling and folding over. Otherwise, if you have a food processor, you can also knead in batches. Cut or shape loaves into the desired shapes without pressing down the dough, or place into 5-6 smaller well-buttered loaf pans. Cut a few slits in the top of the dough, cover it, and allow it to rise for the next 4 to 12 hours, which depends on the room temperature. Bake at 177 degrees Celsius for about an hour. Allow cooling before slicing. The bread will be fresh for up to a week without refrigeration.

Variation:

Sourdough herb and nut bread: During kneading, add 1 tbsp of dill or rosemary to each loaf. At the end of the kneading process, add 25 g of chopped crispy walnuts or pecans.

SOURDOUGH STARTER

Serving size: 1 kg

Calories: 1,820s kcals

Ingredients:

816 g freshly ground rye flour

Cold filtered water

Cheesecloth

Method:

The best outcomes for the sourdough starter are acquired from rye rather than wheat flour, perhaps due to rye containing a lower phytate quantity than wheat.

You will require two gallon-sized bowls. The total time for the starter to be ready is one week.

Grind 204 g flour and allow it to sit for a bit to cool. In one large bowl, mix flour with 475 ml of cold water. The mixture should be pretty soupy. Cover the bowl with a double layer of cheesecloth and secure it with a rubber band to keep out insects and allow bacteria and yeast to enter and act on the mixture. If you live in an unpolluted area with warm weather, you may set the bowl outside in the shade. Or else, keep it in a warm, open place, somewhere indoors or on a patio. The following day and every day for the next seven days, transfer the starter to the other clean bowl and add 102 g of freshly ground rye flour and sufficient cold water to concoct a soupy mixture. Cover it and let it stand. After a couple of days, the starter will start to bubble and develop a wine-like aroma. It should go through a frothy, bubbly stage, and then subside. After seven days, the starter is ready for breadmaking.

Use 667 g for a batch of sourdough bread and save 333 g for the next batch of the starter. If you plan to not use the remaining starter immediately, you may store it in airtight jars in the freezer or the refrigerator.

Avoid the temptation of adding honey to your starter, as some recipes tell you to do that. Honey promotes the proliferation of yeasts at the cost of lactic acid-generating bacteria and may give you an alcoholic fermentation instead.

Place the 333 g of leftover starter in a clean bowl to begin a new starter batch. Add 102 g of freshly ground rye flour and water daily, changing bowls until you end up with 1 kg of the starter.

EASY KEFIR RECIPE

Serving size: 475 ml

Calories: 225 kcal

Ingredients:

470 ml non-homogenized, fresh and preferably raw, whole milk

One packet of kefir powder or 1 tbsp kefir grains

[My recommendations: Zoh Probiotics – Cultures To Love Milk Kefir Starter Culture; Mr. Kefir – Live Milk Kefir Grains (15 Grams)]

Optional: 120 ml good quality cream

Method:

Typically, kefir is thicker than buttermilk or piima milk and has a fantastic tart flavour.

Use a fine strainer to place kefir grains and rinse with filtered water. Use a clean, wide-mouth 950 ml mason jar and place the milk and optional cream. If the milk is cold, place the jar in a pan of simmering water and wait until the milk reaches room temperature. Add kefir powder or grains to the milk, stir well, and cover the jar loosely with a cloth. Place the jar in a warm place (18 to 24 degrees Celsius) for 12 hours to 2 days. The kefir thickens typically in 24 hours and is ready. If you are using grains in your preparation, stir strenuously to redistribute them every now and then, taste the kefir for tartness, which is when you'll know it's ready. Depending on factors such as incubation time, the amount of curd used and the ambient temperature, the kefir may also become effervescent and thick. To remove the grains, pour the kefir through a strainer into another jar and refrigerate it. Finally, the grains that have been strained out can be used to make another batch of kefir. However, if you do not plan to make another batch immediately, then simply prime them for storage by rinsing them well with filtered water and store them in a small jar with approximately 120 ml of filtered water. This can be stored in the refrigerator for many weeks or in the freezer for many months. But if they are stored too long, they may lose their culturing power.

Fahim – Revisited

Remember Fahim, one of my clients whom I mentioned in the first chapter. To recap, Fahim was forty-seven years old when he was diagnosed with type 2 diabetes. He is 5 feet 9 inches and weighed 96 kg. When he came to me, his BMI was over 30. He wanted to lose 25 kg, which he thought was an audacious goal. He had tried everything under the sun – crash diets, cardio and walking – to create a calorie deficit but failed spectacularly to lose weight. His weight fluctuated between 96 and 89 kg and he was frustrated. He also had certain complications from diabetes and was on two oral antihyperglycemic agents along with insulin. When he showed me his blood sugar report, I saw that his fasting blood sugar was higher than normal, and even after two hours post his meals, his blood sugar levels remained higher than normal. This indicated insulin resistance. Additionally, his HbA1c, which indicates how well his body has maintained blood sugar in the last three months, was high, suggesting that it has been poorly managed. Ideally, it should be at 5.7 per cent or below this mark.

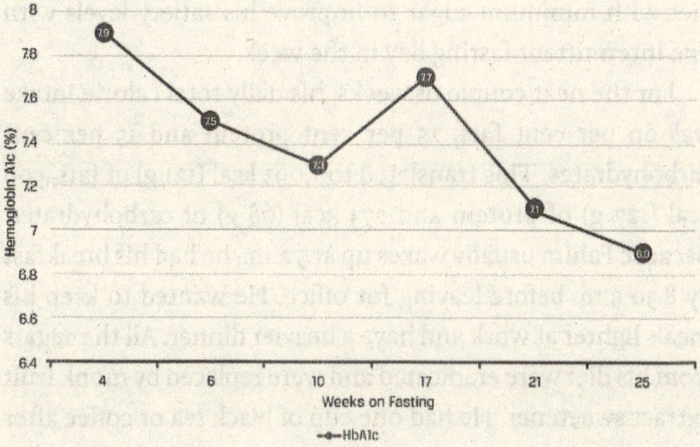

Fahim's HbA1c

He also felt hungry every couple of hours, which indicated that his body was unable to burn fat energy efficiently and required constant feeding to gain food energy. He especially craved foods that gave him instant energy, such as high-sugar comfort foods. I knew I had to address this metabolic deviation and improve his insulin sensitivity, which would quickly clear his blood sugar levels.

For the first two weeks, to control his body's extreme dependence on sugar, I prescribed a very low-carbohydrate diet and 30 g of figs or dates after dinner to address his craving for sweet foods. This hack allowed his body the time to be less dependent on sugar for energy needs throughout the day and switch to fat burning more quickly while not depriving his taste buds of sweet-tasting foods after dinner. His BMR was 1,822 kcal/day. To keep his metabolic health intact, he followed a non-vegetarian, protein-rich, low-carbohydrate diet with minimum sugar to improve his satiety levels with one intermittent fasting day in the week.

For the next couple of weeks, his daily total calorie intake was 60 per cent fats, 25 per cent protein and 15 per cent carbohydrates. This translated to 1,093 kcal (121 g) of fats, 509 kcal (127 g) of protein and 273 kcal (68 g) of carbohydrates. Because Fahim usually wakes up at 5 a.m., he had his breakfast by 8.30 a.m. before leaving for office. He wanted to keep his meals lighter at work and have a heavier dinner. All the sugars from his diet were eradicated and were replaced by monk fruit extract sweetener. He had one cup of black tea or coffee after waking up in the morning and one cup of black tea in the evening. He had preferred to do his one-day fast on Sundays as all his work and social engagements were restricted to the week. Lunch was his only meal on Sunday and during the rest of the day, he would sip on minerals and electrolyte-rich water to keep himself hydrated. Before and after dinner during the

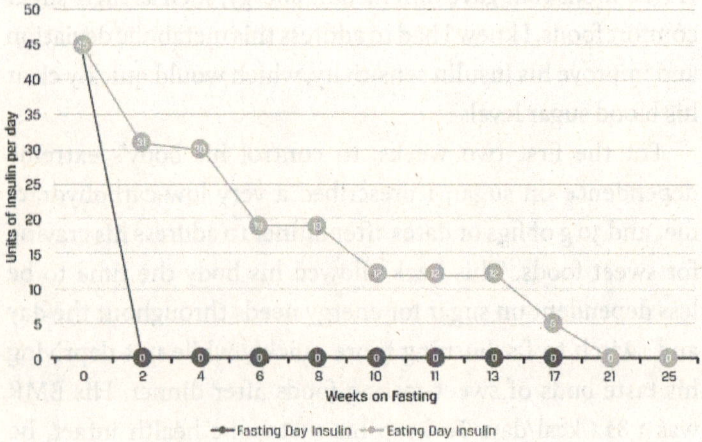

Fahim's insulin and OAH levels post the prescribed diet

weekdays, he would do brisk walking for 15 minutes each, which helped him restore his blood sugar. During this period, with the help of his physician, we tracked his fasting and postprandial blood sugar regularly.

By the end of 2 weeks, he was off his diabetes medication and insulin. I put him on a maintenance diet with 25 per cent carbohydrates and 50 per cent fats that he could sustain, which included a dessert every Sunday with no more than 20 g of carbohydrates. As can be seen in the following figure, Fahim's insulin levels stabilized as a result of this meal plan. This successfully helped Fahim stay off medication and enjoy the desserts he loved once in a while.

Maintenance diet with 25 per cent carbohydrates and 50 per cent fats.

Meal time	*Menu*	*Supplementation*
1st meal 8.30 a.m.	One glass (around 250 ml) of coconut water, one scoop of whey protein, 30 g of nuts and seeds, and 1 butter chiplet (15 g = 1 tbsp) Carbohydrates = 71 kcal, protein = 130 kcal and fats = 257 kcal	Daily: 500 g calcium, vitamin B complex Sunday: 60,000 IU vitamin D
2nd meal 1.30 p.m.	150 g chicken, fish or whole paneer or 5 whole eggs cooked in 15-20 g of ghee (clarified butter) and 200 g salad garnished with extra virgin olive oil (around 2 tsp) Carbohydrates = 48 kcal, protein = 138 kcal and fats = 491 kcal	3 tablets of Krill Oil

Meal time	Menu	Supplementation
3rd meal 7.00 p.m.	100 g chicken or fish or whole paneer or three whole eggs cooked in 15-20 g of ghee (clarified butter), one scoop whey protein in water, one medium chapatti (65 g) made from 70% jowar or naachni and 30% whole wheat or sourdough bread with 50 g cooked vegetable or dal, one small bowl (around 100 g) full fat unflavoured plain Greek yoghurt Carbohydrates = 158 kcal, protein = 241 kcal and fats = 367 kcal	3 tablets of Krill Oil, Zinc, Magnesium and 1 g of vitamin C

2

Exercise Smart, Not More, and Tone Your Body

Regular, intense physical activity will result in two significant alterations that influence our set point weight:

1. Reduction in the cortisol (stress hormone) levels.
2. Lowering of insulin levels facilitated by enhanced insulin sensitivity.

Using your muscles is vital to reduce your insulin levels and fight against recurring weight gain issues. If you are already not exercising and have decided to start it, the first question that would be going through your mind is what kind of exercise is right for you to start with and how to incorporate it into your life? Consistency in doing what you can do should be your first goal. The body requires time to adapt to exercise stress. It is also essential to keep in mind that by choosing to exercise, we are trying to break a sedentary lifestyle habit to build a new pattern of exercising daily. Any new practice only develops once you dedicate time and a place for it, at least in your mind. So go ahead, take a moment and think about how you plan to schedule your active time and place during the day across the week. The second thing you need to do is to do an activity that you really enjoy. Remember today, when you decide to start becoming active, it is not about the best routine you should follow but more about how to make physical activity an enjoyable habit for yourself.

Both cardio and weight training have their own benefits. However, resistance training aids in increasing muscular insulin sensitivity and glucose uptake. The energy that the working muscles use when you weightlift is locally stored muscle glucose.

To appreciate how strength training remarkably improves glucose uptake from the consumption of dietary carbohydrates, it is vital to note that when we exercise, two[1] fundamental types of skeletal muscles get stimulated: type 1 and type 2 muscle fibres. These skeletal muscles surround our joints to allow movement through their contraction and relaxation. For example, when we close the angle of the joint at our elbow and flex our arms, we contract the front muscle of our arms, known as the biceps. All our joints are a mixture of type 1 and 2 muscle fibres.

When we run, walk a long distance or do an activity with a particular muscle group for an extended period, the type 1 muscle fibres are actively recruited to complete the task. As the task is repeated numerous times, the type 1 muscle fibres overcome the activity stress and generate more mitochondria to keep the fuel supply going during the relatively long strenuous activity. Based on the intensity of the activity you

Differences between type 1 and type 2 muscle fibres

Type 1	Type 2
Endurance fibres	*Strength fibres*
These are rich in mitochondrial concentration and thus brownish. The mitochondria concentration in these muscles determines how well they can use oxygen and food energy to allow continuous contraction to perform physical work.	These are not rich in mitochondria and thus whitish.
During prolonged cardio activity, these fibres are recruited at the joints involved in the exercise and essentially produce ATP (cellular currency of energy) in the presence of oxygen, also known as the aerobic method of energy (ATP) production. The class of exercises known as aerobic exercises (dance and spinning) lead to this kind of aerobic energy production in your muscles. This method does not lead to excess lactic acid production, which is a by-product of burning food energy in the absence of oxygen.	These fibres produce energy in the absence of oxygen (anaerobic production) using glucose as fuel and generate the by-product lactic acid. When the production of lactic acid exceeds its clearance, we start feeling the burn in the working muscle and cease the activity to recover.

are performing, the brain decides which fibres are sufficient to do the job at the joint. For instance, when we do an intense workout that will typically last a very short period such as lifting heavy weights and doing a set of biceps curls, chest presses or squats or moving something very fast, both the type 2 and type 1 are actively recruited to do this job. Doing an intense activity depletes muscle glucose and the body feels compelled to adapt by making itself stronger. The muscle will become bigger to store more glucose. The size growth potential of muscle is higher in type 2 muscle fibres than in type 1. Our muscles become more insulin sensitive to help store the carbohydrates we consume in the muscles.

What happens to our muscles when we start ageing?

As we grow older, we do not lose the size of type 1 muscle fibres but progressively lose type 2 muscle fibres. As type 2 muscle fibres are metabolically active tissues, they actively demand energy to consume. The ageing process aims at longevity and survival and thus deems these type 2 muscle fibres a surplus to its survival goals. Thus, it starts to break these muscles down and reduce them in size. At the same time, the body ceases to have adequate ability to build muscles as we age. When we increasingly lead a sedentary lifestyle, are bedridden or have fractured our joints making them immobile under a cast, these type 2 muscle fibres diminish at an accelerated rate, build insulin resistance and result in a fragile body and bones.[2] This is why when the body is not subjected to gravity and resistance, the body ages faster, as also seen in astronauts[3] who travel to space and return with highly fragile, aged bodies and weak musculature. Crucially, these type 2 muscles are necessary to carry out our activities of daily living.[4] In the absence of these muscles, fundamental activities of life such as getting up from the bed or chair and lifting things and carrying them effortlessly become challenging. In addition, the erosion of the bone tissue and joints result in frailty, disability and low quality of life. A fragile body also fails to recover well from falls and often results in compromised physical functionality, strength and independence to move freely without external support from an object or person. Ageing combined with physical inactivity results in a disease condition known as sarcopenia[5] and an increased risk of obesity.[6] Type 2 muscles[7] are also vital endocrine organs (hormone-secreting glands) that secrete myokines, a signalling molecule for the body to reduce inflammation. These muscles are organs of longevity. Thus, the only way to reverse this dreadful condition in old age is to get active starting today. Include some resistance exercises to stimulate the body to keep hold of type 2 muscle fibres for good metabolic health.

If your nearest fitness club is 10 kilometres away, you should walk, jog or do periodic sprints through your neighbourhood. Both cardio and resistance training are effective interventions to improve insulin resistance and reverse the metabolic derailment causing the body to spend more hours in lipogenesis (fat synthesis) than lipolysis (fat breakdown).

Resistance training

In this section, I'll give you some guidance on resistance training. I recommend that you become acquainted with online resources. If you have the budget, do hire a personal trainer to assist you with the correct form of various exercises.

Resistance training is for everyone, especially for women who start at the bare minimum lean tissue curve compared to that of men. Although some women avoid weight training from fear of becoming very bulky, fortunately for most women, this simply does not happen. When a man does resistance training to fatigue, he will amalgamate more muscle size and become stronger and bigger, perhaps tremendously quickly. However, when women engage in strength training to failure, they will undoubtedly get stronger, and their muscles will still be pétit and grow slightly in size, giving the body a much-defined and toned look. You could ask me: Why do men and women have different muscle growth despite doing the same exercises with similar intensity? It is the sex hormones[8] that determine the anabolic capacity of the muscles (muscle building). Women have only one-tenth of the testosterone levels of that of men. Therefore, their muscle building capacity is lower. Irrespective of the muscle size and strength improvements, an average of 60 minutes of resistance exercise per week can improve insulin sensitivity by more than 60 minutes of cardio exercise.[9]

Resistance training comprises three categories of exercises: power, compound and isolation. They should be programmed scientifically into complexes of exercises that involve complementary sets of ancillary muscles and joint stabilizers surrounding and supporting the prime moving muscle. Power and compound exercises have realistic and functional movements. The benefit of this approach is to train and use the muscles in a way that replicates daily life, instead of just doing isolation exercises that produce artificial movement.

Did you know?
The bicep curl or tricep extension with resistance is an artificial movement against resistance. Whenever we pull something towards us, we are not only using our biceps, but we are using our extensive and strong back muscles to do the work more efficiently and powerfully without risking arm or shoulder joint injury. Similarly, when pushing something away, we don't just push it using our triceps, but do so more powerfully and safely by pushing it using our chest, shoulders, and triceps. Bicep curl and tricep extension exercises have no real-world equivalent to how we naturally use them. The only purpose of doing these exercises, whether we admit it or not, is to make our t-shirt fit more tightly around our upper arms. However, to allow strength training to generate the desired results of making our bodies more robust and more insulin sensitive, it is more important to start with exercises that engage the whole body along with the core. These exercises are known as power movements. Some examples are squats, push-ups, lunges, bench press and pull-ups.

Power movements are broadly divided into pulling and pushing complexes. This deceptively simple training framework allows you to adhere to natural movements and encourages complementary muscles that naturally function together to develop and become stronger. So the days that you are pressed for time, focus on power movements. For example, on a back day, skip the bicep curl and focus on rowing and pulling movements because powerful biceps are useless if your shoulder and back muscles are weak as every real-life motion that involves the biceps also involves the shoulder and back muscles.

If you do not want to join a gym, make do with what you have at home. You can use resistance bands, which you can easily carry when you travel. These provide you with the suitable resistance to hit your targeted intensity. You can also focus on body weight exercises such as push-ups, planks, chair squats, lunges, jump squats, sit-ups, single-leg Romanian deadlifts, triceps presses on your furniture like sofa, bed or stable chair and walking around your home while lifting water-filled heavy containers, anything that you can use to fatigue the muscles with these home-friendly routines.

If your circumstances permit, I'd recommend purchasing a weightlifting bench and set of kettlebells or dumbbells that match your strength. Work on expanding your gear over time.

For cardio exercises, high intensity can be achieved by simply performing the movement more vigorously and covering more distance in a given time period. An ideal way to do this is to divide your high-intensity zones into intervals across your training sessions. For instance, you can start by doing the exercise at a lower intensity for a minute and then spring into doing it faster and more intensely close to your maximal capacity for the next 30 seconds and then repeat this drill for the desired number of rounds. In other words, if you go for a walk regularly, don't simply set your watch for 20 minutes and walk however you want. Instead, keep your eye on the clock to mix and introduce intervals of light jogging and heavy sprinting.

For weight training, you can attain higher intensities by performing every exercise to failure. In other words, every time you start a set, you continue that activity irrespective of the number of reps it takes until you can't do it anymore. Just like high-intensity interval training (HIIT) cardio, weight training is an excellent stimulus for your body to adapt and improve its health. In fact, research shows that certain exercises performed for a single set to failure is sufficient[10] to improve insulin sensitivity.

A key benefit of increasing workout intensity in cardio and resistance training is that it makes one exercise type more like the other. When aerobic activities are performed intensely in intervals, they completely tire and strengthen the muscles that are being recruited for the activity. Similarly, if resistance exercises are done more intensely, especially with shorter rest periods in between sets, the cardiopulmonary system is significantly challenged. When the muscles contract repeatedly, they get depleted and pull nutrients, glucose, fat and ketones from the blood. This implies that even if a muscle is insulin resistant, after exercising and repeated muscle contraction, it will still pull the glucose from the blood and become less resistant to insulin. Due to this improved insulin response, our blood insulin levels[11] naturally lower overtime and this improvement occurs even before there is any change[12] in our body weight. Furthermore, another study[13] revealed that an exercise regimen over three months decreased oxidative stress and inflammation markers, even without any weight change. Another fascinating element of exercise[14] as an intervention to improve our metabolic health is that it works universally across all sexes and ages. A study[15] showed that just four months of regular physical activity increased the strength of the test subjects, men in the age bracket of 50 to 65, by nearly 50 per cent, but it also decreased their insulin resistance to less than 80 per cent of preintervention levels. This result was in the absence of any alteration in diet simply by starting an exercise regimen. The regular debate in the exercise science community is whether cardio or weight training helps to improve metabolic health? If you have the time, do both. This way, you would experience a more robust improvement in your health than just aerobic exercise or resistance training alone.

One study tracked approximately 32,000 volunteers for nearly two decades and revealed that engaging in either cardio or resistance exercise for two and a half hours each week yielded equivalent improvements. However, the volunteers who engaged in resistance exercise spent less time for their workout.[16] This means that if you have only an hour or so per day to invest in exercise, engaging in resistance exercises by either moving heavy weights or moving weight very fast, it will give a high return on time investment.

Your body weight is not the only marker of your health. When we think of losing weight, the initial trigger to do so is our inability to fit into the clothes that previously used to fit us well. What we are looking for in this case is inch loss rather than weight loss. The body weight seen on the scale is a combined weight of all the masses we carry in our body including organs, muscles, bones, water and body fat. The first three elements listed are essential and immensely functional aspects of our body. These tissues are denser and leaner compared to body fat, which not only adds weight to the body but also inches and circumference. From a practical point of view, after taking up regular exercise, if you want to assess whether the weight lost is pure fat mass, look at your inch loss. The good news is that if the weight on the weighing scale has not significantly changed, but the inches around the body have reduced, that means the lifestyle that you have adopted by changing your exercise or physical activity regimen, diet and sleep support your lean functional tissue. This is a great predictor of good health and longevity.

Workout intensity

The body uses comparatively more fat as energy with lower intensity exercises.[17] But as the person becomes increasingly more trained and fuels their body with a low carbohydrate diet, the body adapts and burns fat even at high-intensity exercises. Increasing the intensity would mean walking faster than usual, brisk jogging with periodic sprints, an intense jog or a jog with intermittent sprints. The same general principle applies to any other cardio exercises such as swimming and cycling. In fact, for those of us who are pressed for time, increasing the exercise intensity over a shorter period (10 minutes) is equally effective at triggering the metabolic benefit of exercising for a longer duration at lower intensities.[18] This modality of exercise is known as HIIT. Its popularity has exploded; chances are that you or someone you are acquainted with is already doing it. For weight training, a higher-intensity workout implies that each set we are approaching or going to do will be done to muscular failure until the muscle burn is so intense that we cannot do another rep. This is achieved by reducing your dumbbell weight and increasing your reps or vice versa. Weight training requires many years of experience to master as it can be really demanding. But again, this is not something that should be done on your day one of exercising. However, consistency will get you to this stage one day. This should be a gradually progressive process of getting to that point of failure (anywhere between 3-15 reps). The number of sets you perform of the exercise is less important than doing it to failure.

After finishing this chapter, you might think the catchphrase is 'go hard or go home'. A more suitable conclusion would be 'get going as often as you can'. Begin from where you are by doing what you can. Work out six days a week with one rest day. Aim for anything between 40-60 minutes. If you only have 20 minutes, up the intensity.

Workout routines

The anti-ageing dad

My dad is 60 years old. From the time he started working after college, he has been a workaholic, building businesses. However, in his mid-40s, his health started to deteriorate. He got diagnosed with borderline diabetes and hypertension. To add insult to injury, in 2007, he had a major slip disc incident while handling his luggage on one of his business trips. The physician advised him to take painkillers for his intense lower back pain and prescribed complete bed rest for a couple of weeks. This was the time before social media and digital meetings. He felt guilty about missing plans and not achieving his desired projections within the specific timelines. After over two weeks of complete bed rest, I knew that he needed to strengthen his body, especially areas around the damaged region of his lower back. Otherwise, with this weakened condition, the joint degeneration would accelerate, and the pain would resurface again and again, forcing him to be on medication for life. The ordeal would not stop there, and each subsequent episode would be more painful. This state would invariably force him to be inactive and become physically weaker. An inactive lifestyle due to painful and weak joints would initiate the vicious cycle of increased blood sugar and blood pressure problems every decade, confirming his diabetes and hypertension, all of which are risk factors for obesity and heart disease. I counselled him that slipped discs are a part and parcel of today's life and a preventable problem.

The sedentary lifestyle we lead today requires us to have a weak body and tight joints. Thus, with prolonged sitting, the body strives to adapt to and become efficient at modelling a chair sitting posture by tightening the muscles throughout the front side (anterior) of the body involved in the sitting posture and weakening the muscles at the back (posterior) of the body, which are not used and idle during sitting. This finetuning of joints creates a significant imbalance around the neck, shoulders, spine, hips and knees and puts them in poor and vulnerable positions for degeneration, pain and injury. And that adaptation is not great for things we want to do in daily life after work such as standing, walking, exercising, playing sports and lifting objects from the floor.

My dad's conditions with a slipped disc, poorly managed blood sugar, and increasing weight and blood pressure were all a result of this sedentary lifestyle and a high-carbohydrate, low-protein diet. His work required him to sit for long hours. However, to correct that and rehabilitate his injury, I prescribed some exercises to do anytime throughout the day. Doing these exercises would ensure that he would become better at doing activities of daily living such as waking up from bed, getting up from the chair, picking up objects from the floor, walking on an uneven surface and travelling on bumpy roads without risk of significant injury. It's important to realize that it's not always possible to change the outside to suit our weaknesses of the body and health, but we can always work on eradicating our weaknesses and not letting the outside change us and diminish our quality of life. That power to improve ourselves from within and become stronger lies within us. Things never get easier, but you get stronger.

The simple exercise plan given below can be done any time of the day without making you run out of breath or gasping for air. These exercises train the core and deep spinal muscles to get engaged reflexively without conscious thought and adjust the posture of the neck, torso and spine joints by generating torque around the shoulder and hip joints. This torque will brace your joints with their surrounding muscles to protect them from injury.

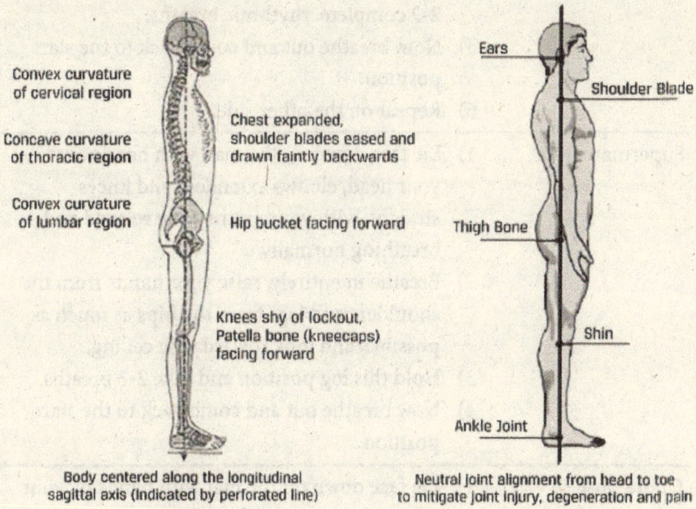

Ideal alignment of shoulder, hips, knees and ankle joints

I have prescribed the following exercise schedule to my dad to rehabilitate his lower back injury. You can follow it too if you sit in a chair for prolonged periods. I would advise doing three sets of five reps of each exercise, with a tempo of 2-3 breaths.

Corrective Exercise	*Exercise Cues*
Alternative deadbug	1) Lie face up on the mat, hands by your side and knees straight, with your entire body relaxed and breathing normally. 2) Bring your legs up with knees bent perpendicular to the hips and arms, straight up at shoulder level. 3) Breathe in entirely and start with your right hand back and left leg down and straight, shy of touching the floor. 4) Breathe out now and hold the position with 2-3 complete, rhythmic breaths. 5) Now, breathe out and come back to the start position. 6) Repeat on the other side.
Superman	1) Lie face down on the mat, with hands over your head, elbows extended, and knees straight, with your entire body relaxed and breathing normally. 2) Breathe in entirely, raise your hands from the shoulders and legs from the hips as much as possible, and look towards the ceiling. 3) Hold this log position and take 2-3 breaths. 4) Now breathe out and come back to the start position.
Cobra pose	1) Lie face down on the mat with hands by your side and knees straight, your entire body relaxed and breathing normally. 2) Now bring your hands next to your chin, palm down. 3) Breathe in entirely and push your upper body away from the floor using your palms, forming an arch position, looking towards the ceiling and ensuring the hips are as close to the floor as possible.

Corrective Exercise	Exercise Cues
	4) Hold the position with 2-3 complete, rhythmic breaths. 5) Now, breathe out and come back to the start position. 6) As you get more comfortable starting the movement with the hands by the side of the chin, eventually, you can take it to the next level. You may bring down the palm next to the collar bone and then the sternum and start the arch from there.

Recollect from our previous chapters that one of the reasons for our hormonal imbalances is insulin resistance. The body does not respond to insulin well due to high cortisol levels under stressful situations when the sympathetic nervous system is dominant. Under stressful conditions, the body quickens its breaths per minute, which are usually shallow, upper thoracic, upper chest or mouth breathing patterns, due to which the lungs absorb oxygen poorly and our core muscles do not engage properly leading to a higher risk of spinal injuries.

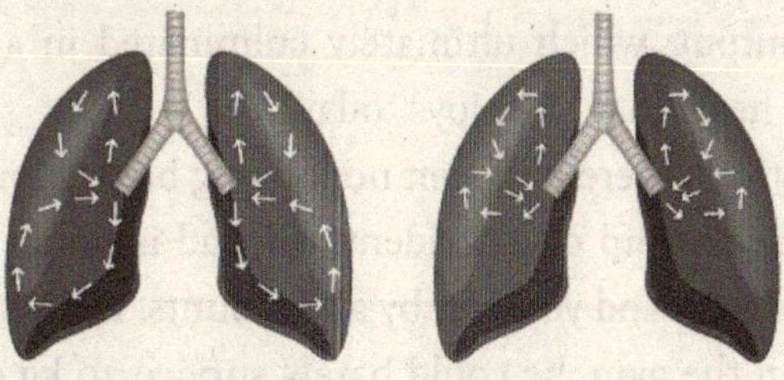

Deep breathing (left) results in complete oxygen absorption, whereas shallow breathing (right) results in incomplete oxygen delivery.

The only way to reduce cortisol and the domination of the sympathetic nervous system on the autonomic nervous system is by driving the parasympathetic nervous system up by consciously using a deep, rhythmic, diaphragmatic breathing pattern from the nose. This completely fills up the lungs with oxygen and improves the oxygen flow to the body. The cortisol levels are reduced and insulin works better to help you burn fat. Such deep, diaphragmatic inhalations also engage the core muscles entirely due to a complete contraction of the diaphragm and help keep your spine and shoulders upright when sitting on the chair.

However, my dad couldn't follow the exercise schedule regularly owing to his business exigencies. We overcame the irregularity by tweaking the time and place of his exercise. Instead of leaving the 'when and where' of these exercises open, we fixed a time. He would do these exercises before bathing every day for 10 minutes in his room. After three weeks of following this routine, the pain was gone and his movement was back in place. He was ready to step into the gym to take his training to the next level and add conditioning exercises to his routine to improve his muscle strength and cardiac output, which ultimately culminated in a stronger body and heart that he enjoys today.

Since then, there has been no looking back. More than 15 years after the slip disc incident, my dad is much stronger, more energetic and younger by all accounts. For instance, on day one in the gym, he could barely survive 20 kg of weight while squatting. But today, I'm proud to say he has improved his overall strength and squats with 140 kg. This is a clear sign of physical regeneration. We know that ageing generally leads to weakening of the body and organs and causes degeneration of joints, making them incapable of performing at the level when the body was younger. However, not in my dad's case. He made lifestyle changes by genuinely understanding the function of different nutrients in foods and their power to regenerate the body. He looked beyond merely the caloric and energy value of foods. Even when it comes to exercising regularly, he knows burning calories is simply a means and a by-product of a good workout. What we are aiming for when exercising is to get stronger and faster, build endurance and flexibility and improve body composition (more lean tissue in the body). Due to this mindset shift, he has stronger bones and muscles and better body composition, heart function and blood sugar than he did at the time of his slipped disc incident.

The official definition of a fitter body is based on five components:

1. Muscular strength: A solid and resilient body that does not easily injure during daily activity.
2. Muscular endurance: The muscles should be able to work for an extended period without quickly fatiguing.
3. Cardiovascular endurance: The heart and lungs should be able to supply nutrients and oxygen-rich blood to the entire body without tiring quickly.
4. Flexibility: The joints should be able to move across their complete range of motion without pain.
5. Ideal body composition: No more than 20 per cent of one's

overall weight should comprise fat mass.

None of the above components of fitness says that burning more calories is the objective of the workout. Yet most individuals, if not all, exercise only to burn calories.

Getting fitter is about having specificity to an exercise regimen. That is why when I deal with individuals who want to start exercising, I focus on their objectives to give a meaningful direction to their workout, whether their primary goal is to improve strength, lean mass, cardiopulmonary output or flexibility. No single workout works on improving all the five components of fitness. There is always a trade-off when we are invested in working out in a certain way or following a particular workout programme. When the programme is continued for a prolonged period, the body quickly adapts to it and ceases to give results. Thus there is no one size fits all and one king exercise for improving fitness. The workouts must change periodically for continuous results in all the fitness components listed above. If the body adapts to a certain workout programme, the returns on our time and effort diminish until we hit a plateau.

Therefore, workout programmes are highly individualized because everyone with the same goal may come from different backgrounds and preferences. These aspects have to be considered to make the outcomes of the workout measurable and sustainable.

The routine my dad has been following ever since his rehabilitation is given on the following page.

SAMPLE TRAINING PROGRAMME TO IMPROVE BODY COMPOSITION		
Strength Training Exercises	**Sets**	**Reps to Failure**
MONDAY – POSTERIOR LOWER-BODY DAY		
The primary goal is to strengthen the back of his body including the lower back, buttocks and hamstrings.		
Bridge hold	2	10 to 20 seconds
Deadlift	3	8-15 reps
Single RDL	2	5-8 reps
Bulgarian split squats	2	8-15 reps
Stiff leg calf raises	2	8-15 reps
Seated calf raises	2	8-15 reps
Seated leg curls	3	8-15 reps
TUESDAY – UPPER BODY PUSHING FUNCTION		
The primary goal is to improve the strength of the upper body pushing complex, which is the chest, shoulders and triceps.		
Flat bench barbell press	3	8-15 reps
Incline dumbbell press	3	8-15 reps
Top pulley cable flyes	2	8-15 reps
Swissball dumbell press	2	8-15 reps
Standing military or single arm dumbbell shoulder press	2	8-15 reps
Cable or dumbbell lateral raises	3	8-15 reps
Cable or machine triceps pushdown	2	8-15 reps
WEDNESDAY – CARDIO & CORE		
The day is strategically included for the general recovery of skeletal muscle tissue, focusing on the heart and lungs and improving the capacity of the core muscles.		
20 minutes of high-intensity interval cardio at targeted 70% of maximum heart rate		
Plank	2	1 to 1½ minutes

Cat and camel	2	5-8 reps
Alternating bird dog	2	5-8 reps
Half kneeling t-spine rotation	2	5-8 reps
Lying down or parallel bar reverse crunches	2	10-15 reps
Crossover sit ups	2	10-15 reps
THURSDAY – ANTERIOR LOWER BODY		
Thigh muscles in the front of the body get very weak with prolonged sitting, making the knee joints vulnerable to degeneration. So it is an important day for individuals who have extended sitting hours.		
Box jumps	3	5-8 reps
Barbell back squats	3	8-15 reps
Lateral shuffle steps	3	8-15 reps
Kettlebell goblet squats	2	8-15 reps
TRX pistol squats	2	8-15 reps
Walking lunges	2	8-15 reps
Step-ups	2	8-15 reps
FRIDAY – UPPER BODY PULLING		
This day focuses primarily on improving the strength of the back muscles for pulling objects towards the body. This is done in two ways – pulling with arms overhead and pulling with arms in front.		
Pull ups	3	8-15 reps
Wide grip barbell rows	3	8-15 reps
Narrow supine grip pulldowns	3	8-15 reps
Single arm dumbbell rows	2	8-15 reps
Cable face pulls	2	8-15 reps
Incline dumbbell supination curls	2	8-15 reps
Preacher's curls	2	8-15 reps
SATURDAY – REST/ LIGHT WALKS/ MASSAGE/ MEDITATION		
SUNDAY – REST/ LIGHT WALKS/ MASSAGE/ MEDITATION		

This is the typical schema of the routine my dad has been following, with minor variations made over time to add challenges and overcome adaptation by working around different volumes of the sets and intensity. If you observe the prime focus of each day of strength training, you can see that we start with an exercise that is a multi-joint movement (compound movement), which involves large muscle groups. These movements mimic real-life movements and result in maximum fat burn, as these exercises are also best for improving insulin sensitivity and regeneration of the body.

You can follow this too and tailor it to suit your lifestyle and fitness goals as you become more knowledgeable about the basic principles of resistance training and a broad range of exercises. If you do not know any exercise or are unfamiliar with it, a simple Google search will show you how to perform the exercise.

In my experience, drastic changes are tough to maintain for long periods, especially during stressful times. Taking baby steps every day towards a long-term goal is easier to maintain and continue. Say your initial goal is to reduce your sugar or fast food intake by 5 per cent, take 500 steps per day, increase daily water intake by 200 ml, or wake up 10 minutes earlier. Tweaking these goals weekly until the larger goal is achieved is sustainable. It may not reap drastic results at the beginning, but over time, half a year, a year, half a decade or a decade down the line, the results will be immense, as is the case with my dad.

The painless wife

As you would have guessed, my wife is a fitness freak like me. Her fitness goals are centred around building a lean body with low-fat composition. Over the years, she has trained regularly using various modalities such as yoga, breathwork, strength training and sometimes cardio. She is not a big fan of regular running but enjoys other aerobic activities such as dancing. The problem came in 2020 when all of us were working from home, and her workload had increased tremendously. Unfortunately, gyms were shut, and she could hardly get any exercise or go for walks amid the lockdown. Suddenly one day, she came to me complaining of a heavy, burning, painful sensation across her entire upper back (the trapezius and rhomboid muscles). She told me that it had been happening for a couple of days, especially after she had long days at work. To understand the root cause of the problem and identify the source of the pain, I ran two tests:

1) Overhead squat with a wooden dowel: As my wife descended into the squat, her hip joint overcompensated by excessively bending forward, and her arms too were falling ahead. This test indicated a very tight upper body.

The end position should appear as in the following image. When mobility (lengthening of muscles) and motor control (mind-muscle connection) across the spine are optimal, it results in a comfortable sitting down position in an overhead squat without excessive hip flexion (torso falling forward) or excessive shoulder flexion (arms falling forward).

2) Reciprocal shoulder mobility test: This was the second test to check for localized restrictions in the shoulder joint and upper back. The subject's thumb should be kept within their fists. One arm is taken overhead with elbows bent (this is the side getting tested) and simultaneously the other hand is taken back from the waist without wiggling or adjusting either arm once placed and the distance between the index finger of overhead arm and index finger of underhand arm is measured. Then the test is repeated on the other side. When the upper back muscles possess good mobility (muscle lengthening capability), the distance between the index fingers is less than the total length of the palm and middle finger. However, if the distance between the fingers is more than that, it indicates a lack of flexibility in the back muscles

and is the source of extreme muscle tightness and pain. In my wife's case, the right-hand side didn't have a problem. The distance between the fingers on the right hand was no greater than the total length of her palm and middle finger. However, her left hand side indicated a red alert as the distance between the index fingers was more than the full length of the palm and middle finger. It also meant an asymmetry and imbalance between the two sides.

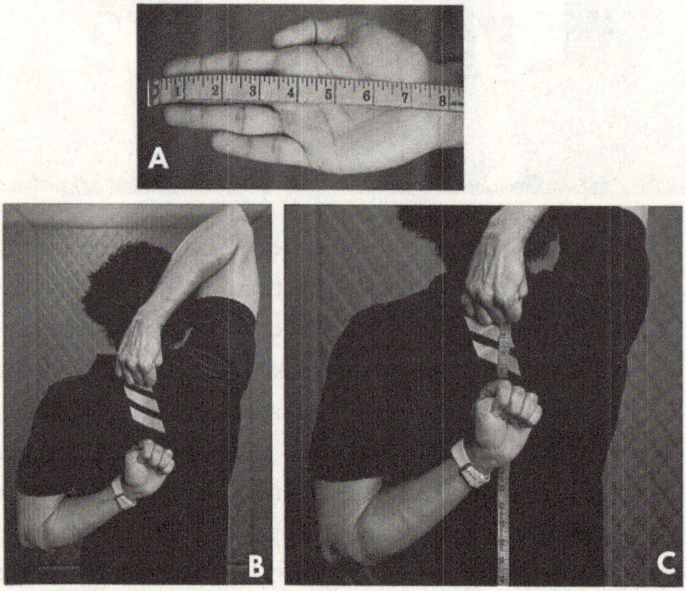

I concluded that the pain was located in her upper back. However, the restrictions were also evident at the root of her spine on the lower back (lumbar region). Her hip flexors, the front part of the hip that forms an 'L-shape' when we sit on a chair, was very tight due to continuous sitting, which may have been contributing to the tight, stiff and painful back. Test 2 clearly showed that there were a lot of restrictions in her shoulders and upper back areas due to continuous work on the keyboard and mouse, which had to be fixed. Her shoulders and neck regions were locked into a flexion position which puts tremendous pressure on her rotator cuff muscles of the shoulders and strains the muscles of the entire upper back, such as the trapezius, latisimus dorsi and rhomboids, due to which they have become very tensed, tight and sensitive to pain.

To resolve this issue, I suggested she do the given exercises (on the following page) three times every day, which she did diligently before getting ready for office, lunch and dinner. Soon, her problem of burning pain in the shoulder and upper back area was gone. Both sides are symmetric, with the index finger distance less than the full length of the palm and middle finger. I would advise doing three sets of five reps of each exercise, with a tempo of 2-3 breaths.

Corrective Exercise	*Exercise Cues*
Alternative deadbug	1) Lie down face up on the mat, with hands by your side and knees straight, with your entire body relaxed and breathing normally. 2) Bring your legs up with knees bent perpendicular to the hips and arms straight up at shoulder level. 3) Breathe in entirely and start with your right hand back and left leg down and straight, shy of touching the floor. 4) Breathe out now and hold the position with 2-3 complete, rhythmic breaths. 5) Now, breathe out and come back to the start position. 6) Repeat on the other side.
Alternative cat & camel	1) Start in a quadruped position with palms underneath the shoulders and knees underneath the hips and breathing normally. 2) Exhale deeply and bring your back up by tucking your chin in and navel towards the chest. 3) Now breathe in completely, take the chin up slowly, and push the belly button out to form an arch in the back.
Arm overhead lat stretch	1) Start with a tall kneeling position next to your sofa, bed, table or chair. 2) Rest your elbows on it, ensuring that this furniture you're using has the strength and required base of support to take the pressure and is well cushioned so that it does not hurt you or scratch your skin. 3) Breathe out and slowly push your hip back till the time your back comes into a tabletop position.

Corrective Exercise	*Exercise Cues*
	4) Stay there for 2-3 breaths and try to push your body down as much as possible to create more arch on your back while feeling the stretch. 5) Now breathe in and slowly return to the start position.
Chest stretch on floor	1) Sit with the legs extended on the floor and breath normally. 2) Place the palms with your arms extended behind the body on the floor, shoulder-width apart. 3) Slowly look up to the ceiling, and push your body forward a couple of inches while feeling the stretch on your arms, front shoulders and chest. 4) With chin up, eyes watching the ceiling, spend time in the position for 2-3 breaths.
Middle shoulder stretch	1) Sit on the floor cross-legged comfortably with your hands by your side and breathe normally. 2) We will start with the right arm, raise it at the shoulder level and place it across your upper chest with elbows up. 3) Place the edge of the left palm just above the right elbow, press the right arm towards your body, and spend some time in the position for 2-3 breaths. 4) Repeat the same steps on the other side.

3

Stress Less, Sleep More

The per capita average daily[1] 'audio-visual' screen time in India was reported to be 4 hours and 48 minutes in 2020. I'm certain that with the advent of affordable internet service, connectivity and growth of YouTube and OTT platforms, our electronic screen time has increased tremendously. The major issue is that it can interfere with our sleep time. After turning off a bright screen with its blue-light radiation, when we finally make it to bed and try to sleep, falling asleep becomes challenging. Typically, the pineal gland in our brain, called our third eye, detects the time when light begins to fade and stimulates the release of the sleep hormone melatonin. When night shift workers try to sleep during the day in the absence of melatonin production, it leads to weight gain. Lack of sleep increases cortisol levels, promotes insulin and leptin resistance, and adjusts your set point weight to a higher number. In addition, we also get cravings for high sugar, processed foods and have sharper appetite.

A study that compared a group who got four and a half hours of sleep and those who got eight and a half hours of sleep showed that those who got lesser sleep consumed 300 calories[2] more than those who got complete sleep. Similar studies showed that a lack of sleep can increase[3] the average blood sugar levels, causing pre-diabetes.

If you are struggling with this issue, here's my advice. Modify your evening routine of relaxation and sleep. To enable good sleep, you should try to get into a schedule that you would have if you were living closer to nature, when your pineal gland would automatically detect nightfall.

1. Avoid screen time and begin to dim the lighting two hours before going to bed. Get lower wattage bulbs, low tabletop lamps and maybe even a dimmer regulator switch installed. Using unscented candles as lighting can perhaps make this step more primaeval and, thus, even more powerful. You will begin to feel sleepy within an hour or two of low lighting. At times, an earlier sleep time may be very challenging to adjust to. However, low-volume soothing music, a relaxing hot bath and some herbal or green tea can assist you in falling asleep quickly.
2. If you never had the habit of reading in bed or have lost the habit, then develop it. Books are powerful in taking you into another world, and reading can frequently have a sedative effect. Even if you do not instantly fall asleep, don't be overly concerned about it. Simply enjoy resting your body and having pleasant thoughts and memories. Sleep will come, and you will feel incredibly refreshed in the morning.

These new habits should become an integral part of your regular life. Of course, there will be moments when you are out and about up until late, but attempt to slip back into and enjoy looking forward to your schedule every other night in. In time, getting 8 hours of sleep will enhance your overall health and metabolism and reduce your set point weight. You will naturally lose weight.

Conclusion

Through this book, I have tried to convey the intricacies involved in the development of human obesity in a structured manner. Discerning the individualistic causes of weight gain profoundly and thoroughly helps one find effective, objective and rational cures for this condition. We can finally start to dream of building a world where obesity and all the associated diseases such as abnormal and uncontrolled blood sugar, increasing waistline, cardiovascular risk factors, and premature mortality are eradicated. That reality, that dream, that universe, and that vision for building a healthier and leaner body that we have always wished to have in the future – all begin from today with the daily application of the knowledge I've presented in this book.

Acknowledgements

I could not have begun the journey that resulted in this book without the inspiration and constant motivation of everyone who is mentioned here.

I want to thank my incredible wife, Poonam. I remember the e-mail she had sent me, along with a fitness book summary in 2011, to motivate me to start writing my first book. I didn't even know she was so impressed with my thoughts. I call it the day when the seed was sown to the day of fruition today, as I write the acknowledgements. You are my best half, and I wouldn't be half the author I am today without your encouragement and consistent support.

To my lovely parents, Hema and Dinesh, and my adorable brother, Vinay – you all believed in me at every single step, in all my ups and downs, you embraced my failures as yours, and you cheered with me in all my successes like yours. That's what matters the most. I love you all!

To my mentor Mr Kaizzad Capadia, who lives in our hearts and will always be there with me as a guiding light forever. All the development and research in this book were only possible because of his mentorship on how to think and write clearly about health, fitness, exercise and nutrition, when I started my writing stints more than a decade ago. I will always remain grateful to him for his mentorship. If the ideas in this book influence and improve the health and well-being of even one per cent of the population across the globe, it will be a tribute to his excellence and contribution to the fitness industry in India.

A special thank you to my teachers Rob Griffiths and Andy Evans, for giving me the immense learning opportunity in research as a student while completing my master's in Sports Management at the University of South Wales. I'm grateful for your trust and for allowing me to pursue my passion for sports and public health policies.

To all my clients, you got results only because you believed in my research and tools. I can't thank each one of you enough for motivating me to pen down my thoughts in the book every single time I discussed new research with you to improve your health. And thank you for trusting me to experiment with new ideas on your fitness and nutrition which helped me corroborate my academic research presented in this book.

To all my business associates, partners, and friends on social media, you have been a huge motivation; it feels like yesterday when you all encouraged me to write this book.

To all my workout partners and friends (it's a long list, so you know who you are), thank you for your friendship and insightful discussions and debates on exercise and nutrition, which I've always enjoyed during our workouts. This kept me going to get more clarity and look at the literature more objectively.

I can't even begin to thank my colleagues and various team members involved in this book journey of over two years now.

Shiv Shivakumar and Radhika Marwah, for your invaluable guidance through the book's journey.

Trisha Bora, thank you for putting up with me as you went through my drafts multiple times, your every input enriched my writing skills.

Poulomi Chatterjee and Swarnima Narayan for believing in the research and the book.

Amol Ghotkar and Sagar Madhavi for the interesting illustrations and making complicated diagrams look easy. Sagar Thakur for digital support.

Dominica Aranha for managing my office, everyone at 48 Fitness, everyone at Brand VTF, all the social media teams, Prashant Pankaj, Tanya Haldar, Vijeta Dahiya, Hitesh Purohit, Aditya Kamble, Pratyusha Kedare, Chirag Rajput, Sanil Nair, Sushmita Ghosh, Anish Kajrolkar, Alnawaz Shaikh and various other agency partners for their constant support.

Most importantly, my heartfelt thanks to the whole team at Hachette India, who worked with me tirelessly and guided me at every single step to make this book happen. I can't thank you enough, Thomas Abraham, Swetha Nisthala, Sonali Jindal, Riti Jagoorie and Naina Tripathi. Writing and publishing this book has been the most enriching journey of my life and Hachette India has been the best publisher to work with.

Lastly, my immense gratitude to all the esteemed personalities who gave their precious time to the book:

Hrithik Roshan
Anil Kapoor
Ranbir Kapoor
Tiger Shroff
Yasmin Karachiwala
Kris Gethin

Dr Shriram Nene
Warda Sajid Nadiadwala
Anand Pandit
Priti Srivastava
Shiv Shivakumar
Surendra Tipparaju
Dr Tanaya Mishra
Mukesh Ralhan
Prof Preeti Shroff Mehta
Olga Tellis
Ashutosh Sinha
Dr Niraj Vora

Notes

Introduction

1. 'Lifestyle Diseases the Biggest Killer in India Today', *CSE India*, 27 November 2017.
2. Jude Isabella, 'Why We Need To Go Beyond Corn, Wheat, and Rice', *GreenBiz*, 15 May 2014.
3. Sharon Begley, 'Insight: America's Hatred of Fat Hurts Obesity Fight', Reuters, 11 May 2012.

PART I: WHY WE GAIN FAT

1. The Big Fat Lie

1. Herman Pontzer, et al., 'Hunter-Gatherer Energetics and Human Obesity,' *PLoS One*. 7, (2012). doi:10.1371/journal.pone.0040503.
2. J. Diamond, *Guns, Germs, and Steel: The Fates of Human Societies* (W.W. Norton & Company, 2004).
3. J.A. Brillat-Savarin, *The Physiology of Taste* (London: Penguin, 2004).
4. William Banting, 'Letter on Corpulence, Addressed to the Public', *Obesity Research* 1, no. 2 (March 1993).
5. Erin Brodwin, 'Our Obsession with Calories Can Be Traced Back 100 Years — And It Hides a Bigger Problem', *Yahoo*, 30 May 2017.
6. 'Years of Compassion 1914–1923', *Herbert Hoover Presidential Library and Museum*.
7. John Yudkin, *Pure, White and Deadly: How Sugar is Killing Us and What We Can Do to Stop It* (London: Penguin Life, 2012).
8. United States, Congress, Senate, and Select Committee on Nutrition and Human Needs, 'Dietary Goals for the United States' (1977): 83.
9. Jason Gillespie, 'USDA ERS – Commodity Costs and Returns', *Economic Research Service*, USDA, 3 October 2022.; M. Shahbandeh, 'Rice Yield Per Harvested Acre in the U.S. from 2000 to 2021,' *Statista*, 21 Feb 2022.; Heather Hamilton, 'The Relationship Between Cow Size & Production', *Beef*, 27 December 2011.
10. *No-fad Diet: A Personal Plan for Healthy Weight Loss* (United States: Clarkson Potter/Publisher, 2005).

11. Jean-Pierre Flatt, 'Misconceptions in Body Weight Regulation: Implications for the Obesity Pandemic', *Critical Reviews in Clinical Laboratory Sciences* 49, no. 4 (2012): 150–165. https://doi.org/10.3109/10408363.2012.712904.
12. 'Obesity and Overweight', *World Health Organisation*, 9 June 2021.
13. G.W. Wilson, 'Overweight and Underweight: The Psychosomatic Aspects', in *In Your Weight and How to Control It*, edited by Morris Fishbein, rev. ed., (Garden City, N.Y.: Doubleday, 1963): 113–26.
14. L.H. Newburgh and M.W. Johnston, 'Endogenous Obesity—A Misconception', *Annals of Internal Medicine* 8, no. 3 (February 1930): 815–25.
15. Edwin B. Astwood, 'The Heritage of Corpulence', *Endocrinology* 71, (August 1962): 337–41.; Jerome Groopman, 'Is Fat Killing You, or Is Sugar?', *New Yorker*, 27 March 2017.
16. CSE India, 'Lifestyle Diseases the Biggest Killer in India Today'.
17. 'National Family Health Survey 5 201–0', Ministry of Health and Family Welfare, Government of India.
18. Richard Laursen, 'Why We Should Be Eating More Meat, Not Less', *Sapien*, 8 Mar 2020.
19. Astwood, 'The Heritage of Corpulence'.; Roxane Gay, *Hunger: A Memoir of (My) Body* (New York: HarperCollins, 2017).
20. 'Alcohol Use in Families,' *American Academy of Child & Adolescent Psychiatry*, May 2019.

2. Calories Don't Count

1. Edwin F. Du Boi, *Basal Metabolism in Health and Disease*, 2nd ed (Philadelphia: Lea & Febiger, 1936).
2. Jeffrey M. Friedman, 'Modern Science Versus the Stigma of Obesity', *Nature Medicine* 10, (2004): 563–569. https://doi.org/10.1038/nm060-63.
3. Today Study Group, 'A Clinical Trial to Maintain Glycemic Control in Youth With Type 2 Diabetes', *New England Journal of Medicine*.
4. *Arteriosclerosis, Thrombosis, and Vascular Biology* 35, no. 1 (2015). doi:10.1161/ATV.0000000000000016.
5. Barbara V. Howard, et al., 'Low-Fat Dietary Pattern and Weight Change Over 7 Years: The Women's Health Initiative Dietary Modification Trial', *JAMA*, 295, no. 1 (2006): 39–49. doi:10.1001/jama.295.1.39.
6. Ibid.
7. Alison Fildes, et al., 'Probability of an Obese Person Attaining Normal Body Weight: Cohort Study Using Electronic Health Records', *American Journal of Public Health* 105, no.9 (2015): e54–9. doi:10.2105/AJPH.2015.302773.

8. Elliott P. Joslin, *Joslin's Diabetes Mellitus* (Lippincott Williams and Wilkins; 14th edition, 2007).
9. Bray George, Claude Bouchard and W.P. James, *Handbook of Obesity* (New York: Marcel Dekker, 1998).
10. Ancel Keys, et al., *The Biology of Human Starvation* 2 (Minneapolis: University of Minnesota Press, 1950).
11. 'The Great Starvation Experiment, 194–945', *Mad Science Museum*.

3. Metabolism Matters

1. D.L. Johannsen, et al., 'Metabolic Slowing with Massive Weight Loss Despite Preservation of Fat-Free Mass', *Journal of Clinical Endocrinology and Metabolism* 97, no. 7 (2012): 489–2496. doi:10.1210/jc.201–444.
2. Gina Kolata, 'After The Biggest Loser, Their Bodies Fought to Regain Weight', *The New York Times*, 20 May 2016.
3. C. von Noorden and Adolf Magnus-Levy, 'The Physiology of Metabolism', *Metabolism and Practical Medicine* 1, (1907).
4. Max Rubner, *The Laws of Energy Consumption in Nutrition* (United States: U.S. Army Research Institute of Environmental Medicine, 1968).
5. 'Metabolism', *Better Health*.
6. Jeffrey M. Friedman, 'Modern Science Versus the Stigma of Obesity', *Natural Medicine* 10, (2004): 563–569. https://doi.org/10.1038/nm060-63.

4. Our Bodies Don't Like Change

1. 'Homeostasis, Better Health', *Biology Online*.
2. Denis Noble, 'Claude Bernard, the First Systems Biologist, and the Future of Physiology', *Experimental Physiology* 93, (2008): 16–26. https://doi.org/10.1113/expphysiol.2007.038695.
3. Walter B. Cannon, *The Wisdom of the Body* (New York: W.W. Norton, 1939).
4. C.P. Richter, 'Ingestive Classics Curt Richter and the Behavioral Control of Homeostasis', *Harvey Lecture Series* 38, (1943): 63–103.
5. Johan H. Koeslag, 'The Human Biology of Obesity, And its Relevance to Insurers', *Journal of Insurance Medicine*, 22, no. 1 (Spring 1990).
6. Ana Julia Fereira, 'The Minnesota Starvation Experiment – How it Happened and What it Taught Us', *Maze*, 4 May 2021.
7. Jou Chin, 'The Biology and Genetics of Obesity — A Century of Inquiries', *New England Journal of Medicine* 370, (2014): 1874–1877. https://doi.org/10.1056/NEJMp1400613.
8. Priya Sumithran, et al., 'Long-Term Persistence of Hormonal Adaptations to Weight Loss', *The New England Journal of Medicine* 365, no. 17 (2011): 1597–604. https://doi.org/10.1056/NEJMoa1105816.

5. The Calorie Hysteria

1. Y-H Yu, et al., 'Metabolic Vs. Hedonic Obesity: A Conceptual Distinction and Its Clinical Implications', *Obesity Reviews* 16, no. 3 (2015): 234–247. https://doi.org/10.1111/obr.12246.
2. Max Rubner, *The Laws of Energy Consumption in Nutrition* (United States: U.S. Army Research Institute of Environmental Medicine, 1968).
3. Andrea C. Buchholz and Dale A. Schoeller, 'Is a Calorie a Calorie?', *The American Journal of Clinical Nutrition* 79, no 5 (2004): 899S–906S. https://doi.org/10.1093/ajcn/79.5.899S.
4. M. Schwartz, et al., 'Obesity Pathogenesis: An Endocrine Society Scientific Statement', *Endocrine Reviews* 38, no. 4 (2017): 26–96. https://doi.org/10.1210/er.201–0111.
5. Hilde Bruch and Grace Touraine, 'Obesity in Childhood: V. The Family Frame of Obese Children*', *Psychosomatic Medicine* 2, no. 2 (1940): 141–206.
6. Ibid.
7. Hilde Bruch, *The Importance of Overweight* (New York: W. W. Norton, 1957).
8. Russell Baker, 'American Fat', *New Yorker*, 4 January 1973.
9. Hugo R. Rony, 'Obesity and Leanness', *Obesity* 3, no. 6 (1995): 60–24. https://doi.org/10.1002/j.1550-8528.1995.tb00197.x.
10. John Valentine and George Andrew Durrin, *Energy, Work and Leisure* (London: Heinemann Educational Books, 1967).
11. Susan Sontag, *Illness as Metaphor and AIDS and Its Metaphors* (New York: Penguin, 1991).
12. J.P. Delany, et al., 'High Energy Expenditure Masks Low Physical Activity in Obesity', *International Journal of Obesity* 34, (2013): 1006–1011. https://doi.org/10.1038/ijo.2012.172.
13. P.S. Shetty, 'Adaptation to Low Energy Intakes: The Responses and Limits to Low Intakes in Infants, Children and Adults', *European Journal of Clinical Nutrition* 53, no. 1 (1999): 1–3. https://doi.org/10.1038/sj.ejcn.1600741.
14. Keith N. Frayn, *Metabolic Regulation: A Human Perspective*, (Wiley-Blackwell, 2010).
15. Rony, 'Obesity and Leanness'.

6. Are Genetics Or Toxic Food Environment To Be Blamed?

1. 'Why We Overeat', *Harvard T.H. Chan School of Public Health.*
2. 'Obesity and Overweight', *World Health Organization*, 9 June 2021.
3. Dirk Schroeder and Reynaldo Martorell, 'Poor Fetal and Child Growth

and Later Obesity and Chronic Disease: Relevance for Latin America', *Obesity and Poverty, A New Public Health Challenge*, (2004): 10–15.

4. Mariel Pressler, et al., 'Dietary Transitions and Health Outcomes in Four Populations – Systematic Review', *Nutritional Epidemiology* 9, (Feb 2022). https://doi.org/10.3389/fnut.2022.748305.
5. C. Slome, et al., 'Weight, Height and Skinfold Thickness of Zulu Adults in Durban', *South African Medical Journal* 34, no. 24 (1960): 50–09.
6. G.D. Campbell, 'Diabetes in Asians and Africans in and around Durban', *South African Medical Journal* 37, no. 48 (1963): 119–208.
7. J. Wardle and D. Boniface, 'Changes in the Distributions of Body Mass Index and Waist Circumference in English Adults, 1993/1994 to 2002/2003', *International Journal of Obesity* 32, (2008): 527–532. https://doi.org/10.1038/sj.ijo.0803740.
8. Jose G.B. Derraik, et al., 'Large-For-Gestational-Age Phenotypes and Obesity Risk in Adulthood: A Study of 195,936 Women', *Scientific reports* 10, no. 1 (2020). https://doi.org/10.1038/s4159-2-882.
9. Pamela J. Surkan, et al., 'Reasons For Increasing Trends In Large For Gestational Age Births', *Obstetrics & Gynecology* 104, no. 4 (2004): 72–26. https://doi.org/10.1097/01.aog.0000141442.59573.cd.
10. Jimmy Célind, et al., 'Secular Trends of Birthweight in Boys from 1950 to 2010', *Pediatrics & Neonatology* 60, no. 5 (2019): 54–48. https://doi.org/10.1016/j.pedneo.2019.01.012.
11. Juhee Kim, et al., 'Trends in Overweight from 1980 Through 2001 Among Preschool-Aged Children Enrolled in a Health Maintenance Organization', *Obesity* 14, no. 7 (2006): 110–112. https://doi.org/10.1038/oby.2006.126.
12. 'Epigenetics Between The Generations: We Inherit More Than Just Genes', *ScienceDaily*, 17 July 2017.; Abeer M. Mahmoud, 'An Overview Of Epigenetics In Obesity: The Role Of Lifestyle And Therapeutic Interventions', *International Journal of Molecular Sciences* 23, no. 3 (2022): 1341. https://doi.org/10.3390%2Fijms23031341.
13. 'Somatype', *Britannica*.
14. Robert C. Klesges, et al., "The Memphis Girls' Health Enrichment Multi-Site Studies (GEMS): An Evaluation of the Efficacy of a 2-Year Obesity Prevention Program in African American Girls', *Archives of Pediatrics & Adolescent Medicine* 164, no. 11 (2010): 100–014. https://doi.org/10.1001/archpediatrics.2010.196.
15. G.D. Campbell, 'Cleave the Colossus and the History of the "Saccharine Disease" concept', *Nutrition and Health*, 11, no. 1 (1996).
16. Ibid.
17. Martin Hult, et al., 'Hypertension, Diabetes and Overweight: Looming Legacies of the Biafran Famine', *PloS* one 5, no. 10 (Oct. 2010). doi:10.1371/journal.pone0013582.

18. Nady El Hajj, et al., 'Epigenetics and Life-Long Consequences of an Adverse Nutritional And Diabetic Intrauterine Environment', Reproduction 148, no. 6 (2014): R111-R120, https://doi.org/10.1530/REP-1-334.; Robert A. Waterland and Randy L. Jirtle, 'Transposable Elements: Targets for Early Nutritional Effects on Epigenetic Gene Regulation', *Molecular and Cellular Biology* 23, no. 15 (2003): 5293–5300. doi:10.1128/MCB.23.15.
19. J. Le Magnen, 'Is Regulation of Body Weight Elucidated', *Neuroscience Biobehavior Review* 8, no. 4 (1982): 51–22. doi:10.1016/014–634(84)9000.
20. Claude Bouchard, et al., 'The Response to Long-Term Overfeeding in Identical Twins', May 1990). https://doi.org/10.1056/NEJM199005243222101.
21 J. Levine, N. Eberhardt, M. Jensen, 'Role of Nonexercise Activity Thermogenesis in Resistance to Fat Gain in Humans', *Science* 283, no. 5399 (Jan 1999): 211–214. https://www.science.org/doi/10.1126/science.283.5399.212.
22. F. Du Bois, *Basal Metabolism in Health and Disease* (Lea & Febiger, 1936).
23. Elisa, 'Overshooting Set Point Weight in Eating Disorder Recovery', *Follow the Intuition*, 12 January 2017.
24. John R. Speakman, et al., 'Set Points, Settling Points and Some Alternative Models: Theoretical Options to Understand How Genes and Environments Combine to Regulate Body Adiposity', *Disease Models & Mechanisms*, 4, no. 6 (2011): 733–45. https://doi.org/10.1242/dmm.008698.
25. P. Tataranni, et al., 'Body Weight Gain in Free-Living Pima Indians: Effect of Energy Intake Vs Expenditure', *International Journal of Obesity* 27, (2003): 1578–1583. https://doi.org/10.1038/sj.ijo.0802469.
26. J. Grundlingh, '2,4-dinitrophenol (DNP): A Weight Loss Agent with Significant Acute Toxicity and Risk of Death', *Journal of Medical Toxicology* 7, no. 3 (2011): 205–212. https://doi.org/10.1007/s1318-1-16.
27. Emma Bleasdale, Sam N. Thrower, and Andrea Petroczi, 'Would You Use it with a seal of Approval? Important Attributes of 2,4-Dinitrophenol (2,4-DNP) as a Hypothetical Pharmaceutical Product', *Frontiers in Psychiatry* 9, no. 124 (April 2018). https://doi.org/10.3389/fpsyt.2018.00124
28. A. Da Poian, et al., 'Nutrient Utilization in Humans: Metabolism Pathways', *Nature Education* 3, no. 9 (2010):11.
29. Muthu Periasamy, et al., 'Skeletal Muscle Thermogenesis and its Role in Whole Body Energy Metabolism', *Diabetes & Metabolism Journal* 41, no. 5 (2017): 327–336. https://doi.org/10.4093/dmj.2017.41.5.327.; Julia Nowack, et al., 'Muscle Non-shivering Thermogenesis and Its Role in the Evolution of Endothermy', *Frontiers in physiology* 8, no. 889.

(2019). https://doi.org/10.3389/fphys.2017.00889.; B.F. Palmer and D.J. Clegg, 'Non-Shivering Thermogenesis as a Mechanism to Facilitate Sustainable Weight Loss', *Obesity Reviews* 188, (2017): 819–831. https://doi.org/10.1111/obr.12563.; Naresh C. Bal, et al., 'The Role of Sarcolipin in Muscle Non-Shivering Thermogenesis', *Frontiers in Physiology* 9 (2018), https://doi.org/10.3389/fphys.2018.01217.

30. S. Goya Wannamethee and Janice L. Atkins, 'Muscle Loss and Obesity: the Health Implications of Sarcopenia and Sarcopenic Obesity', *Proceedings of the Nutrition Society* 74, no. 4 (2015): 405–12. https://doi.org/10.1017/S002966511500169X.; Rita Rastogi Kalyani, et al., 'Age-Related and Disease-Related Muscle Loss: The Effect of Diabetes, Obesity, and Other Diseases', *The Lancet. Diabetes & Endocrinology* 2, no. 10 (2014): 819–29. https://doi.org/10.1016/S2213-587(14)7003-.; E. Run and K. Mook Choi, 'Health Consequences of Sarcopenic Obesity: A Narrative Review', *Frontiers in Endocrinology* 11, no. 332 (2020).
31. J Nauru-1, 'The Astonishing Story of Nauru, the Tiny Island Nation with the World's Highest Rates of Type 2', *Diabetes*.; 'Adult Obesity Facts', *Centers for Disease Control and Prevention*, May 2022.

7. Understand Your Hormones for Weight Loss

1. F.G. Benedict, 'Human Vitality and Efficiency Under Prolonged Restricted Diet', *Carnegie Institution of Washington*.
2. I.P. Pavlov and S. Koshtoyants, *I.P. Pavlov: Selected works* (Foreign Languages Publishing House, 1955).
3. David Cumming, et al., 'Plasma Ghrelin Levels after Diet-Induced Weight Loss or Gastric Bypass Surgery', *New England Journal of Medicine* 346, (May 2002): 1623–1630. https://doi.org/10.1056/NEJMoa012908.
4. Sebely Pal and Vanessa Ellis, 'The Acute Effects of Four Protein Meals on Insulin, Glucose, Appetite and Energy Intake in Lean Men', *British Journal of Nutrition* 104, no. 8 (2010): 1241–48. https://doi.org/10.1017/S0007114510001911.
5. Sumithran, et al., 'Long-Term Persistence of Hormonal Adaptations to Weight Loss', *New England Journal of Medicine* 365, no. 17(2011): 1597–1604. doi:10.1056/NEJMoa1105816.
6. Y. Zhang, et al., 'Positional Cloning of the Mouse Obese Gene and Its Human Homologue', *Nature* 374, no. 6521, (1995): 479–479. https://doi.org/10.1038/374479a0.
7. Milan Obradovic, et al., 'Leptin and Obesity: Role and Clinical Implication.' *Frontiers of Endocrinology 18,* (May 2021), https://doi.org/10.3389/fendo.2021.585887

8. R.H. Lustig, et al., 'Obesity, Leptin Resistance, and the Effects of Insulin Reduction', *International Journal of Obesity* 28, (2004): 1344–1348. https://doi.org/10.1038/sj.ijo.0802753.
9 E. Fryk, et al, 'Hyperinsulinemia and Insulin Resistance in the Obese May Develop as Part of a Homeostatic Response to Elevated Free Fatty Acids: A Mechanistic Case-Control and a Population-Based Cohort Study', *EBioMedicine 65*, 103264. https://doi.org/10.1016/j.ebiom.2021.103264.; Paula Bautista, et al., 'Insulin Resistance and β-Cell Function of Lean versus Overweight or Obese Filipino Patients with Newly Diagnosed Type 2 Diabetes Mellitus', *Asean-endocrinejournal, Journal of the ASEAN Federation of Endocrine Societies* 34, no. 2 (2019): 164–70. https://doi.org/10.15605/jafes.034.02.07.
10. Y.T. Wondmkun, 'Obesity, Insulin Resistance, and Type 2 Diabetes: Associations and Therapeutic Implications', *Diabetes Metabolic Syndrome and Obesity* 13, (2020): 361–616. https://doi.org/10.2147/DMSO.S275898.
11. S. Quarta, et al, 'An Exploratory Critical Review on TNF-α as a Potential Inflammatory Biomarker Responsive to Dietary Intervention with Bioactive Foods and Derived Products', *Foods* 11, no. 2524, (2022). https://doi.org/10.3390/foods11162524.
12. Antonio Pérez-Pérez, et al., 'Role of Leptin in Inflammation and Vice Versa', *International Journal of Molecular Sciences* 21, no. 16 (2020): 5887. https://doi.org/10.3390/ijms21165887.
13. Judith A. Whitworth, et al., 'Hyperinsulinemia Is Not a Cause of Cortisol-Induced Hypertension', *American Journal of Hypertension* 7, no. 6 (1994): 56–65. https://doi.org/10.1093/ajh/7.6.562.
14. G. Pagano, et al., 'An In Vivo and In Vitro Study of the Mechanism of Prednisone-Induced Insulin Resistance in Healthy Subjects', *Journal of Clinical Investigation* 5, (1983): 181–90. https://doi.org/10.1172/JCI111141.
15. Rizza A. Roberta, Lawrence J. Mandarino, and John E. Gerich, 'Cortisol-Induced Insulin Resistance in Man: Impaired Suppression of Glucose Production and Stimulation of Glucose Utilization due to a Postreceptor Defect of Insulin Action', *Journal of Clinical Endocrinology and Metabolism* 54, no. 1 (1982): 13–38. https://doi.org/10.1210/jcem-5-131.
16. Heather Ferris and C. Ronald Kahn, 'New Mechanisms of Glucocorticoid-Induced Insulin Resistance: Make No Bones About It', *Journal of Clinical Investigation* 122, no. 11 (Nov. 2012): 3854–3857. https://doi.org/10.1172/jci66180.
17. R.P. Stolk, et al., 'Gender Differences in the Associations Between Cortisol and Insulin In Healthy Subjects', *Journal of Endocrinology* 149, no. 2 (1996): 313–318. https://doi.org/10.1677/joe.0.1490313.

18. M. Salvadori, et al., 'Post-Transplant Diabetes Mellitus', *Journal of Nephrology* 5, (2003): 62–4.
19. Libuse Tauchmanovà, et al., 'Patients with Subclinical Cushing's Syndrome Due to Adrenal Adenoma Have Increased Cardiovascular Risk', *The Journal of Clinical Endocrinology & Metabolism* 87, no. 11 (2002): 4872–4878. https://doi.org/10.1210/jc.200-11766.
20. Catherine Prince, 'Putting Down Your Phone May Help You Live Longer', *The New York Times,* 24 April 2019.
21. Jennifer Daubenmier, et al., 'Mindfulness Intervention for Stress Eating to Reduce Cortisol and Abdominal Fat among Overweight and Obese Women: An Exploratory Randomized Controlled Study', *Journal of Obesity,* (2011). https://doi.org/10.1155/2011/651936.
22. W.B. Webb and H.B. Agnew Jr., 'Are We Chronically Sleep Deprived?', *Bulletin of the Psychonomic Society* 6, (1975): 4–8. https://doi.org/10.3758/BF03333140.
23. Karine Spiegel, Rachel Leproult and Eve Van Cauter, 'Impact of sleep debt on metabolic and endocrine function', *The Lancet* 354, (1999): 143–439.
24. E.L. Sweeney, et al., 'Skeletal Muscle Insulin Signaling and Whole-Body Glucose Metabolism Following Acute Sleep Restriction in Healthy Males', *Physiology Reports* 23, (Dec 2017): e13498. https://doi.org/10.14814/phy2.1349.
25. E.Y. Joo, et al., 'Adverse Effects of 24 Hours of Sleep Deprivation on Cognition and Stress Hormones', *Journal of Clinical Neurology* 2, (Jun 2012): 14–20. https://doi.org/10.3988/jcn.2012.8.2.146.
26. R. Leproult, et al., 'Sleep Loss Results in an Elevation of Cortisol Levels the Next Evening', *Sleep* 20, no. 10 (1997): 86–70.
27. Norito Kawakami, Naoyoshi Takatsuka and Hiroyuki Shimizu, 'Sleep Disturbance and Onset of Type 2 Diabetes', *Diabetes Care* 27, no. 1 (2004): 282–283. https://doi.org/10.2337/diacare.27.1.282.
28. Ibid.
29. J.P. Chaput, et al., 'Findings from the Quebec Family Study on the Etiology of Obesity: Genetics and Environmental Highlights', *Current Obesity Reports* 3, no.1 (Jan 2014): 5–6. https://doi.org/10.1007/s1367-1-08-3
30. Shahrad Taheri, et al., 'Short Sleep Duration is Associated with Reduced Leptin, Elevated Ghrelin, and Increased Body Mass Index', *PLoS Medicine* 3 (Dec 2004): e62. https://doi.org/10.1371/journal.pmed.0010062.
31. A.V. Nedeltcheva, et al., 'Insufficient Sleep Undermines Dietary Efforts to Reduce Adiposity', *Annals of International Medicine* 153, no. 4 (Oct 2010): 435–441. https://doi.org/10.7326/000-81-5--20101005-0006.

32. Guan Qingyun, et al., 'Mechanisms of Melatonin in Obesity: A Review', *International Journal of Molecular Sciences* 23, no. 1 (2021): 218.
33. Achim Peters, 'Why Do We Crave Sweets When We're Stressed?' *Scientific American*, 27 February 2019
34. N.D. Volkow, 'Reward, Dopamine And The Control of Food Intake: Implications for Obesity', *Trends in Cognitive Science* 15, no. 1 (Jan 2011): 3–6. https://doi.org/10.1016/j.tics.2010.11.001.
35. M. You and G.E. Arteel, 'Effect of Ethanol on Lipid Metabolism', *Journal of Hepatology* 70, no. 2 (February 2019): 23–48. doi: 10.1016/j.jhep.2018.10.037.; J.L. Price and Jo Nixon S. 'Retrospective Hair Cortisol Concentrations from Pretreatment to Early Recovery in Alcohol Use Disorder', *Alcohol and Alcoholism* 56, no. 2, (March 2021): 181–184. https://doi.org/10.1093/alcalc/agaa127.

8. Fats at the Heart of It All

1. J. Yerushalmy and H.E. Hilleboe, 'Fat in the Diet and Mortality from Heart Disease; A Methodologic Note', *New York State Journal of Medicine* 57, no. 14: 2343–54. PMID: 13441073.
2. J.P.A. Ioannidis, 'Why Most Published Research Findings Are False', PLoS Medicine 2, no. 8 (2005): e124. https://doi.org/10.1371/journal.pmed.0020124.; JPA Iaonnidis, 'The Role of Bias in Nutritional Research', *Youtube*, 20 June 2018.
3. Giovanni Giorgi and Agostino Di Ciaccio, 'Statistics in the Big Data Era', *Rivista Italiana di Economia, Demografia e Statistica* 70, (2016).
4. 'What to Know About Lipoproteins, Cholesterol, and Diet', *Medical News Today*, 22 December 2021.
5. E.H. Ahrens Jr., 'Carbohydrate-Induced and Fat-Induced Lipemia', *Transactions of the Associations of American Physicians* 74, (1961): 134–146.
6. J.L. Goldstein, 'Hyperlipidemia in Coronary Heart Disease: I. Lipid Levels in 500 Survivors of Myocardial Infarction', *Journal of Clinical Investigation* 52, no. 7 (July 1973): 1533–1543. https://doi.org.10.1172/JCI107331.
7. Andrew Mente, et al., 'Association of Dietary Nutrients with Blood Lipids and Blood Pressure in 18 Countries: A Cross-Sectional Analysis from the PURE Study', *The Lancet Diabetes & Endocrinology* 5, no. 10 (2017): 77–87.
8. Here is a very good article talking about how National Institute of Health, American Heart Association and American Diabetes Association embraced the low-fat, high carbohydrates paradigm as a treatment for weight gain and preventing heart disease:

Ann F. La Berge, 'How the Ideology of Low Fat Conquered America', *Journal of the History of Medicine and Allied Sciences* 63, no. 2(2008): 139–177. https://doi.org/10.1093/jhmas/jrn001.
9. P.S. MacLean, et al., 'Biological Control of Appetite: A Daunting Complexity', *Obesity (Silver Spring)* 25, no. 1 (March 2017): S8-S16. https://doi.org/10.1002/oby.21771.
10. 'EXPLAINED: Why is France's 35-Hour Week Such a Sacred Cow?', *The Local Fr*, 26 May 2020.
11. National Inst. Of Nutrition, Hyderabad. *Dietary Guide for Indians – A Manual*, 2nd Ed. (Hyderabad: National Institute of Nutrition, 2011).

9. Obesity – A Nutrient Deficiency Disease

1. Zeen Cindy, ed., *Vegetable Oils in Food Technology* (Blackwell Publishing, 2011).
2. ET Bureau, 'Indians Wish to Prioritise Eating Healthy in 2021, Says Survey by Habbit', *The Economic Times*, 14 January 2021.
3. F. Catalan, 'Cold-Pressed Olive Oil: All You Need To Know', *O-Live & Co*, 06 December 2019.
4. Julia Belluz, 'Americans are Eating Way More Fat', *Vox*, 31 July 2018.
5. I. Rahkovsky, S. Martinez and Fred Kuchler. 'New Food Choices Free of Trans Fats Better Align U.S. Diets With Health Recommendations', *Economic Research Service*, April 2012.
6. Rohan Kumar, B. Yamanura, and B. Boraiah, 'Rice Bran Oil – A Silver Lining to Indian Edible Oil Economy: A Review', *Agricultural Reviews*, April 2021. doi.org/10.18805/ag.R-2140.
7. Eoin Connolly, 'Cargill Foods Latches on to Rising Pune Supergiants', *SportsPro Media*, 5 April 2016.
8. H. Okuyama, 'Medicines and Vegetable Oils as Hidden Causes of Cardiovascular Disease and Diabetes', *Pharmacology* 98, (2016): 13–70. https://doi.org/10.1159/000446704.
9. E. Nelson and Kavitha Ramachandra, 'The Impact of the Green Revolution on Indigenous Crops of India', *Journal of Ethnic Foods* 6, no.8, https://doi.org/10.1186/s4277-1-01-9.
10. Manika Sharma, et al., 'A Comparison of the Indian diet with the EAT-Lancet Reference Diet', *BMC Public Health* 20, 812 (2020). https://doi.org/10.1186/s1288-2-895-.
11. I. Qadeer, S.M. Ghosh, and A.P. Madhavan, 'India's Declining Calorie Intake: Development or Distress?', *Social Change*, *46*, no. 1 (2016): 1–26. https://doi.org/10.1177/0049085715618474.; Angus Deaton and Jean Druze, 'Food and Nutrition in India: Facts and Interpretations', *Economic and Political Weekly* 44, no. 7 (Feb 2019): 42–65.

12. Drew DeSilver, 'What's on Your Table? How America's Diet has Changed Over The Decades', *Pew Research Center,* 13 October 2016.
13. C. Candela, L.M. Lopez, V. Kohen, 'Importance of a Balanced Omega 6/Omega 3 ratio for the Maintenance of Health. Nutritional Recommendations', *Nutricional Hospitalria* 26, no. 2 (2011): 323–329. 04. lomo –011:lomo 3/09 (uam.es).; A.P. Simopoulos, 'An Increase in the Omega-6/Omega-3 Fatty Acid Ratio Increases the Risk for Obesity', *Nutrients.* 8, no. 3 (2016): 128. https://doi.org/10.3390/nu8030128.; J.J. Di Nicolantonio and J.H. O'Keefe, 'Omega-6 Vegetable Oils as a Driver of Coronary Heart Disease: The Oxidized Linoleic Acid Hypothesis', *Open Heart* 5, 2018: e000898. https:doi.org/0.1136/openhrt-201-00898.
14. Nutrition and Diseases--1973 [-1974]: Hearings, Ninety-third Congress, First[-second] Session. United States: U.S. Government Printing Office, 1973.
15. Carl Voegtlin, 'Recent Work on Pellagra', *Public Health Reports (189-970)* 35, no. 25 (1920): 1435–52. https://doi.org/10.2307/4575618.
16. F. Luca, G.H. Perry, and A Di Rienzo 'Evolutionary Adaptations to Dietary Changes', *Annual Review of Nutrition* 30, (2010): 29–14. https://doi.org/10.1146/annurev-nutr-08050-41048.
17. G. Rose, 'Strategy of Prevention: Lessons from Cardiovascular Disease', *British Medical Journal* 282, no. 6279, (1981). doi:10.1136/bmj.282.6279.1847.
18. Diego Ortiz, 'How the Humble Potato Changed the World', *BBC,* 4 March 2020.
19. Raizman N. Scurvy, 'How a Surgeon, a Mariner, and a Gentleman Solved the Greatest Medical Mystery of the Age of Sail', *Journal of Clinical Investigation* 114, no. 12 (2004): 1690. https://doi.org10.1172/JCI23917.
20. James Lind, *Treatise of the Scurvy*, 1753.
21. C. Will, Julie, Ph.D., M.P.H, Tim Byers, M.D., M.P.H, 'Does Diabetes Mellitus Increase the Requirement for Vitamin C?', *Nutrition Reviews* 54, no. 7 (July 1996): 193–202. https://doi.org/10.1111/j.175-887.1996.tb03932.x.
22 G.N. Dakhale, H.V. Chaudhari, M. Shrivastava, 'Supplementation of Vitamin C Reduces Blood Glucose and Improves Glycosylated Hemoglobin in Type 2 Diabetes Mellitus: A Randomized, Double-Blind Study', *Advances in Pharmacological and Pharmaceutical Sciences*, (2011). https:doi.org/10.1155/2011/195271.
23. C. Malo and J. X. Wilson. 'Glucose Modulates Vitamin C Transport in Adult Human Small Intestinal Brush Border Membrane Vesicles', *The Journal of Nutrition* 130, no. 1 (January 2000): 63–69. https://doi.org/10.1093/jn/130.1.63.; S.J. Padayatty and M. Levine 'Vitamin C: The

Known and the Unknown and Goldilock,' *Oral Diseases* 22, no. 6, (2016): 46–93, https://doi.org/10.1111/odi.12446.

24. Francisco J. Nualart et al., 'Recycling of Vitamin C by a Bystander Effect*', *Journal of Biological Chemistry* 278, no 12 (2003): 1012–1033. https://doi.org/10.1074/jbc.M210686200.
25. R. Wilson, 'Inadequate Vitamin C Status in Prediabetes and Type 2 Diabetes Mellitus: Associations with Glycaemic Control, Obesity, and Smoking', *Nutrients* 9, no. 9 (2017): 997. https://doi.org/10.3390/nu9090997
26. Smaer Basoul, et al., 'Vitamin C in Health and Disease', *Journal of Contemporary Dental* Practice 5, no. 2 (May 2004): 1–14.
27. Linus Pauling Institute – Micronutrient Information Center. 'Vitamin C', *Oregon State University.*
28. Pennington, 'Treatment of Obesity: Development of the Past 150 years'.
29. C.P. Richter, 'Ingestive Classics Curt Richter and the Behavioral Control of Homeostasis', *Harvey Lecture Series* 38, (1943): 63–103.
30. Edward F. Adloph, 'Urges to Eat and Drink in Rats', *American Journal of Physiology 187–976* 151, no.1 (1947): 11–25. https://doi.org /10.1152/ajplegacy.1947.151.1.110.

10. Obesity and Omega Fats

1. Katalin Nagy and Tiuca Ioana-Daria, 'Importance of Fatty Acids in Physiopathology of Human Body', In *Fatty Acids*, edited by Angel Catala (London: IntechOpen, 2017). https://doi.org/10.5772/67407.
2. 'The Importance of Omega-3 and Omega-6 Fatty Acids', *Food-facts for Healthy Choices*, 27 March 2019.
3. Research Institute, 'Fat: the New Health Paradigm', *Credit Suisse. docView (credit-suisse.com)*
4. Stephan J. Guyenet and Susan E. Carlson, 'Increase in Adipose Tissue Linoleic Acid of US Adults in the Last Half Century', *Advances in Nutrition* 6, no. 6 (November 2015): 660–664. https://doi.org/10.3945/an.115.009944
5. Jayashree Bhosale, 'India's Cooking Oil Imports Expected to Grow at 3.4% per Annum Till 2030, says Economic Survey', *Economic Times*, 31 January 2022.
6. Radheshyam Jadhav, 'Edible Oil Production Not in Sync with Growth in Consumption', *The Hindu Business Line*, 17 March 2022.
7. Harish Damodaran, 'The Other Oil: How a Product Almost Entirely Imported Has Defied Food Inflation', *The Indian Express*, 3 July 2016.
8. Stephan Guyenet, 'Seed Oils and Body Fatness – a Problematic Revisit', *Whole Health Source*, 21 August 2011.

9. C.E. Ramsden, et al., 'Use Of Dietary Linoleic Acid for Secondary Prevention of Coronary Heart Disease and Death: Evaluation of Recovered Data from the Sydney Diet Heart Study and Updated Meta-Analysis', *BMJ* 346, (2013): e8707. doi.org/10.1136/bmj.e8707.
10. Sarah Rehkamp. 'A Look at Calorie Sources in the American Diet', *USDA*, December 5, 2016.
11. R. Mensink and Martjin Katan, 'Effect of Dietary Trans Fatty Acids on High-Density and Low-Density Lipoprotein Cholesterol Levels in Healthy Subjects', *The New England Journal of Medicine* 323, (1990): 43–45. doi.org/10.1056/NEJM199008163230703.; D. Mozaffarian, 'Trans Fatty Acids and Cardiovascular Disease', *The New England Journal of Medicine* 354, (2006): 1601–1613. https://doi.org/10.1056/NEJMra054035.
12. A.P. Simopoulos, 'An Increase in the Omega-6/Omega-3 Fatty Acid Ratio Increases the Risk for Obesity', *Nutrition* 8, no. 3 (2016): 128. doi:10.3390/nu8030128.
13. E. Patterson, et al., 'Health Implications of High Dietary Omega-6 Polyunsaturated Fatty Acids,' *Journal of Nutrition and Metabolism* 2012, 539426. https://doi.org/10.1155/2012/539426.
14. Slavko Komarnytsky, et al., 'Endocannabinoid System and Its Regulation by Polyunsaturated Fatty Acids and Full Spectrum Hemp Oils', *International Journal of Molecular Sciences* 22, no. 11 (2021): 5479. https://doi.org/10.3390/ijms22115479.
15. T.T. Le, T.B. Huff and J.X. Cheng, 'Coherent anti-Stokes Raman Scattering Imaging of Lipids in Cancer Metastasis', *BMC Cancer* 9, (2009): 42. https://doi.org/10.1186/147-40-2.; University of Illinois at Urbana-Champaign, 'Study in Mice Examines Impact of Reused Cooking Oil on Breast Cancer Progression', *ScienceDaily*, 21 March 2019.; Seymour Daton, et al., 'A Controlled Clinical Trial of a Diet High in Unsaturated Fat in Preventing Complications of Atherosclerosis', *Circulation* 1, no. 2 (July 1969).; Pearce M, Seymour Dayton. 'Incidence of Cancer in Men on a Diet High in Polyunsaturated Fat', *The Lancet* 297, no. 7697 (March 1971).
16. Wanda J.E. Bemelmans, et al., 'Effect of an Increased Intake of α-Linolenic Acid and Group Nutritional Education on Cardiovascular Risk Factors: The Mediterranean Alpha-linolenic Enriched Groningen Dietary Intervention (MARGARIN) Study', *The American Journal of Clinical Nutrition* 75, no. 2 (February 2002): 221–227. https://doi.org/10.1093/ajcn/75.2.221.; C.E. Ramsden, et al., 'Re-Evaluation of the Traditional Diet-Heart Hypothesis: Analysis of Recovered Data from Minnesota Coronary Experiment (196–3)', *BMJ* 353, (2016): i1246. https://doi.org/10.1136/bmj.i1246.

17. Simopoulos, 'An Increase in the Omega-6/Omega-3 Fatty Acid Ratio Increases the Risk for Obesity'.
18. Ibid.
19. Clémentine Bosch-Bouju and Sophie Layé, 'Dietary Omega-6/ Omega-3 and Endocannabinoids: Implications for Brain Health and Diseases', In *Cannabinoids in Health and Disease,* edited by Rosaria Meccariello, Rosanna Chianese. (London: IntechOpen, 2016). https://. doi.org/10.5772/62498.
20. Susan Allport,*The Queen Of Fats: Why Omega-3s Were Removed from the Western Diet and What We Can Do to Replace Them* (Univ of California Press, 2008), 15.
21. 'America's Most Widely Consumed Oil Causes Genetic Changes in the Brain', *Science News*, 17 January 2020.; 'Canola Oil Linked to Worsened Memory and Learning Ability in Alzheimer's', *Science News*, 7 December 2017.; Floyd H. Chilton 'Depression and Altered Serum Lipids in Cynomolgus Monkeys Consuming a Western Diet', *Physiology & Behavior* 104, no. 2 (2011): 22–27. https://doi.org/10.1016/j.physbeh.2011.01.013.
22. Neal Colgrass, 'Vegetable Oils Can Actually Kill You', *Newser,* 8 Nov 2015.'; Chilton, 'Depression and Altered Serum Lipids'.
23. W.C. Willett, 'Dietary Fat Lays a Major Role in Obesity: No', *Obesity Reviews* 3, no. 2 (2002): 5–8. https://doi.org/10.1046/j.146-89x.2002.00060.x.
24. 'Consumption of Saturated Animal Fats in the Diet of Humans May Decrease the Rate of Heart Disease in the Future', *International Journal of Research – Granthaalayah* 5, no. 1 (January 2017).
25. S.L. Malhotra, 'Epidemiology of Ischaemic Heart Disease in India with Special Reference to Causation', *Heart* 29, no. 6, (1967): 89–05. https://doi.org/10.1136/hrt.29.6.895.
26. S.L. Malhotra, 'Geographical Aspects of Acute Myocardial Infarction in India with Special Reference to Patterns of Diet and Eating', *Heart* 29, no. 3 (1967): 33–44. https:/doi.org/10.1136/hrt.29.3.337.
27. Sears Barry and Mary Perry, 'The Role of Fatty Acids in Insulin Resistance', *Lipids in Health & Disease* 14, (2015): 121. https://doi.org/10.1186/s1294-1-12-.
28. R. Akilen et al., 'The Effects of Potatoes and Other Carbohydrate Side Dishes Consumed with Meat on Food Intake, Glycemia and Satiety Response in Children', *Nutrition & Diabetes* 6, no. 2 (2016): e195. https:doi.org/10.1038/nutd.2016.1.
29. Ibid.
30. Kyle Mamounis, Ali Yasrebi, and Troy Aroepke, 'Linoleic Acid Causes Greater Weight Gain Than Saturated Fat Without Hypothalamic

Inflammation in the Male Mouse', *The Journal of Nutritional Biochemistry* 40, (2014): 12–31. https://doi.org/10.1016/j.jnutbio.2016.10.016.

31. Angela Castoldi et al., 'The Macrophage Switch in Obesity Development', *Frontiers in Immunology,* (January 2016). https://doi.org/10.3389/fimmu.2015.00637.
32. E. Patterson, et al., 'Health Implications of High Dietary Omega-6 Polyunsaturated Fatty Acids', *Journal of Nutrition and Metabolism* 2012, (2012). https://doi.org/10.1155/2012/539426.
33. Nehemiah Cox and Frederic Geissmann, 'Macrophage Ontogeny in the Control of Adipose Tissue Biology', *Current Opinion in Immunology* 62, (2020): 1–8. https://doi.org/10.1016/j.coi.2019.08.002.
34. Sait Bulut, et al., 'Seasonal Variation in the Fatty Acid Composition and ω6/ω3 Ratio of the Pike (Esox lucius) Muscle Living in Karamik Lake, Turkey', *Freseius Environment Bulletin* 19, no. 10 (2010): 222–231.; Gregory L. Florant, 'Lipid Metabolism in Hibernators: The Importance of Essential Fatty Acids', *American Zoologist*, 38, no. 2 (1998): 33–40.; Thomas Ruf and Walter Arnold, 'Effects of Polyunsaturated Fatty Acids on Hibernation and Torpor: A Review and Hypothesis', *American Journal of Physiology-Regulatory, Integrative and Comparative Physiology* 294, (2008): 3; S. Giroud, et al. 'Seasonal Changes in Eicosanoid Metabolism in the Brown Bear', *The Science of Nature* 105, no. 58 (2018). https://doi.org/10.1007/s0011-1-58-.; A.L. Evans, et al., 'Drivers of Hibernation in the Brown Bear', *Frontiers in Zoology* 13, no. 7 (2016). https://doi.org/10.1186/s1298-1-14-.
35. Sylvain Giroud, et al., 'Dietary Lipids Affect the Onset of Hibernation in the Garden Dormouse (Eliomys quercinus): Implications for Cardiac Function', *Frontiers in Physiology* 9, (2018): 1235. https://doi.org/10.3389/fphys.2018.01235.; V. Diedrich, S. Steinlechner, and Frank Scherbarth, 'Effects of Unsaturated Fatty Acids on Torpor Frequency and Diet Selection in Djungarian Hamsters (Phodopus sungorus)', *The Journal of Experimental Biology* 217, no. 24 (August 2014): 4313-9. doi:10.1242/jeb.113217.
36. Jennifer Prince, 'Omega-6 Fatty Acids May Increase Fat Accumulation, Insulin Resistance in Subjects with Type 2 Diabetes, Study Suggest', *Nutritional Outlook*, 7 January 2019.

11. Insulin Resistance – The Hidden Player in Obesity

1. Wilcox G, 'Insulin and Insulin Resistance', *The Clinical Biochemist* 26, no. 2, (2005):1–9.
2. L.J. Anderson, J.M. Tamayose and J.M. Garcia, 'Use of Growth Hormone, IGF-I, and Insulin for Anabolic Purpose: Pharmacological

Basis, Methods of Detection, and Adverse Effects', *Mol Cell Endocrinol*, 464 (2018): 6–4. https://doi.org/10.1016/j.mce.2017.06.010.

3. Andy Coghlan, 'Athletes May be Increasing Abusing Insulin', *New Scientist*, 8 August 2001.
4. Michael Ormsbee, 'Does the Window of Opportunity Exist for Post-Exercise Nutrition?', *Wondrium Daily*, 16 September 2020.
5. J.C. Brand-Miller, et al., 'Glycemic Index, Postprandial Glycemia, and the Shape of the Curve in Healthy Subjects: Analysis of a Database of More Than 1,000 Foods', *The American Journal of Clinical Nutrition* 89, no. 1 (2009): 9–05. https://doi.org/10.3945/ajcn.2008.26354.
6. Davide Gnocchi and Giovannella Bruscalupi, 'Circadian Rhythms and Hormonal Homeostasis: Pathophysiological Implications', *Biology* 6, no. 1 (2017): 10. https://doi.org//10.3390/biology6010010
7. Francesca Amati, et al., 'Physical Inactivity and Obesity Underlie the Insulin Resistance of Aging', *Diabetes Care* 1 32, no. 8 (August 2009): 1547–1549. https://doi.org/10.2337/dco-267.
8. Hannah Grossland, et al., 'The Impact of Immobilisation and Inflammation on the Regulation of Muscle Mass and Insulin Resistance: Different Routes to Similar End-Points', *The Journal of Physiology* 597, no. 5, (2019): 125–0. https://physoc.onlinelibrary.wiley.com/doi/pdfdirect/10.1113/JP275444.
9. Raymond I. Fink et al., 'Mechanisms of Insulin Resistance in Ageing', *The Journal of Clinical Investigation* 71, (June 1983): 152–5.
10. P. Myllynen, V.A. Koivisto and Esko A. Nikkila, 'Glucose Intolerance and Insulin Resistance Accompany Immobilization', *Journal of Internal Medicine* 222, no. 1 (1987): 7–1.
11. 'MyD88 Regulates Physical Inactivity-Induced Skeletal Muscle Inflammation, Ceramide Biosynthesis Signaling, and Glucose Intolerance', *American Journal of Physiology-Endocrinology and Metabolism* 309, no. 1 (1 July 2015): E11–21. https://doi.org/10.1152/ajpendo.00124.2015.
12. Oh Sung Kwon, et al., 'MyD88 Regulates Physical Inactivity-Induced Skeletal Muscle Inflammation, Ceramide Biosynthesis Signaling, and Glucose Intolerance', *American Journal of Physiology-Endocrinology and Metabolism* 309, no. 1 (2015), https://doi.org/10.1152/ajpendo.00124.2015.
13. Thomas Yates, et al., 'Self-Reported Sitting Time and Markers of Inflammation, Insulin Resistance, and Adiposity', *American Journal of Preventive Medicine* 42, no. 1, (2012): 1–7.
14. Ananya Mandal, 'History of Diabetes', *News Medical Life Sciences*, 4 June 2019,
15. K.S. Polonsky, B.D. Given and E. Van Cauter, 'Twenty-Four-Hour Profiles and Pulsatile Patterns of Insulin Secretion in Normal and

Obese Subjects', *The American Society for Clinical Invesitgation* 81, (1988): 44–48. https://doi.org/10.1172%2FJCI113339.

16. Elle Ferrannini, et al., 'Insulin Resistance and Hypersecretion in Obesity', *The Journal of Clinical Investigation* 100, no. 5 (1997): 116–173. https://doi.org/10.1172/JCI119628.
17. The Diabetes Control And Complications Trial Research Group, 'Influence of Intensive Diabetes Treatment on Body Weight and Composition of Adults with Type 1 Diabetes in the Diabetes Control and Complications Trial', *Diabetes Care.* 24, no. 10 (2001): 171–721. https://doi.org/10.2337/diacare.24.10.1711.
18. UK Prospective Diabetes Study (UKPDS) Group, 'Intensive Blood-Glucose Control With Sulphonylureas Or Insulin Compared with Conventional Treatment and Risk of Complications in Patients with Type 2 Diabetes (UKPDS 33)', *The Lancet* 352, no. 9131 (September 1998): 83–53.
19. Robert R. Henry, et al., 'Intensive Conventional Insulin Therapy for Type II Diabetes: Metabolic Effects During a 6-mo Outpatient Trial', *Diabetes Care* 16, no.1 (1993): 21–31. https://doi.org/10.2337/diacare.16.1.21.
20. Paraskevi Sapountzi, et al., 'Case Study: Diagnosis of Insulinoma Using Continuous Glucose Monitoring System in a Patient With Diabetes', *Clin Diabetes* 23, no. 3 (July 2005): 140–143. https://doi.org/10.2337/diaclin.23.3.140
21. 'Results of a Prospective Strategy to Diagnose, Localize, and Resect Insulinomas', *Surgery* 110, no. 6, (December 1991): 98–7. https://doi.org/10.5555/uri:pii:003960609190341l.
22. M. Ravnik-Oblak, A. Janez and A. Kocijanicic, 'Insulinoma Induced Hypoglycemia in a Type 2 Diabetic Patient', *Wiener Klinische Wochenschrift* 113, no. 9 (2001): 33–41. PMID: 11388080.
23. P.A. Velasquez-Mieyer et al., 'Suppression of Insulin Secretion is Associated with Weight Loss and Altered Macronutrient Intake and Preference in a Subset of Obese Adults', *International Journal of Obesity and Related Metabolic Disorders* 27, no. 2 (2003): 21–26. https://doi.org/10.1038/sj.ijo.802227.
24. Stephen C. Benoit et al., 'Insulin and Leptin as Adiposity Signals', *Recent Progress in Hormone Research* 59, no. 1 (2004): 267–85. https://doi.org/10.1210/rp.59.1.267.
25. Lifestyle Desk, 'Study Suggests Snacks Are Increasingly Replacing Meals in India: Here's Why', *The Indian Express*, 5 December 2019.
26. Sagar Malviya, 'Indians Turn to Snacks for Meals, Seek Convenience and Comfort Over Health: Study', *Economic Times*, 11 February 2022.
27. 'What is Wrong With the Indian Diet? Apparently a Lot, Claims UK-Based Cardiologist Dr Aseem Malhotra', *Times of India*, 15 May 2020.

28. Louise Petty, 'Changes in Eating Habits Over the Years: Comparing Diets Now & Then', *High Speed Training*, 5 June 2017.
29. Jameason D. Cameron, Marie-Josée Cyr, and Éric Doucet, 'Increased Meal Frequency Does Not Promote Greater Weight Loss in Subjects Who Were Prescribed an 8-Week Equi-Energetic Energy-Restricted Diet', *British Journal of Nutrition* 103, no. 8 (2010): 1098–1101. https://doi.org/10.1017/S0007114509992984.
30. Kiyah J. Duffey and Barry M. Popkin, 'Energy Density, Portion Size, and Eating Occasions: Contributions to Increased Energy Intake in the United States, 1977–2006', *PLoS Medicine* 8, no. 6: e1001050. https:/doi.org/10.1371/journal.pmed.1001050.
31. Ibid.
32. Kiyah J. Duffy and Barry M. Popkin, 'Does Hunger and Satiety Drive Eating Anymore? Increasing Eating Occasions and Decreasing Time Between Eating Occasions in the United States', *The American Journal of Clinical Nutrition* 91, no. 5 (2010): 134–347. https://doi.org/10.3945/ajcn.2009.28962.
33. Jessica Roekenes and Catia Martins, 'Ketogenic Diets and Appetite Regulation', *Current Opinion in Clinical Nutrition and Metabolic Care*, 24, no. 4 (July 2021): 35–63. https://doi.org/10.1097/MCO.0000000000000760.
34. Daisie Johnson and Ernst J. Drenick, 'Therapeutic Fasting in Morbid Obesity: Long-term Follow-up', *Archives of Internal Medicine* 137, no. 10 (1977): 1381–1382.

12. Carbohydrates and the Glycaemic Index Mania

1. Statement of American Medical Association Council on Foods and Nutrition, 'A Critique of Low-Carbohydrate Ketogenic Weight Reduction Regimens: a Review of Dr. Atkins' Diet Revolution Statement of American Medical Association Council on Foods and Nutrition', *Nutrition Reviews* 32, no. 1 (July 1974): 15–23. https://doi.org/10.1111/j.175-887.1974.tb05180.x.
2. Holly Reiland and Joanne Slavin, 'Systematic Review of Pears and Health', *Nutrition today* 50, no.6, (2015): 30–05. https://doi.org/10.1097/NT.0000000000000112.
3. J.M. Rippe, and T.J. Angelopoulos, 'Added Sugars and Risk Factors for Obesity, Diabetes and Heart Disease,' *International Journal of Obesity* 40, no. 1, (2016): S22-S27.
4. 'A Brief History of High Fructose Corn Syrup', *Clark Street Press*, 2 November 2020.
5. Maulishree Jhawer, 'High Fructose Corn Syrup and Obesity', *Medindia*, accessed 21 November 2022.

6. Anushree Gupta, 'Which Foods Contain High Fructose Corn Syrup? Here is How it Affects Your Weight Loss', *Times Now News*, 4 October 2019.
7. Seema Gulati, and Anoop Misra, 'Sugar Intake, Obesity, and Diabetes in India', *Nutrients* 6, no. 12 (2014): 595–4. https:/doi.org/10.3390/nu6125955.
8. Czapp, 'Where next for Indian sugar consumption?', *Chinimandi*, 28 October 2021.
9. Gulati and Misra, 'Sugar Intake, Obesity, and Diabetes'.
10. 'India Encourages Nation to Eat More Sugar', *Diabetes.co.uk*, 12 November 2020.
11. Gulati and Misra, 'Sugar Intake, Obesity, and Diabetes'.
12. Manu Raj Mathur, et al., 'Determinants of Sugar-Sweetened Beverage Consumption among Indian Adults: Findings from the National Family Health Survey-4', *Indian journal of community medicine : official publication of Indian Association of Preventive & Social Medicine* 45, no.1 (2020): 6–5. https://doi.org/10.4103/ijcm.IJCM_201_19.
13. 'Glycemic Load', *Diabetes.co.uk*, 10 June 2022.
14. Liangyou Rui, 'Energy Metabolism in the Liver', *Comprehensive Physiology* 4, no. 1 (2014): 17–7. https://doi.org/10.1002/cphy.c130024.
15. Frank B. Hu and Vasanti S Malik. 'Sugar-Sweetened Beverages and Risk of Obesity and Type 2 Diabetes: Epidemiologic Evidence', *Physiology & Behavior* 100, no. 1 (2010): 47–54. https://doi.org/10.1016/j.physbeh.2010.01.036.
16. Cherry Law, et al., 'Changes in Take-Home Aerated Soft Drink Purchases in Urban India After The Implementation of Goods and Services Tax (GST): An Interrupted Time Series Analysis', *SSM-Population Health* 14, (2021). https://doi.org/10.1016/j.ssmph.2021.100794.
17. Czapp, 'Where Next for Indian Sugar Consumption?'
18. Louis Hue and Heinrich Taegtmeyer, 'The Randle Cycle Revisited: A New Head for an Old Hat,' *American Journal of Physiology-Endocrinology and Metabolism* 297, no. 3 (2009): E578–91. https://doi.org/10.1152/ajpendo.00093.2009.
19. P.H. Weinstock et al., 'Lipoprotein Lipase Controls Fatty Acid Entry into Adipose Tissue, but Fat Mass Is Preserved by Endogenous Synthesis in Mice Deficient in Adipose Tissue Lipoprotein Lipase,' *Proceedings of the National Academy of Sciences* 94, no. 19 (1997): 10261–66. https://doi.org/10.1073/pnas.94.19.10261.
20. R.B. Simsolo, J.M. Ong, and P.A. Kern, 'The Regulation of Adipose Tissue and Muscle Lipoprotein Lipase in Runners by Detraining,' *Journal of Clinical Investigation* 92, no. 5 (1993): 2124–30. doi.org/10.1172/JCI116813.; Hong Wang and Robert H. Eckel, 'Lipoprotein

Lipase: From Gene to Obesity', *American Journal of Physiology-Endocrinology and Metabolism* 297, no. 2 (2009): E271–88. doi.org/10.1152/ajpendo.90920.2008.; Barbara J. Nicklas, et al., 'Responses of Adipose Tissue Lipoprotein Lipase to Weight Loss Affect Lipid Levels and Weight Regain in Women', *American Journal of Physiology-Endocrinology and Metabolism* 279, no. 5 (2000): E1012–19. doi.org/10.1152/ajpendo.2000.279.5.E1012.; Adrianne E. Hardman and Sara L. Herd, 'Exercise and Postprandial Lipid Metabolism', *Proceedings of the Nutrition Society* 57, no. 01 (1998): 63–72. doi.org/10.1079/PNS19980011.

21. Yoshitaka Hayashi, Regulates Lipolysis and Fatty Acid Oxidation through Inositol Triphosphate Receptor 1 in the Liver', *Journal of diabetes investigation* 12, no. 1 (2021): 3–4. https://doi.org/10.1111/jdi.13315
22. Shireesh Srivastava, et al., 'Mitochondrial Biogenesis and Increased Uncoupling Protein 1 in Brown Adipose Tissue of Mice Fed a Ketone Ester Diet', *The FASEB Journal* 26, no. 6 (2012): 2351–62. https://doi.org/10.1096/fj.11-200410.; The DCCT Research Group, 'Weight Gain Associated With Intensive Therapy in the Diabetes Control and Complications Trial', *Diabetes Care* 11, no. 7 (1988): 567–73. https://doi.org/10.2337/diacare.11.7.567.; Shireesh Srivastava, et al., 'A Ketogenic Diet Increases Brown Adipose Tissue Mitochondrial Proteins and UCP1 Levels in Mice', *IUBMB Life* 65, no. 1 (2013): 58–66. https://doi.org/10.1002/iub.1102.; Bonnie J. Brehm, et al., 'A Randomized Trial Comparing a Very Low Carbohydrate Diet and a Calorie-Restricted Low Fat Diet on Body Weight and Cardiovascular Risk Factors in Healthy Women,' *The Journal of Clinical Endocrinology & Metabolism* 88, no. 4, (2003): 1617–1623. https://doi.org/10.1210/jc.200–21480.
23. C.B. Ebbeling, et al., 'Effects of a Low Carbohydrate Diet on Energy Expenditure During Weight Loss Maintenance: Randomized Trial', *BMJ* 363, (2018): k4583. https://doi.org/10.1136/bmj.k4583.
24. Kelsey Miller, 'The Starvation Study That Changed The World', *Refinery29*, 11 July 2016,

PART 2: HOW TO LOSE WEIGHT AND MAINTAIN IT

1. Diabetes Prevention Program Research Group, '10-year Follow-Up of Diabetes Incidence and Weight Loss in the Diabetes Prevention Program Outcomes Study', *The Lancet* 374, no. 9702, (2009): 1677–1686. https://doi.org/10.1016/s014-736(09)61457-4.

1. Eat Well, Not Less

1. L. Douyon and D.E. Schteingart, 'Effect of Obesity and Starvation on Thyroid Hormone, Growth Hormone, and Cortisol Secretion', *Endocrinology & Metabolism Clinics of North America* 31, no. 1, (2002): 173–189. https://doi.org/10.1016/S0889-8529(01)00023-8
2. Ibid.
3. R. Vettor, 'The Right Nutrition for the Nutrition Related Diseases', *Reviews in Endocrine and Metabolic Disorders* 21, 293–296 (2020). https://doi.org/10.1007/s11115-2-9582-5.
4. Kiyah J. Duffey and Barry M. Popkin, 'Does Hunger and Satiety Drive Eating Anymore? Increasing Eating Occasions and Decreasing Time Between Eating Occasions in the United States', *The American Journal of Clinical Nutrition* 91, no. 5 (2010): 1342–1347.
5. David Loxterkamp, 'Fasting: The History, Pathophysiology and Complications', *The Western Journal of Medicine* (1982).
6. Ibid.
7. Nicole Jacqueline Jensen, Helena Zander Wodschow, Malin Nilsson, and Jørgen Rungby, 'Effects of Ketone Bodies on Brain Metabolism and Function in Neurodegenerative Diseases', *International Journal of Molecular Sciences* 21, no. 22, (2020): 8767. https://doi.org/10.3390/ijms21228767.
8. Oliver E. Owen et al., 'Liver and Kidney Metabolism', *The Journal of Clinical Investigation* 48, (1969).
9. Kian Y. Ho, et al., 'Fasting Enhances Growth Hormone Secretion and Amplifies the Complex Rhythms of Growth Hormone Secretion in Man', *The Journal of Clinical Investigation* 81, (1988): 96–75.
10. Ernst J. Drenick et al., 'Prolonged Starvation as Treatment for Severe Obesity', *JAMA* 187, no. 2 (1964): 10–05.
11. A. Zakaria, I. Sabry, and Amal El Shehaby, 'Ramadan-Like Fasting Reduces Carbonyl Stress and Improves Glycemic Control in Insulin Treated Type 2 Diabetes Mellitus Patients', *Life Science Journal* 10, no. 2, (2013): 384–90.
12. M.N. Harvie, et al., 'The Effects of Intermittent or Continuous Energy Restriction on Weight Loss and Metabolic Disease Risk Markers: A Randomized Trial in Young Overweight Women', *International Journal of Obesity (Lond)* 35, no. 5, (2011): 71–27. https://doi.org/10.1038/ijo.2010.171.
13. Benjamin D. Horne, et al., 'Relation of Routine, Periodic Fasting to Risk of Diabetes Mellitus, and Coronary Artery Disease in Patients Undergoing Coronary Angiography', *The American Journal of Cardiology* 109, no. 11 (2012): 1558–1562.

14. Suleiman Furmli et al., 'Therapeutic Use of Intermittent Fasting for People with Type 2 Diabetes as an Alternative to Insulin', *BMJ Case Rep* 2018, https://doi.org/10.1136/bcr-201-21854.
15. Surabhi Bhutani, et al., 'Improvements in Coronary Heart Disease Risk Indicators by Alternate-Day Fasting Involve Adipose Tissue Modulations', *Obesity* 18, no.11, (2012): 2152–2159. https://doi.org/10.1038/oby.2010.54.
16 Leonie K Heilbronn, et al., "Alternate-Day Fasting in Nonobese Subjects: Effects On Body Weight, Body Composition, and Energy Metabolism', *The American Journal of Clinical Nutrition* 81, no. 1 (2005): 69–73. https://doi.org/10.1093/ajcn/81.1.69.
17. Christian Zauner, et al., 'Resting Energy Expenditure in Short-Term Starvation is Increased as a Result of an Increase in Serum Norepinephrine', *The American Journal of Clinical Nutrition* 71, no. 6 (2000): 1511–1515. https://doi.org/10.1093/ajcn/71.6.1511.
18. A.M. Johnstone, et al., 'Effect of an Acute Fast on Energy Compensation and Feeding Behaviour in Lean Men and Women', *International Journal of Obesity* 26, (2002): 162–628.
19. Michael N. Clifford, 'Chlorogenic Acids and Other Cinnamates – Nature, Occurrence and Dietary Burden', *Journal of the Science of Food and Agriculture* (2019).
20. Jose Angel Gomez-Ruiz, Davis S. Leake, and Jennifer M. Ames, 'In Vitro Antioxidant Activity of Coffee Compounds and Their Metabolites', *Journal of Agricultural and Food Chemistry* 55, no. 17 (2007): 6962–69. doi.org/10.1021/jf0710985
21. Ivon E.J. Milder, et al., 'Lignan Contents of Dutch Plant Foods: A Database Including Lariciresinol, Pinoresinol, Secoisolariciresinol and Matairesino', *British Journal of Nutrition* 93, (2005): 393–402. https://doi.org/10.1079/BJN20051371.
22. G. Webster Ross, et al., 'Association of Coffee and Caffeine Intake With the Risk of Parkinson Disease', *JAMA* 283, no. 20 (2000): 267–679, https://doi.org/10.1001/jama.283.20.2674.
23. Catarina Santos, et al., 'Caffeine Intake and Dementia: Systematic Review and Meta-Analysis', *Journal of Alzheimer's Disease* 20, (2010): S187–S204.
24. Susanna C. Larsson and Alicja Wolk, 'Coffee Consumption and Risk of Liver Cancer: A Meta-Analysis', *Gastroenterology* 132, no. 5 (2007): 1740–45. https://doi.org/10.1053/j.gastro.2007.03.044.
25. Ibid.
26. Yoko Kabayashi, et al., 'Green Tea Polyphenols Inhibit the Sodium-Dependent Glucose Transporter of Intestinal Epithelial Cells by a Competitive Mechanism', *Journal of Agricultural and Food Chemistry* 48, no. 11 (2000): 5618–5623. doi.org/10.1021/jf0006832.

27. Vanessa Crespy and Gary Williamson, 'A Review of the Health Effects of Green Tea Catechins in In Vivo Animal Models', *The Journal of Nutrition* 134, no. 12, (2004): 3431S–3440S. https://doi.org/10.1093/jn/134.12.3431S.
28. Rick Hursel and Margriet S. Westerterp-Plantenga, 'Catechin- and Caffeine-Rich Teas for Control of Body Weight in Humans', *The American Journal of Clinical Nutrition* 98, no. 6, (2013): 1682S–1693S, https://doi.org/10.3945/ajcn.113.058396.
29. A.G. Dulloo, et al., 'Green Tea and Thermogenesis: Interactions between Catechin-Polyphenols, Caffeine and Sympathetic Activity', *International Journal of Obesity* 24, no. 2, (2000): 25–58.
30. Michelle C. Venables, et al., 'Green Tea Extract Ingestion, Fat Oxidation, and Glucose Tolerance in Healthy Humans', *The American Journal of Clinical Nutrition* 87, no. 3, (2008): 778–784. https://doi.org/10.1093/ajcn/87.3.778.
31. Abdul G. Dulloo, et al., 'Efficacy of a Green Tea Extract Rich in Catechin Polyphenols and Caffeine in Increasing 24-H Energy Expenditure and Fat Oxidation in Humans', *The American Journal of Clinical Nutrition* 70, no. 6 (1999): 1040–1045. https://doi.org/10.1093/ajcn/70.6.1040.
32. Marcel W.L. Koo and Chi H. Cho, 'Pharmacological Effects of Green Tea on the Gastrointestinal System', *European Journal of Pharmacology* 500, (2004): 17–85. https://doi.org/10.1016/j.ejphar.2004.07.023.
33. Loren Cordain, et al., 'Influence of Modern Chronic Wine Consumption on Insulin Sensitivity and Other Correlates of Syndrome X in Moderately Obese Women', *Metabolism* 49, no. 11 (2000): 147–8.
34. Ibid.
35. Raffaele Napoli, et al., 'Red Wine Consumption Improves Insulin Resistance but not Endothelial Function in Type 2 Diabetic Patients', *Metabolism* 49, no. 3 (2005): 31–3. https://doi.org/10.1016/j.metabol.2004.09.010.
36. Davide Grassi, et al., 'Cocoa Reduces Blood Pressure and Insulin Resistance and Improves Endothelium-Dependent Vasodilation in Hypertensives', *Hypertension* 46, (2005): 398–405. https://doi.org/10.1161/01.HYP.0000174990.46027.70.
37. Luc Djousse, et al., 'Chocolate Consumption is Inversely Associated with Prevalent Coronary Heart Disease: The National Heart, Lung, and Blood Institute Family Heart Study', *Clinical Nutrition* 30, no.2, (2011): 182–187. https://doi.org/10.1016%2Fj.clnu.2010.08.005.
38. Davide Grassi, et al., 'Blood Pressure is Reduced and Insulin Sensitivity Increased in Glucose-Intolerant, Hypertensive Subjects after 15 Days of Consuming High-Polyphenol Dark Chocolate,' *The Journal of Nutrition* 138, no. 9, (2008): 1671–1676, https://doi.org/10.1093/jn/138.9.1671.

39. David Jenkins et al., 'Possible Benefit of Nuts in Type 2 Diabetes', *The Journal of Nutrition* 138, no 9, (2008): 1752S–1756S. https://doi.org/10.1093/jn/138.9.1752S.
40. Joan Sabate and Michelle Wien, 'Nuts, Blood Lipids and Cardiovascular Disease', *Asia Pacific Journal of Clinical Nutrition* 19, no. 1, (2010): 13–36.
41. Pablo Hernandez Alonso, et al., 'Beneficial Effect of Pistachio Consumption on Glucose Metabolism, Insulin Resistance, Inflammation, and Related Metabolic Risk Markers: A Randomized Clinical Trial', *Diabetes Care* 7, no. 11 (2014), https://doi.org/10.2337/dc1–431.
42. H. Walter Lack and Susy Fuentes, 'The Discovery, Naming and Typification of Chenopodium quinoa (Chenopodiaceae)', *Wildenowia* 43, no. 1, (2013): 14–49. https://doi.org/ 10.3372/wi.43.43117.
43. Nicoletta Maestri, 'Amaranth The Origin and Use of Amaranth in Ancient Mesoamerica', *ThoughCo*, 16 January 2020.
44. 'Benefits of B17', *ITC Community Therapy Center*, 15 March 2021.
45. Jessica Gavin, 'Chia Seeds Health Benefits & Uses', Jessica Gavin, 1 December 2020.
46. Patty W. Siri-Tarino, Qi Sun, Frank B Hu, and Ronald M Krauss, 'Meta-analysis of Prospective Cohort Studies Evaluating the Association of saturated fat with Cardiovascular Disease,' *The American Journal of Clinical Nutrition* 91, no. 3, (2010): 535–546, https://doi.org/10.3945/ajcn.2009.27725.
47. Naomi Fukugawa, et al., 'High-Carbohydrate, High-Fiber Diets Increase Peripheral Insulin Sensitivity in Healthy Young and Old Adults', *The American Journal of Clinical Nutrition* 52, (1990): 524–528, https://doi.org/10.1093/ajcn/52.3.524.
48. So-Yeon An, et al., 'Beneficial Effects of Fresh and Fermented Kimchi in Prediabetic Individuals', *Annals of Nutrition and Metabolism* 63 (2013): 11–19.
49. Dae Kwon, et al., 'Long-term Consumption of Fermented Soybean-Derived Chungkookjang Enhances Insulinotropic Action Unlike Soybeans in 90% Pancreatectomized Diabetic Rats', *European Journal of Nutrition* 46, no. 1 (2007): 4–2.
50. Jeong-Mu Cheong, Dae-Ik Kim, and Kil Soo-Kim, 'Insulin Sensitivity Improvement of Fermented Korean Red Ginseng (*Panax ginseng*) Mediated By Insulin Resistance Hallmarks in Old-aged *ob/ob* Mice', *Journal of Ginseng Research* 39, no. 4 (2015): 33–37. https://doi.org/10.1016/j.jgr.2015.03.005.
51. Sandor Katz, 'Making Sauerkraut', *Wild Fermentation*, 27 April 2012.
52. Carol S. Johnston, Andrea M. White, and Shannon M Kent, 'Preliminary Evidence That Regular Vinegar Ingestion Favorably Influences

Hemoglobin A1c Values in Individuals with Type 2 Diabetes mellitus', *Diabetes Research and Clinical Practice* 84, no. 2 (2009): e15-e17. doi.org/10.1016/j.diabres.2009.02.005.

53. Andrea M. White and Carl S. Jonhston, 'Vinegar Ingestion at Bedtime Moderates Waking Glucose Concentrations in Adults With Well-Controlled Type 2 Diabetes', *Diabetes Care* 30, no. 11, (2007).
54. Yuting Ruan, et al., 'Effect of Probiotics on Glycemic Control: A Systematic Review and Meta-Analysis of Randomized, Controlled Trials', *Plos One* 10, no. 7, (2015): e0132121. doi.org/10.1371/journal.pone.0132121
55. 'Evaluating the Public Health Significance of Micronutrient Malnutrition', 2009. gff-part-2-en.pdf (who.int)
56. Araceli Muñoz-Garach, et al., 'Nutrients and Dietary Patterns Related to Osteoporosis', *Nutrients* 12, no. 7, (1986). doi:10.3390/nu12071986
57. Meera Sangaramoorthy, et al., 'Intake of Bean Fiber, Beans, and Grains and Reduced Risk of Hormone Receptor-Negative Breast Cancer: The San Francisco Bay Area Breast Cancer Study', *Cancer Medicine* 7, no. 5 (2018): 213–144. doi.org/10.1002/cam4.1423; Rocio Campos-Vega, et al., 'Common Beans and Their Non-Digestible Fraction: Cancer Inhibitory Activity-An Overview', *Foods (Basel, Switzerland)* 2, no. 3, (2013): 37–92. doi.org/10.3390/foods2030374.
58. Nongnuch Sutivisedsak, et al., 'Physical Properties and Fatty Acid Profiles of Oils from Black, Kidney, Great Northern, and Pinto Beans', *Journal of Oil & Fat Industries* 88, (2011): 19–00. doi.org/10.1007/s11746-010-1669-8.
59. Bill Lands, PhD, 'Dietary Omega-3 and Omega-6 Fatty Acids Compete in Producing Tissue Compositions and Tissue Responses', *Military Medicine* 179, no. 11, (2014): 76–81. doi.org/10.7205/MILMED-D-1-0149.
60. R.L. Divi, et al., 'Anti-Thyroid Isoflavones from Soybean: Isolation, Characterization, and Mechanisms of Action', *Biochemical Pharmacology* 54, no. 10 (1997): 108–6. DOI: 10.1016/s0006-2952(97)00301-8.
61. Beatrice L. Hunter, 'The Downside of Soybean Consumption', http://superiorsites3.com/NNF01SoyBeatrice.htm
62. James Spounlas, '"Gender Issues" Tied to Soy Consumption?' *American Free Press*, 12 July 2016.
63. Elin M. Östman, Helena G.M. Liljeberg Elmståhl, and Inger M.E. Björck, 'Inconsistency Between Glycemic and Insulinemic Responses to Regular and Fermented Milk Products,' *The American Journal of Clinical Nutrition* 74, no. 1 (2001): 96–100. DOI: 10.1093/ajcn/74.1.96.
64. Alireza Ostadrahimi, et al., 'Effect of Probiotic Fermented Milk (Kefir) on Glycemic Control and Lipid Profile in Type 2 Diabetic Patients: A Randomized Double-Blind Placebo-Controlled Clinical Trial', *Iranian Journal of Public Health* 44, no. 22 (2015): 22–7.

65. Y. Rhee and A. Brunt, 'Flaxseed Supplementation Improved Insulin Resistance in Obese Glucose Intolerant People: A Randomized Crossover Design', *Nutrition Journal* 10, no. 44 (2011). doi.org/10.1186/147-89-4
66. Lisa E. Heaton, et al., 'Selected In-Season Nutritional Strategies to Enhance Recovery for Team Sport Athletes: A Practical Overview', *Sports Medicine (Auckland, N.Z.)* 47, no. 11 (2017): 220–218. doi.org/10.1007/s40279-017-0759-2.
67. Linda Heller, 'The Chicken Soup Cure', *Chicago Tribune*, 14 April, 1992.
68. Amy Blaszyk, 'Taking Stock Of Bone Broth: Sorry, No Cure-All Here', *The Salt*, 10 February 2015.
69. Doug Cook, 'Is Bone Broth Healthy?' *CDHF*, 14 November 2022.
70. D. Yulan Lin, et al., 'Therapeutic Potential of Amino Acids in Inflammatory Bowel Disease', *Nutrients* 9, no. 9, (2017): 920. doi/org/10.3390/nu9090920; Ibid.
71. M.J. Lopez and S.S. Mohiuddin, 'Biochemistry, Essential Amino Acids', In *StatPearls, Treasure Island (FL)*, StatPearls Publishing, 2022.
72. Walter A. Muller, Gerald Faloona, and Roger H. Unger, 'The Effect of Alanine on Glucagon Secretion', *The Journal of Clininal Investigation* 50, no. 10 (1971): 2215–18. doi.org/10.1172/JCI106716.
73. Daniel A. Traylor, Stefan H.M. Gorissen, Stuart M. Phillips, 'Perspective: Protein Requirements and Optimal Intakes in Aging: Are We Ready to Recommend More Than the Recommended Daily Allowance?', *Advances in Nutrition* 9, no. 3, (2018): 171–182. doi.org/10.1093/advances/nmy003.
74. Jay R. Hoffman, and Michael J. Falvo, 'Protein – Which is Best?', *Journal of Sports Science & Medicine* 3, no. 3, (2004): 11–0.
75. Tino Just, et al., 'Cephalic Phase Insulin Release in Healthy Humans After Taste Stimulation?', *Appetite* 51, (2008): 62–7.
76. D. Jakubowicz, et al., 'Incretin, Insulinotropic And Glucose-Lowering Effects of Whey Protein Pre-Load in Type 2 Diabetes: A Randomised Clinical Trial', *Diabetologia* 57, (2014): 1807–1811. doi.org/10.1007/s0012-1-305-x.
77. Ralph A. DeFronzo, et al., 'Effects of Exenatide (Exendin-4) on Glycemic Control and Weight Over 30 Weeks in Metformin-Treated Patients With Type 2 Diabetes', *Diabetes Care* 28, no. 5, (2005): 1092–1100. doi.org/10.2337/diacare.28.5.1092.
78. Nicole M. Avena et al., 'Evidence for Sugar Addiction: Behavioral And Neurochemical Effects of Intermittent, Excessive Sugar Intake', *Neuroscience and Biobehavioral Reviews* 32, no. 1 (2008): 2–9. doi.org/10.1016/j.neubiorev.2007.04.019.
79. Chase M. Walton, et al., 'Nontraditional Therapy of Diabetes and Its Complications', *Journal of Diabetes Research* 2019, (2019): 1–6. doi.org/10.1155/2019/8681959.

2. *Exercise Smart, Not More, and Tone Your Body*

1. 'Muscle Fibre Types', *Physiopedia*, accessed November 2022.
2. Daisy Wilson, et al., 'Frailty and Sarcopenia: The Potential Role of an Aged Immune System', *Aging Research Reviews* 36, (2007): 1–10. doi.org/10.1016/j.arr.2017.01.006
3. 'Bone and Muscle Loss in Microgravity', *NASA*, accessed November 2022.
4. H. Vikne, et al., 'Human Skeletal Muscle Fiber Type Percentage and Area After Reduced Muscle Use: A Systematic Review and Meta-Analysis', *Scandinavian Journal of Medicine & Science in Sports* 30, (2020): 1298–1317. doi.org/10.1111/sms.13675
5. Emanuelle Marzetti and Christian Leeuwenberg, 'Skeletal Muscle Apoptosis, Sarcopenia and Frailty at Old Age', *Experimental Gerontolgy* 41, no. 12, (2006): 123–238. doi.org/10.1016/j.exger.2006.08.011
6. Matteo Cesari, et al., 'Frailty Syndrome and Skeletal Muscle: Results From the Invecchiare in Chianti Study', *The American Journal of Clinical Nutrition* 83, no. 5 (2006): 1142–1148. doi.org/10.1093/ajcn/83.5.1142
7. Fabio Demontis, et al., 'The Influence of Skeletal Muscle on Systemic Aging and Lifespan', *Aging Cell* 12, no. 6 (2013): 943–9. doi.org/10.1111/acel.12126
8. David J. Handelsman et al., 'Circulating Testosterone as the Hormonal Basis of Sex Differences in Athletic Performance', *Endocrine Reviews* 39, no. 5 (2018): 80–29. doi.org/10.1210/er.201–0020
9. A. Grøntved, et al., 'A Prospective Study of Weight Training and Risk of Type 2 Diabetes Mellitus in Men', *Arch Intern Med* 172, no. 17, (2012): 1306–1312. doi.org/10.1001/archinternmed.2012.3138
10. Ahmed D. Ismail, 'The Effect of Short-Duration Resistance Training on Insulin Sensitivity and Muscle Adaptations in Overweight Men', *Experimental Physiology* (2018). doi.org/10.1113/EP087435
11. B.C. Bergman, et al., 'Muscle Sphingolipids During Rest and Exercise: A C18:0 Signature for Insulin Resistance in Humans', *Diabetologia* 59, (2016): 785–798. doi.org/10.1007/s0012–1–850-y
12. V.A. Hughes, et al., 'Exercise Increases Muscle GLUT-4 Levels and Insulin Action in Subjects with Impaired Glucose Tolerance', *AJP – Endocrinology and Metabolism* 264, (1993): E855.
13. Sechang Oh, et al., 'Exercise Reduces Inflammation and Oxidative Stress in Obesity-Related Liver Diseases', *Medicine & Science in Sports & Exercise* 45, no. 12 (2013): 221–222. https://doi.org/10.1249/MSS.0b013e31829afc33
14. John P. Miller, et al., 'Strength Training Increases Insulin Action in Healthy 50- to 65yr-old Men', *Hurley Journal of Applied Physiology* 77, no. 3, (1994): 112–127.

15. Ibid.
16. Grøntved, et al., 'A Prospective Study of Weight Training'.
17. Juul Achten, et al., 'Determination of the Exercise Intensity that Elicits Maximal Fat Oxidation', *Medicine & Science in Sports & Exercise*, 34, no. 1, (2004): 92.
18. J.A. Babraj, et al., 'Extremely Short Duration High Intensity Interval Training Substantially Improves Insulin Action in Young Healthy Males', *BMC Endocrine Disorders* 9, no. 3 (2009). https://doi.org/10.1186/147-82--3

3. Stress Less, Sleep More

1. Gaurav Laghate, 'India Records Highest TV Consumption in a Week with Total Time Spent of 1.27 Trillion Minutes', *Economic Times*, 9 April 2020.
2. King's College London, 'Sleep Deprivation May Cause People to Eat More Calories', *Science Daily*, 2 November 2016.
3. Teresa Arora, and Shahrad Taheri, 'Sleep Optimization and Diabetes Control: A Review of the Literature', *Diabetes Therapy: Research, Treatment and Education of Diabetes and Related Disorders* 6, no. 4 (2015): 425–468, https://doi.org/10.1007/s1330-1-141-z.

Index